The Lukács Reader

To Iris Murdoch

THE LUKÁCS READER

Edited by

Arpad Kadarkay

BLACKWELL
Oxford UK & Cambridge USA

First published 1995

Blackwell Publishers Ltd
108 Cowley Road
Oxford OX4 1JF

Blackwell Publishers Inc.
238 Main Street
Cambridge, Massachusetts 02142
USA

British Library Cataloguing in Publication Data
A CIP catalogue record for this book is available from the British Library.

Library of Congress Cataloging-in-Publication Data
The Lukács reader / edited by Arpad Kadarkay.
    p. cm.
Includes bibliographical references and index.
ISBN 1-55786-570- 1. ISBN 1-55786-571-X
1. Lukács, György, 1885–1971—Contributions in criticism.
2. Lukács, György, 1885–1971—Aesthetics. 3. Lukács, György, 1885–1971. 4.
Marxist criticism. 5. Aesthetics, Modern—20th century.
        I. Kadarkay, Arpad, 1934- .
    PN75.L8L85 1995
                                                                94–47944
    199'.439–dc20   CIP
Typeset in 11 on 13 pt Plantin by Pure Tech India Ltd, Pondicherry
Printed in Great Britain by Hartnolls Ltd, Bodmin, Cornwall

This book is printed on acid-free paper.

Contents

91899

Preface

The literary career of Georg Lukács (1885–1971) spanned nearly seven decades of twentieth-century European thought, politics and culture. He was not only one of the most important intellectuals of this century, but as a Marxist, rising from the chaos of 'Old Europe' torn by war and revolutions, he became a philosopher of the first Marxist state. He stood at the epicentre of almost every major historical event of the turbulent twentieth century, from the Russian revolution of 1917 to the Hungarian revolution and its aftermath in 1956.

As a philosopher and representative of his own ideals, Lukács took up a position, often as adversary, on all the great events, ideas and personalities of his long and fascinating career. In this selection of his writings, conveniently structured by topic, Arpad Kadarkay presents the breadth and depth of Lukács's thought.

Whether he is putting on a Socratic mask in pursuit of Eros, or analysing the essence of Shakespeare, Ibsen, Wilde or Shaw, Lukács is always thought-provoking and often startling. We see a mind grappling with the fundamental issues of human existence, centred on love and work, striving to extend the boundaries of thought. If we want to gain a deeper understanding of the human condition and consider life at the limits, *vita in extremis*, we should read Lukacs's essays in autobiography.

The *Lukács Reader* is the most comprehensive introduction to Lukács's work yet published in English. The essays chosen encompass every aspect of his thought: his early autobiographical essays, written under the influence of Socrates, Plato and Kierkegaard; his original reflections on Shakespeare, Ford, Strindberg, Ibsen, Wilde and Shaw; his pioneering essays on aesthetics, art and modernism; the rich and subtle essay on 'Class Consciousness' and, finally, his attempt to turn the tables on Nietzsche and Heidegger as he examines their ideas.

Given the vast range of this material, each section has been prefaced by a brief introduction describing the basic issues and the essential background. Editorial intervention has otherwise taken the form of providing extensive explanatory notes at the ends of chapters. All these notes are by the editor unless otherwise indicated.

While working on the *Reader*, I enjoyed the sustained and sustaining support of archivists, librarians, friends and colleagues. I am indebted to the Bodleian Library, the Hungarian Academy of Sciences Library, and the Lukács Archive in Budapest for access to published and unpublished material.

The following colleagues of mine at the University of Puget Sound provided me with stimulus and help: Michael Curley, Mott Greene, David Lupher, Lisa Neil, Ted Taranovski and Mike Veseth.

I wish to thank Lee Congdon, Professor of History, James Madison University, whose friendship and many acts of kindness eased my search for elusive documents. As always, Leszek Kolakowski, whose friendship I enjoyed many summers and many winters, supported my labours. I am most grateful to David Frisby, University of Glasgow, for the rare materials he sent me which proved valuable and helpful. It is a pleasure to thank Martin Jay at the University of California for being a conversation partner and lively correspondent. I am singularly fortunate to benefit from George Steiner's work whose presence in the *Reader*, as well as his correspondence, I gratefully acknowledge. I want also to record my particular gratitude to James McFarlane, Emeritus Professor of European Literature at the University of East Anglia, for reading and commenting on Lukács's essays on Strindberg and Ibsen. Professor McFarlane's monumental work, the eight volumes of *The Oxford Ibsen*, the standard English text of the plays, proved invaluable during my long labours on the *Reader*.

Alison Truefitt is a demon of a copy editor; the flicker of flags fluttering at the right margin of my manuscript, the painstaking scrutiny of every single word, her tough-minded way of correcting slips and offering improvements and felicitous reformulations have left me with a debt that seems impossible to discharge. She earned my admiration and gratitude.

Finally, I should like to thank my editors at Basil Blackwell, Stephan Chambers, John Davey and Andrew McNeillie, for the advice, support and professionalism which they brought to the production of this volume.

Acknowledgements

The editor and the publishers would like to thank the following for permission to include the material collected in this edition: for 'Integrated Civilizations' and 'Class Consciousness', the MIT Press; for 'Ideology of Modernism', HarperCollins Publishers; for 'Friedrich Nietzsche' and 'Martin Heidegger' Humanities Press, for the rest of the material included, in parts I-IV, the Philosophical Institute of the Hungarian Academy of Sciences, Lukács Archive and Library, and Artijus, Agency for Literature and Theatre in Budapest.

The publishers apologize for any errors or omissions in the above list and would be grateful to be notified of any corrections that should be incorporated in the next edition or reprint of this book.

PART I

Essays in Autobiography

Introduction

Essays in Autobiography

The beautiful woman of my mind.

Dante

I have died, but she lives in me.

Lukács

'A youth like mine', Lukács once wrote, 'cannot be forgotten.' The greatest Marxist intellectual of the twentieth century was born in 1885 into a Jewish family of privilege and wealth in Budapest. His father, József Löwinger, a leading banker in the Austro-Hungarian empire, changed the family name to Lukács. Lukács's father, a self-made man with little formal education, showered his precocious son with attention and money. In recognition for his services to the monarchy, Lukács's father was ennobled in 1901 and later became court councillor and a personal friend and adviser of István Tisza, the arch-conservative statesman and prime minister. Lukács himself affixed 'von' to his name and signed himself, up to 1918, as Georg von Lukács.

Despite his gilded youth, Lukács was a born 'radical' and dissenter. To begin with, this took the form, as he put it, of 'unripe' socialism. Brilliant and gifted, Lukács attended the best private school, the Evangelical Gymnasium, in Budapest that attracted many converted Jews like Lukács. In its heyday, the school produced the mathematician and godfather of the computer John von Neumann, the physicist Eugene Wigner, the conductor Antal Doráti and the composer Imre Kalman. Lukács's explosive talent manifested itself early, but it also estranged him from his family. Indeed, his most marked talent, at first, was the staging of 'spontaneous rebellions' against social norms and conventions, including his father's own marriage. Lukács openly resented his father's showing respect for his wife: 'My father had great respect for my mother. I valued my father for his hard work and intelligence. But his high esteem for my mother offended me, and, at times, I despised him for it. In fact, we only developed a close relationship when my father, largely at my urging, became more critical of my mother.'[1]

An extraordinary statement, as was Lukács's deliberate attempt as a Marxist to annihilate and suppress his early development. Leaving Heidelberg in 1916, where he belonged to Max Weber's famed circle, Lukács, in a surge of despair, made a radical departure and returned to Budapest where he joined the newly formed communist party in 1918. But before leaving Heidelberg for good, Lukács packed the evidence of his aesthetic, ethical and erotic experiences, that make up the *Essays in Autobiography*, into a suitcase, and deposited it for safekeeping at the Deutsche Bank of Heidelberg. Discovered after his death (1971), it contained various manuscripts, drafts, notes, letters and diary (*Reader* chapters 2 and 4), and material for an incomplete work on Dostoevsky (*Reader* chapter 15). Lukács considered his earlier life, his pre-Marxist stage, of no value, better buried and forgotten.

But in old age, as death closed in on him, Lukács did remember his youth and, sketching the outline of his biography, he acknowledged that his unhappy love affair with Irma Seidler (1883–1911) touched the 'very centre' of his life. Lukács's autobiographical sketch contains this revealing passage:

> My Kierkegaard phase. It is not without Regine Olsen [the subject of Kierkegaard's unhappy love affair]: Irma Seidler. The *Soul and Form* is dedicated to her memory. She was its inspiration, but without realizing it. Those strict bourgeois conventions: if you break an engagement – you're an outcast. In my case, only marriage could have offered a solution to sexual need. But in my case, there is an absolute and therefore silent rejection [of marriage] for the sake of an independent and productive life.[2]

What Lukács meant by 'conventions' is that he, born to wealth and gifted, was destined to attain greatness. Lukács's intellectual virtuosity did not conceal his near-Olympian disdain for ordinary mortals, including Irma Seidler, to whom he wrote:

> There are those who understand me yet do not live and there are those who live but do not understand me . . . You madam can hardly understand this. And because I sincerely wish you happiness, I am glad you don't understand me, for I can hardly expect from you any spiritual understanding of my spiritual state of the mind.[3]

To attain a spiritual state of the mind, Lukács read widely and was wealthy enough to sample the best of what Europe offered in culture and learning. Disgusted with the chaotic, prosaic and life-denying bourgeois world, he domiciled himself in philosophy and sought refuge in pure spirit. Irma Seidler on the other hand, born into a poor Jewish family, was a struggling artist who barely managed to eke out a living. As Lukács expressed it in a letter to his close friend, 'What shall I do? Imagine, a lovely talented young woman accustomed to hunger. Is it not monstrous? What I can do to help her amounts to nil.' And as was his habit, Lukács modelled his life, even his love, on philosophical precedents. Reflecting on his own relationship with Irma Seidler, Lukács wrote, quoting Socrates, 'Eros is truly the child of wealth and poverty.'[4] Of course the child of wealth – Lukács – could have kept the child of poverty – Irma Seidler – as his mistress or married her. He rejected both categories as bourgeois conventions. A rich man keeping a mistress reminded him of his own father's friends with expensive mistresses set up in villas, and marriage symbolized his own mother whom he hated.

Since Irma Seidler could neither be his mistress nor his wife, he turned her into a philosophical experiment, whose object was to discover himself and the transcendental meaning of life. To the Socratic Lukács (*Reader* chapter 4) Irma symbolized life. The recurring refrain, 'Irma is life', in Lukács's diary (*Reader* chapter 2) is a prelude to tragedy. It is a prelude because Lukács, living a lifeless life of the mind, placed Eros 'in the middle'. Love stood between the philosopher and his work. And so Lukács, having chosen the Socratic path, let Irma Seidler go. By going out of his life, and marrying a fellow artist, she gave Lukács a new loneliness. He had always been lonely, but this was a new loneliness, for it yielded a tragic knowledge: in the erotic struggle between man and woman there are no victors only victims. But in such a tragedy, as Lukács put it in analysing Strindberg (*Reader* chapter 7) 'the light falls on the man and the shadow on the woman.'

Just how Lukács distributes the light and shadow of his own unhappy love affair makes engrossing reading. Here, too, Lukács's effort to create an artwork out of himself, a literary character who is also a philosopher, is influenced by Plato and Kierkegaard. Plato held that the lover is likely in a state of elation and gratified pride to publish the fact that his efforts have not gone unrewarded [*Phaedrus*, 232]. Kierkegaard, taking his cue from Plato, said joy is 'communicative, social, open, wishes to express itself'. Sorrow is reserved, 'silent, solitary, and seeks to return into itself'.[5] Disappointed love prefers to hide in the secret recesses of the soul and therefore cannot be depicted artistically, for it lacks repose, is not at one with itself, does not come to rest in any one definite expression.

Lukács, however, confounded both Plato and Kierkegaard, renowned exponents of the ethics and aesthetics of love, by making public his unrewarded love, under whose dominion he lost the mastery of his proud, Socratic self. Lukács's reflective grief and sorrow, contrary to Kierkegaard, move not inward but outward and become the subject of aesthetic–philosophic portrayal.

Many great minds have entered the dominion of love and, grappling with Eros, have left us masterpieces that make an irreplaceable contribution to our understanding of love and life. Plato's Socrates, discoursing on love's mysteries, has a god-like detachment. We can almost see the ivy in his hair, his crown of violets. But Lukács, who presents himself as a love-sick Socrates, is bereft both of ivy and violets. Reading the self-portrait in the autobiography, it is tempting to think of Lukács as Socrates writing, in violation of his own edict (*Phaedrus*, 275) what it means to Know Thyself when in love.

Following their first infatuating weeks in December 1907, Irma Seidler and Lukács made their obligatory tour of Italy, chaperoned by Lukács's closest friend, the polyglot genius Leo Popper (1886–1911), featured prominently in Lukács's diary. The star-crossed lovers managed to 'kiss in the dark' on the Ponte Vecchio, and heard the 'streets sing' in Florence. No doubt, Popper teased Lukács, the walls also 'danced to Dionysus' and his torch-lit procession of Eros.[6]

Visiting the Uffizi, the two friends discussed Irma's artistic talent and wondered whether the 'inner light' really burned in her. Since Lukács's amorous trip was unknown to his wealthy parents, who were unhappy with Irma's age and background, the lovers returned in separate trains to Budapest. By June 1908, they had quarrelled and Lukács's first autobiographical essay, concealed behind Kierkegaard's unhappy love affair with Regine Olsen, appeared in Hungary's leading literary journal, *Nyugat* [The West] in 1910. In the essay Lukács argues about marriage pro and con, but mostly con. While falling in love has the immediacy of divinity, marriage is based on resolution, which lacks the spontaneity of erotic love.

Falling in love is something simple, but marriage! – marriage is a civic duty, it translates passion into formality, and binds you to the society of ordinary men with common concerns. Instead Lukács, taking his clue from Nietzsche, celebrated the fatal solitude of 'great men' who, despite Eros, remain 'servants and fanatics of their own development'.[7] Lukács faced the seductive possibilities both of Nietzsche, who claimed that none of the great philosophers – Plato, Spinoza, Kant, Schopenhauer – were married because marriage is an obstacle to fulfilment, and Goethe, whose love, as Lukács never failed to point out, gave birth to *Iphigenié*.

The philosopher's 'tragic sorrow' is that his wife never understands what he is talking about. Lukács's essays in *Soul and Form*, inspired by Irma Seidler to whom the book is dedicated, so many pearls of misunderstanding strung on an unconsummated love, illuminated also the fate of lovers who belonged to different 'castes' – a term favoured by Lukács and his circle. Like Goethe's Gretchen in *Faust*, Irma came from the lower strata of society. Her letters to Lukács were sent to the post office, and never to his family villa. Trying to use the language Lukács understood best, Irma, quoting Faust, who courts the spirit as long as it continues to appear, added: 'There is no need to court if we can capture it.' The message was plain: Don't worship me; take me.

Lukács's flirtation with roles in his essays – an ascetic, Faust, a Silenic-featured Socrates – stood in sharp contrast to the assumed uniformity of female nature. Irma's power as a woman, in relation to him, was that of consenting and being captivated by a 'higher man' – more restless than lustful. As long as she was the object of his essays (see Lukács's comments on Ibsen's *When We Dead Awaken, Reader* chapter 8), she could enjoy this power. Her role was to please and be desirable. She was, in essence, an experiment for a philosopher who approached Eros for the conquest of the spirit, not the flesh. As an artist, however, Irma had negated her purpose as a woman. As Kant would say, art is indifferent to its object and cares not whether it pleases or repels. Translated from aesthetics to ethics, this meant that Irma held no interest for Lukács as an object of real sexual desire. Although she awakened Eros in him, Lukács was separated from her by a deep metaphysical chasm.

Even Lukács's friend Popper advised him to get over his Socratic '*Liebe-zum-Gegenteil*' – love in opposition. But to no avail. And poor Irma, who dreamt of marriage, had to read Lukács's essays on the 'higher' eroticism of Socratic souls. Growing irritated with the barren shores of philosophy and, not surprisingly, weary of Lukacs's divinatory excursions into Socratic 'love', Irma in an act of desperation married a fellow artist, Karoly Reti.

Lukács referred to Irma's marriage as a 'bourgeois deformity' and, predictably enough, it ended in divorce. From Florence, Lukács informed Irma that his essays, *Soul and Form*, were to be dedicated to her. Though grateful, she had misgivings about Lukács's attempt to 'fictionalize' their relationship. 'I am afraid that through the dedication', she wrote to Lukács, 'or otherwise, I could be identified.'[8] In April 1911, Béla Balázs (1884–1949), Lukács's spiritual twin and famed librettist of Béla Bartók, visited Lukács in Florence. Through him Lukács forwarded to Irma an inscribed copy of *Soul and Form* and a copy of Charles-Louis Philippe's *Marie Donadieu* (1904), which celebrates truly 'free' – inwardly liberated – erotic love. Balázs, the Don Juan of Budapest, saw the book's joyous endorsement of the erotic as a gateway to paradise on earth. In his view, 'Every man ought to read it to see woman as fate without hating or punishing her for her sins.'[9]

Balázs's return to Budapest bearing Lukács's 'gift' to Irma was a prelude to tragedy. For Lukács, Irma Seidler was merely a 'school for self-recognition'. To Balázs, Irma was a woman and therefore his latest victim. It was May (1911) and she was the 'new woman'. In the words of Don Giovanni:

> tonight she will come
> To my house of pleasure. Hush, I am certain
> I caught a scent of woman here! (Mozart, *Don Giovanni* I iv)

On the day that Irma was to come to Balázs's house of pleasure, he caught the scent of another woman. Let us not forget that Balázs is the author of *Bluebeard's Castle*. It was more than Irma could bear. Having passed through all the stages of unconsummated love with Lukács, a latter day Socrates, Irma, humiliated and shamed by Balázs, committed suicide on 18 May 1911. And so, Irma became a black cross in Lukács's diary with the entry:

> I have forfeited my right to life . . . I still cannot accept her death.

We have translated most of Lukács's diary, containing entries from 25 April 1910 to 24 May 1911. The few entries left out are either excessively obscure or bear no direct relation to the most crisis-ridden period of his life. The translation is based on the Hungarian version of the diary, found in the famous Heidelberg suitcase in 1973.

It was under the shadow of his eternal beloved's death that Lukács, suspended between 'sin and frivolity', found himself in Dante's first ring of hell whose lost souls live with desire, though without hope. It was here that Lukács composed 'On Poverty of Spirit', a philosophical confession of his own responsibility for Irma's death. In this dialogue, Lukács appears as a legitimate son of Kierkegaard. Indeed, 'On Poverty of Spirit' invites close comparison with Kierkegaard's *Fear and Trembling*, on which it was modelled. We can get to the core of Lukács's dialogue by comparing it with Kierkegaard's interpretation of Abraham's trial-and-temptation to sacrifice Isaac. Abraham's willingness to sacrifice Isaac is supposed to be the test of faith. In the end, Abraham does not sacrifice his beloved son. But Lukács did sacrifice Irma Seidler, the eternal beloved of his soul. Whereas Kierkegaard's *Fear and Trembling* is an allegory of religious consciousness,

Lukács's 'On Poverty of Spirit' is the true confession of a philosopher at the gates of hell.

There are other crucial differences between the two works. In *Fear and Trembling*, Abraham must be silent; he cannot speak, for what could he really say to Isaac? By contrast, Lukács, having sacrificed his own love, does speak, and speaks from the hidden depth of his soul as death broods over his words. And when he speaks, standing at the gates of hell, it is worth listening to. Had Lukács chosen to be silent in the deepest crisis of his life, he would have weakened the impact of his writings. Consider Lukács's superhuman effort – overwhelmed by guilt and responsibility – to make himself intelligible to others. Above all to Martha in the dialogue, who is no other than Emma Seidler, the wife of Emil Lederer, a professor at Heidelberg and Max Weber's friend.

No wonder that Max Weber and his wife Marianne, to whom Lukács sent the manuscript 'On Poverty of Spirit', were deeply moved by his 'profoundly artistic' essay on the poor in spirit. The English translation is based on the Hungarian version originally published in Lukács's own journal, *A Szellem* [The Spirit] in December 1911. The essay also appeared in *Neue Blätter* in 1912, where Lukács joined such contributors as Martin Buber, Rudolf Kassner, Soloviev, Yeats and Rilke, whose cycle of poems from *Das Mariannleben* appeared in the same issue, next to Lukács. The joint appearance of Lukács and Rilke in *Neue Blätter* is illuminating. Not only did Lukács greatly admire Rilke, whose poems he and Leo Popper frequently discussed in their letters, but Rilke's poems and Lukács's essays are products of an era when the supersensitive self had either to find redemption or justify a new kind of human existence.

Indeed, Weber himself agreed with Lukács's argument in 'On Poverty of Spirit' that Kantian ethics suffers from 'poverty of spirit' and that bourgeois life, dominated by law and judicial norms, inhibits human intercourse. Lukács was reluctant to place human relations under legal rules, but felt that the ethical code inherent in a system of law should prescribe and substantiate the human communion that would terminate man's 'eternal loneliness'. Kant conceived of law as the expression of the universal moral law, and as a coercive order confined to men's external relations. In contrast, Lukács in 'On Poverty of Spirit' argues that the moral decisions of the inner man cannot find outward expression in legality or the performance of duty. Kantian law, blind to an individual's particular inner moral life, cannot distinguish between tragic responsibility and moral fault. But for Lukács the concept of 'duty' no longer exerted any claim at all. He held that what contingently happens to an agent can force him morally to violate duty.

Lukács agreed with Weber that the sphere of erotic relations is a sphere of such moral conflict. For Lukács and Weber, erotic relations were intimately coercive because the stronger partner, the male, subordinates the less 'brutal partner', as Weber put it, to the mysterious workings of fate. We know from Marianne Weber's biography of her husband Max that he, like his friend Lukács, had in him the amoral hedonism and intellectual superiority to 'ruthlessly' subject others to his ends. We should not be surprised that Weber, who apparently never consummated his marriage with Marianne, took more than an academic interest in Lukács's philosophical confession 'On Poverty of Spirit', a work which delineates Lukács's own sense of guilt for ruthlessly exploiting his love affair with Irma by placing her between the erotic and ascetic spheres of life.

Both Marianne and Max Weber, desperate refugees from the ruins of failed marriage, were hardly indifferent to Lukács's existential confession concerning the 'joyless barrenness' of a man who, caught between a driving compulsion to work and the erotic sphere, leads a tormented personal life.

Not surprisingly, the ethical hero of 'On Poverty of Spirit' shoots himself. This act symbolizes Lukács's own denouement as the agent of Kant's categorical imperative that unequivocally condemned suicide as self-murder. Kant was explicit, 'To destroy the subject of morality in one's person is to root out the existence of morality itself from the world.' But in the midst of his feeling of guilt and his grief Lukács dissented from Kant – erstwhile arbiter of the metaphysics of morals.

NOTES

[1] Lukács, *Curriculum Vitae*, ed. Janos Ambrus (Budapest: Magvetö, 1982), p. 12.

[2] *Ibid.*, p. 18.

[3] Lukács to Irma Seidler, 23 March 1908, Philosophical Institute of the Hungarian Academy of the Sciences, Lukács Archive and Library, Budapest. Hereafter: LAK.

[4] Lukács, *Soul and Form*, tr. Anna Bostock (London: Merlin Press, 1974), p. 93.

[5] Kierkegaard, *Either/Or*, ed. and tr. Howard V. Hong and Edna H. Hong (New Jersey: Princeton University Press, 1987), I, p. 169.

[6] Popper to Lukács, 7 October 1910, LAK.

[7] Lukács, *Soul and Form*, p. 48.

[8] Irma Seidler to Lukács, 8 February 1911, LAK.

[9] Béla Balázs, *Naplo* [Diary] (2 vols, Budapest: Magvetö, 1982), vol. 2, p. 376.

1

Soren Kierkegaard and Regine Olsen

Fair youth, beneath the trees, thou canst not leave
Thy song, nor ever can those trees be bare;
Bold Lover, never, never canst thou kiss,
Though winning near the goal – yet, do not grieve;
She cannot fade, though thou has not thy bliss,
For ever wilt thou love, and she be fair!

Keats Ode on a Grecian Urn

The value of gesture! In other words: the value of form in life, the life-creating, life-enhancing value of forms. A gesture is perhaps only an unambiguous expression of movement, and form is perhaps the absolute's only road in life; the only thing which is self-sufficient, what is real and more than mere possibility.

The gesture alone expresses life – but is it possible to express life? Is not this the tragedy of every art of life, that it wants to build a crystal palace out of air, that it wants to forge realities from the soul's ethereal possibilities? That it wants to construct the bridges of forms, spanning inter-human relations, from the meeting and parting of souls? Are there gestures at all, and has the concept of form any meaning viewed from the perspective of life?

Kierkegaard once said that reality has nothing to do with possibilities, and yet he wagered his whole life on a gesture [of breaking off his engagement to Regine Olsen]. Every piece of his writings, every struggle and adventure of his forms are in some way the back-drop to that gesture, whose function perhaps was to stand out more clearly against the chaotic multiplicity of life. Why did he do it? How could he do it? Of all men, Kierkegaard saw more clearly than anyone else the thousand facets and thousand-fold variability of every motive. He saw with such clarity how every object passes into the other, into its opposite, and what unbridgeable abysses yawn – if we really look closely – between barely discernible transitions. Why did he do it?

Perhaps because gesture is still a primitive life-necessity. Perhaps because a man who wants to be 'honest' (one of Kierkegaard's most frequently used words) must force life to yield up its single meaning. He must seize that ever-changing Proteus so firmly that, unable to move, it will divulge the truth. Perhaps the gesture – to express myself in Kierkegaard's dialectics – is the paradox: the point where reality and possibility, matter and air, the finite and the infinite, form and life intersect. Or to express this more accurately and in Kierkegaard's terminology: the gesture is the leap by which the soul passes from one into the other, and by which, leaving the ever relative facts of life, it reaches the eternal certainty of forms. In short, the gesture is that unique leap by which the absolutes become possible in life. The gesture is the great paradox of life, because only its fixed eternity can contain and turn into reality the evanescent moments of life.

Whoever does more than merely play with life needs the gesture to make his life more real than a Protean game. But can there really be a gesture *vis-à-vis* life? Is it not a self-delusion on the part of everyone – heroically appealing as it may be – to believe that an action, a turning towards something or a turning away constitutes the gesture, which is as solid and self-contained as a statue?

In September 1840, Soren Aaby Kierkegaard, Master of Arts, became engaged to Regine Olsen, State Councillor Olsen's eighteen-year-old daughter. Less than a year later he broke off the engagement. He left for Berlin, and when he returned to Copenhagen he lived there as a noted eccentric. His strange ways made him a constant target for the humourous papers, and although his writings – published under various pen-names[1] – found some admirers on account of their wit, the majority hated their 'immoral' and 'frivolous' contents. His later works made still more open enemies for him. Namely, the whole Protestant Church. It was during his strenous fight with the church, contending that the whole protestant establishment of his time was non-Christian, and indeed destroyed the very possibility of anyone becoming a Christian, that he died.

A few years earlier Regine Olsen had married one of her old admirers.

What really happened here? The number of possible explanations is endless. And the very appearance of Kierkegaard's writings, of his letters and of his diary made the explanations easier and, at the same time, made it harder to understand what really happened, and to comprehend its full significance for Soren Kierkegaard and Regine Olsen and their life.

Kassner – who describes Kierkegaard in unforgettable and unsurpassable terms – discards every explanation. 'Kierkegaard', he writes, 'made a poem of his relationship with Regine Olsen, and when Kierkegaard makes a poem of his life he does so not in order to conceal the truth but in order to be able to reveal it.'

There is no explanation, for what is there is more than an explanation: it is a gesture. Kierkegaard said: I am a melancholic. He said: I was a whole eternity too old for her. He said: my sin is that I dragged her with myself into the great flood. He said:

> If I had not been a penitent, had not had my *vita ante acta*, had not been melancholy, my union with her would have made me happier than I had ever dreamed of being.[2]

He left Regine Olsen and said he did not love her, he never really loved her, he was a man whose fickle spirit required new people and new relationships at every moment. For the most part his writings proclaimed this loudly, and the way he spoke and the way he lived merely served to underscore and confirm Regine Olsen's belief in it.

When Regine married one of her old admirers, Kierkegaard wrote in his diary:

> I saw a pretty girl today – it does not interest me any more – I do not wish it – no husband can be more faithful to his wife than I am to her.[3]

The gesture: to make unambiguous the many causes and consequences of the inexplicable. To depart in such a way that it leaves only sorrow, only tragedy – once their encounter became tragic – or perhaps only a collapse, but no vacillation, no disintegration of every reality into possibility. If Regine Olsen had lost that which seemed to signify life to her, then let her lose the meaning of life; if the one whom Regine Olsen loved had to leave her, let the one who left her be a scoundrel and a seducer, so that, for her, every road towards life would still be clear. And since Kierkegaard had to leave life in the name of penitence, let that penitence grow with the chivalrously worn sinner's mask, which disguises his real sin.

Regine Olsen's marriage was a necessity for Kierkegaard. 'She fully understood the point', he wrote, 'that she had to get married.' She had to, so that there would be no uncertainty, no equivocation, no further 'possibility' in this relationship, only this: the seducer and the jilted girl. The girl consoles herself and finds the way back to life. And the seducer's mask conceals the ascetic, whose asceticism moulded him into a gesture. But the transformation of the girl is unilinear from the beginning, and behind the seducer's fixedly smiling mask, the ascetic's real face is just as fixed. The gesture is pure and expresses everything. 'Kierkegaard made a poem of his life.'

The only essential difference between one life and another is the extent to which it is absolute or merely relative; the extent to which a life's mutually incompatible opposites diverge sharply, and cannot coexist even for a moment, for they preclude each other. The opposites that life-problems are subsumed under – the dichotomies of 'either–or' – truly represent that stage when the roads appear to diverge. Kierkegaard was always saying: I want to be honest. And this honesty could not mean anything less than the duty – in the purest sense – to live a life according to poetic principles; the duty to choose and the duty to travel to the very end of every chosen road at every crossroad.

But when a man looks around he may fail to see roads and cross-roads, or to find any sharply distinct choices anywhere because all things flow into each other and become one. Only when we divert our gaze from something and then much later look at it again, only then do we find that one thing has become another; perhaps not even then. The whole substance of Kierkegaard's philosophy is to find the fixed points in the ceaseless pendulum movements of life, and establish the absolute, qualitative differences among life's chaotic, converging nuances. And, having found certain things to be different, he sought to make them so unambiguous and profoundly different that the interaction between them, the possibility of developing from one to the other could never again efface that which separated them. In so many words, Kierkegaard's honesty entails a paradox. Namely, what-ever has not already grown into a new, organic unity which cancels out all former differences, must remain divided forever. Man must choose among the different things, he must not seek 'middle roads' or 'higher unities' which might resolve the 'merely apparent' contradic-tions. Consequently, there is no system anywhere, for it is not possible to live a system. The system is always a vast palace, whose creator can only withdraw into a modest corner.[4] Life can never fit into the logical system of thought. From this perspective, the starting point for such a system is always arbitrary, it is absolute only in itself, and what it builds, from the perspective of life, is only relative, a mere possibility. Life has no system. In life only the individual and concrete exist. To exist is to be different. The absolute is intransigent, and the individual is unambiguous and concrete. Truth is only subjective – perhaps; but subjectivity is quite certainly truth. The individual thing is the only thing that exists; the individual is the real man. Hence life contains a few typical, fixed spheres of possibilities, or, as Kierkegaard put it, stages: the aesthetic, the ethical, the religious stages. Each is distinct from the other with a sharpness that allows of no nuances, and the connection between each is the miracle, the leap, the sudden meta-morphosis of the entire being of a man.

Kierkegaard's honesty then is the clarity of his ability to draw a sharp distinction between things: the system from life, human being from human being, stage from stage. To see the absolutes in life without any shallow compromises.

But is it not a compromise to see life without compromise? Is not such nailing down of the absolute merely a disguise for the imperative to observe everything. Is not a stage a 'higher unity'? Is not the life-denying system itself a system? Is not the leap merely a sudden transition? Is there not, after all, a rigorous choice involved in every expediency, a compromise concealed in every vehement denial? Can one be 'honest' toward life, and yet still attempt to romanticize life's events?

The inner honesty of Kierkegaard's gesture of breaking his engagement can only be that it was done for Regine Olsen's sake. The letters and diary-entries fully confirm that, had they stayed together, Regine would have been destroyed. Her light hearted laughter would have proved ineffective against the terrifying sadness of his dark melancholy. Eventually, her laughter would have become fainter and its soaring spirit, grown weary and heavy, would have been crushed into the stony ground below. And her sacrifice would have benefited no one. Consequently it was his duty – irrespective of what it cost him from the perspective of human happiness, and human existence – to save Regine Olsen's life.

But the question is whether Regine Olsen's life was the only thing he saved? The question is whether the very thing which, in his view, made it necessary for them to part, formed an essential part of his life? Did he not give up a struggle, a struggle that eventually might have succeeded, against his great melancholy because he loved his melancholy, loved it more than anything else, and couldn't have lived without it? 'My sorrow is my castle,' he once wrote, and elsewhere (to quote one example from the many) he said:

And yet in that melancholy I loved the world, for I loved my melancholy. Everything has helped to heighten the tension of my position, her sufferings, all my exertions, and finally the fact that I was derided has, with the help of God, contributed to my breaking through now, finally, when I am obliged to worry about my livelihood.[5]

Reflecting on Regine and himself, he wrote:

She would have been ruined and presumably she would have wrecked me, too, for I should constantly have had to strain myself trying to raise her up. I was too heavy for her, she too light for me, but either way there is most certainly a risk of overstrain.

There are human beings to whom – for the sake of their greatness – anything which even remotely resembles happiness and sunshine must always be forbidden. Karoline [Schelling] once wrote to Friedrich Schlegel: 'Some thrive under oppression, and Friedrich is one of them – if he were to enjoy the full glory of success even once, it would destroy what is finest in him.' And Robert Browning recaptured this tragedy, Friedrich Schlegel's tragedy, in Chiappino's sad story, who was strong and noble, refined and full of deep feelings, so long as he always remained in the shadow and his life was confined to unhappiness and sterile longing. And when misfortune raised him higher than he ever had hoped in his wild, bitter dreams, he became empty, and the pain of that emptiness – an emptiness that arrived with 'happiness' – his cynical words can barely disguise. (Browning called this disaster a soul's tragedy.)

Perhaps Kierkegaard knew this, perhaps he sensed its truth. Perhaps it was the fury of his great creative instinct, released by the pain he felt immediately after breaking the engagement, which demanded – in advance – this form of outlet. Perhaps something inside him knew that happiness – if it was attainable – would paralyse and make him sterile forever. Perhaps he was afraid that happiness is not unattainable, that Regine's lightness of spirit could have after all redeemed his great melancholy and that both of them might have been happy. But what would have become of him if life deprived him of his unhappiness?[6]

Kierkegaard presented himself as the sentimental Socrates: 'Loving is the only thing I'm an expert in,' he proclaimed. Socrates wanted only to recognize, to understand human beings who loved, and therefore the central problem in Kierkegaard's life presented no problem for Socrates. Kierkegaard said.

> Loving is the only thing I'm an expert in. Just give me an object for my love, only an object. But here I stand like an archer whose bow is stretched to the uttermost limit and who is asked to shoot at a target five paces ahead of him. This I cannot do, says the archer, but put the target two or three hundred paces further away and you will see!

This is similar to Keats's prayer to nature:

> A theme! a theme! great nature! give a theme;
> Let me begin my dream.

To love! Who can be loved in such a way that the object of love would not stand in love's way? Who is strong enough and able to contain everything within himself, so that his love will become absolute and stronger than anything else? Who stands so high above all others that whoever loves him can never make demands on him, never be proved right against him? So that the love by which he is loved will be an absolute one?

To love: try never to be proved right. This is how Kierkegaard described love. For the cause of the enduring relativity of all human relationships, of their fluctuation and its pettiness is that each day someone else is right. Today one thing is better, nobler, and more beautiful, tomorrow the other. There can be constancy and clarity only if the lovers are qualitatively different from one other, if one stands so high above the other that the question of right and wrong – in the broadest sense – can never be posed, even as a question.

This expresses the ascetic medieval knights' notion of ideal love, but it is more romantic here than it ever was. Kierkegaard's keen psychological insight strips away the knights' naive faith – naive compared to his own – to reveal that the beloved woman whom the troubadours renounced in order to idealize her (or even an idealized woman) could never and nowhere have a dream image strong enough and distinct enough from reality to become an object of their absolute love. In my view, the root of Kierkegaard's religiosity is this. God can be loved in such way; no one else but God. He once wrote that God is the postulate that we hang on to by necessity in order to endure life. Yes, but Kierkegaard's God is enthroned so high above everything human, is separated from everything human by such a deep chasm – how could he help man to endure his life? My feeling is that God helped Kierkegaard in this way. Kierkegaard needed the absoluteness of life, its undisputed stability, and the opportunity to spread his all embracing love. He needed a love devoid of problems, a love in which it was not now the one, now the other that was better, now the other that was right. The only certainty and unambiguity is that man is never right, and God alone can give me this assurance. 'You love a man', he wrote, 'and you want always to be proved wrong against him, but, alas, he has been unfaithful to you, and however much this may pain you, you are still in the right against him and wrong to love him so deeply.' The soul turns to God because it cannot exist without love, and God gives everything to the lover his heart desires. 'Never shall tormenting doubts pull me away from him, never shall the thought appeal to me that I might prove right against him; before God I can never be right.'

Kierkegaard was a troubadour and a Platonist, and he was both these things romantically and sentimentally. Deep down in his soul there burn sacrificial flames for the ideal woman – and the same flames burn at the stake to which the same woman is condemned. When man stood face to face with the world for the first time, everything was his that surrounded him, and yet each separate thing vanished before his eyes and every step led him past each separate thing. He would have starved to death, tragically, absurdly, in the midst of all the world's riches, had there been no woman, who at the very first moment knew how to grasp things and recognized their use and immediate significance. And the woman saved man for life – in the sense of Kierkegaard's parable – but only in order to confine him to life, to chain him to its finiteness. The real woman, the mother, is the most profound opposite of any longing for infinity. Socrates married and was happy with Xanthippe only because he considered marriage as an obstacle on the way to the Ideal, and he rejoiced at overcoming difficulties. Socrates' joy recalls Suso's God saying: 'You have always found obstacles in all things; and that is the sign of my chosen one, whom I want to have for myself.'

Kierkegaard did not accept this challenge. Perhaps he backed away from it, perhaps he no longer needed it. Who knows? For the world of human communion, the ethical world (whose typical form is marriage) stands between two worlds that are close to Kierkegaard's soul: the world of pure poetry and the world of pure faith. And if the foundation of his ethical life, 'duty', appears firm and secure compared with the 'possibilities' of poet's life, still his poetic judgements, though forever fluctuating, contain permanent values close to his absolute religious feelings. But the substance of his religious certainties is just as imaginary as is the substance of his poetic possibilities – where then is the dividing line between the two?

But it hardly matters. At least it hardly matters here. For Kierkegaard, Regine Olsen was no more than a step on his way to the icy temple of nothing-but-the-love-of-God. That he felt guilty towards her only deepened his relationship with God; that he loved her through suffering and caused her suffering only helped him to intensify his ecstasies and channel them.[7] Everything that would have stood between them, if they really wanted to belong to each other, gave wings to his flight. 'I thank you for never having understood me,' he wrote to her in a letter which he never sent, 'for it taught me everything. I thank you for being so passionately unjust towards me, for that determined my life.'

For Kierkegaard, even the jilted one, the ideally unattainable Regine Olsen could only be a step towards his goal. But it was the safest step leading to the heights. Reminiscent of the Provençal troubadours' Woman, glorifying poetry, Kierkegaard's great faithlessness served as a base for his great faithfulness. The woman had to belong to another in order to be idealized and loved with real love. But Kierkegaard's faithfulness went deeper than the troubadours', and consequently it was more faithless. Because even the most beloved woman was but a road towards the great, the only absolute love, the love of God.[8]

Whatever may have been the reasons for what he did, Kierkegaard acted only to save Regine Olsen for life. The gesture of rejection, irrespective of its inner meanings, outwardly – in Regine Olsen's eyes – had to be unequivocal. Kierkegaard believed that Regine only faced one great danger: uncertainty. Since Regine's life could not grow out of her love for him, he had to strive with all his power – sacrificing his good name – to incur her permanent hatred. He wanted Regine to consider him as a scoundrel and her whole family to despise him as an infamous seducer. For if Regine hated him, she was saved.

But the engagement was broken suddenly, although foreshadowed by long and violent scenes. Now Regine was obliged to see a different man in Kierkegaard than she had previously known. She had to re-evaluate every minute, every word, and every silence of their to-getherness if she was to feel that the new and old Kierkegaard were connected, that they were one and same. From that moment on-wards, she had to see whatever he might do in a new light. Kierke-gaard did everything to make it easier for her to channel the flood of newly formed images in a single direction. In the direction he wanted, the only one he considered proper for Regine: the channelling of hate against himself.

This is the background, swathed in the light of life, of Kierkegaard's erotic writings, especially 'The Seducer's Diary'.[9] Prominent features of these writings are an incorporeal sensuality and a wearisome, programmatic ruthlessness. The erotic life, the beautiful life, a life given to pleasure appear as a world view – and no more than that. It seems that Kierkegaard only sensed inwardly the possibilities inherent in world views, which neither his subtle reasoning nor his analysis could render corporeal. The seducer's chance, the seducer *in abstracto* as it were, needs only the chance for seduction, only a situation which he created and enjoyed; he does not really need women as objects of pleasure. He embodies the Platonic idea of the seducer, who is a seducer in such a profound sense that he almost ceases to be one. A man so remote from others, so far above all human thought, that what he desires from them is no longer their concern, or if it is, it erupts into their life like an incomprehensible natural disaster. The absolute seducer, who invokes in every woman he approaches an anxious sense of the eternally strange, yet who (Kierkegaard was unable to see this side of the seducer), precisely because he is so infinitely remote, borders on the comic in the eyes of every woman who is not destroyed when he looms on the horizon of her life.

As we have already said, Kierkegaard's gesture towards Regine Olsen was that of a seducer. But Kierkegaard also possessed the real potential of a seducer, and the gesture always reacts back upon the soul that directed it. There are no empty comedies in life: this is perhaps the saddest ambiguity of human relationships. One cannot just play. One can play only with what is there, and one cannot play at anything without it somehow becoming an integral part of real life, a life from which one anxiously, carefully wants to remove play.

Regine, of course, could only see the gesture. Under its impact – at least that's what Kierkegaard wanted and wagered everything on it – she had to retranslate everything in her life into its opposite. But something that has been lived physically can, at most, only be poisoned by the realization that it was but a game. In fact, one can never completely and unequivocally re-evaluate anything. One can only re-evaluate opinions about things and their values. For what Regine lived through with Kierkegaard was life, a living reality. And this reality could only be shaken and inescapably confounded in retrospect by the arbitrary re-evaluation of motives. For if the present forced Regine to see Kierkegaard in a different light, then this way of seeing him was a sensual reality only for the present. The reality of the past spoke in a different voice, and refused to be silenced by the fainter voice of her new knowledge.

Soon after breaking off the engagement, Kierkegaard wrote to Emil Boesen, his only close friend. If Regine knew, he wrote, with what anxious care he had arranged everything and executed it, once he had decided they had to part, she would recognize his love for her in his careful preparation.[10] We know little about Regine's life, but we know that she sensed this. After Kierkegaard's death, she read his posthumous writing and wrote to his nephew Dr Henrik Lund:

> These writings shed a new light on our relationship. It is a light in which I too saw it sometimes; but . . . my modesty forbade me to think that it was the true light, and yet my unshakable faith in him made me see it like that again and again.

Kierkegaard himself felt something of this ambiguity. He felt that his gesture remained, after all, a mere possibility in Regine's eyes, just as Regine's gesture had in his own eyes. The gesture proved insufficient to create a solid reality between them. If there was a road to the real truth, it could only have been the road to Regine. However, any attempt to travel that road would have destroyed everything that he had accomplished so far. He had to remain uncertain inwardly and immobile outwardly, for what if everything was settled in her already, in which case his gesture of moving towards her would intrude on a living reality. The doubt remained. Ten years after breaking off the engagement he still did not dare to meet her. What if her whole marriage was only a mask, and she loved him as before? A meeting would have destroyed everything.

It is impossible to maintain the rigid certainty of one's gesture – if indeed it ever has a real certainty at all. Much as one may want to, one cannot disguise forever as play, so deep a melancholy as that of Kierkegaard, or continue the disguise for any length of time. Nor can such passionate love as that of Kierkegaard ever masquerade as faithlessness. Yes, the gesture reacts back upon the soul, but the soul in turn reacts upon the gesture which seeks to hide it. The soul shines forth from that gesture and neither of the two, neither gesture nor soul, is capable of remaining hard and pure and separate from the other throughout a lifetime.

The only thing which the outward purity of a gesture can produce is that an individual, having abandoned his own unambiguous stand, will inevitably misunderstand the actions of the other. Consequently, chance movements, innocent remarks and careless words acquire life-determining significance; and the gesture's life-awakening reflex is still strong enough to return to its original stance. When they parted, Regine asked Kierkegaard, almost childishly between tearful pleas and questions, whether he would still think of her from time to time – and this question became the leitmotif of Kierkegaard's whole life.[11] And when she became engaged, she greeted him in the street, expecting approval. But it triggered quite another train of thought in the unsuspecting Kierkegaard. Unable to bear the weight of his mask, Kierkegaard thought that the time had arrived, the wounds being healed, for mutual explanations. However Regine, in agreement with her husband, returned his unopened letter with the certainty of a gesture that ensured every question remained uncertain for ever more. Moreover, this uncertainty became her question. Once Kierkegaard was dead, she would also grieve deeply over the uncertainty brought on by the absence of clearly spoken words. Whether they actually met or not, it produced the same inadequacy: an abrupt dislocation following the gesture and then a forced return to uncertainty on the one hand, and the failure to understand both on the other.

Where psychology begins, monumentality ends: perfect clarity is only a modest expression of a striving for monumentality. Where psychology begins, there are no more deeds but only motives for deeds; and whatever requires explanation, whatever can bear explanation, has already ceased to be solid and clear. Even if something remains under the pile of debris, the flood of explanations will inexorably wash it away. For nothing is more inconstant in the world than causes and their explanations. Whatever exists for any reason may have been its opposite for other reasons, or, under slightly different circumstances, for the same reason. Even when the reasons remain the same – but they never do – they can never be constant. Because what seemed to sweep the whole world away in a moment of great passion becomes ridiculously small once the storm is over and, conversely, what was once negligible becomes gigantic in the light of later knowledge.

The kingdoms of Lilliput and Brobdingnag, with their continual shifts of life dominated by motives, are one of the most submerged and the most vanishing of all kingdoms because they belong to the soul's domain, the insubstantial realm of psychology. Once psychology assumes a role in life, it puts an end to gestures that encompass life and life situations. The gesture is unambiguous only as long as every psychological explanation of human behaviour remains fixed.

Here poetry and life part with a tragic, decisive finality. The psychology of poetry is always unambiguous, for it is always an *ad hoc* psychology; even if it appears to spread out in several directions, its multiplicity is always unambiguous, and it merely imparts more complexity to the balance of the final unity. But in life nothing is unambiguous. In life there is no *ad hoc* psychology. Because in life it is not only motives which have been adopted for the sake of unity that play a role, and not every note that has once been struck must necessarily resonate to the end. In life, psychology cannot be conventional. But in poetry, it always is – however subtle and complex the convention. In life, only a hopelessly limited mind can believe in the unambiguous. In poetry, only the completely failed work can be ambiguous in this sense.

This is why, of all the lives, the poet's life is the most profoundly unpoetic, the most profoundly empty of profile and gesture. (Keats was the first to see this.) That which gives life to life becomes conscious in the poet. In a real poet there can be no limitation against life, nor can he entertain any illusions about his own life. Consequently, life is only a raw material for the poet. Only his strong, spontaneous hands can knead something unambiguous from the chaos, create symbols from incorporeal phenomena, and give form (draw the boundary and give meaning) to the boundless and the fluid. That is why a poet's own life can never serve as the raw material to which he will give form.

Kierkegaard's heroism was that he wanted to create forms from life. His honesty was that he saw the crossroads and journeyed to the end of the road he had chosen. His tragedy was that he wanted to live what cannot be lived. 'I am struggling in vain,' he wrote, 'I am losing the ground under my feet. My life will, after all, have been a poet's life and no more.'[12] The poet's life has no meaning and value because it is never absolute, never a thing in itself and for itself. A poet's life is always defined in relation to something, and this relation is meaningless and yet it completely consumes his life – for a moment at least; but then life is made up of nothing but such moments.

It is against this necessity that Kierkegaard's boundless life waged its majestically limited struggle. And life – it could be said cunningly – gave him everything that could be given, and all that he could ask for. Yet life's every gift was mere deception. After all, life could never give him reality; it could only lure him deeper and deeper, with the mirage of victory and success – like Napoleon in Russia – into the all-devouring desert.

His heroism did achieve the appearance of victory and success. He fought for it in life as in death. He lived in such a way that every moment of his life enclosed a statue-like, solid gesture maintained to the end. And he died in such a way that death came at the right time, exactly when and how he wanted it. When we look at it closely, we know how confident was his most confident gesture. And even if death overtook him at the climax of his most real, most profound struggle, just as he wanted it, so that, dying, he could be a martyr to his own struggle, yet he could not stand witness to his own mortality. For, despite everything, his death pointed at several possibilities. In life, everything points to different possibilities, and only *post facto* realities can exclude a few possibilities (never all of them, with the exception of one reality). But even these few possibilities open the way to a million new ones.

He was fighting the Christians of his time when death overtook him. He stood in the midst of a violent struggle. He had nothing to seek in life outside that struggle, and he could no longer intensify his struggle. (Some incidental factors made his death fateful also. Kierkegaard had lived off his capital all his life. Reminiscent of the Middle Ages, he considered interest a usury. When he died, his fortune was just running out.) When he collapsed in the street and they took him to hospital, he said he wanted to die because the cause he served needed his death.[13]

Thus, he died. But his death left every question open. Where would the path have led that came to an end at his tombstone? Where was he going when he encountered death? An inner need for death is only one among an endless series of possible explanations. And if his death did not come in answer to an inner and final call, then we cannot view the end of his path as an end, and must try to imagine its further meandering. Then Kierkegaard's death acquires a thousand meanings, becomes accidental and devoid of destiny. And then Kierkegaard's purest and most unambiguous gesture of his life – vain effort! – was not a gesture after all.

NOTES

1 Kierkegaard's sustained use of pseudonyms compounds the problem of establishing his own views on any given issue. Kierkegaard's authorship therefore must be studied in conjunction with his fascinating and enigmatic persona. He predicted that the time will come 'when not only my writings but my whole life, the intriguing secret of the whole machinery, will be studied and studied'. Gregor Malantschuk, *Kierkegaard's Thought*, ed. and tr. by Howard V. Hong and Edna H. Hong (Princeton University Press, 1971), p. 4.

2 *The Journals of Kierkegaard*, tr. Alexander Dru (Harper and Row, 1958), pp. 71–2.

3 *Ibid.*, p. 77.

4 As Kierkegaard once put it:

In relation to their systems most systematizers are like a man who builds an enormous castle and lives in a shack close by; they do not live in their own enormous systematic buildings. But spiritually that is a decisive objection. Spiritually speaking a man's thought must be the building in which he lives – otherwise everything is topsy-turvy. *Journals*, p. 98.

5 *Journals*, p. 138.

6 Kierkegaard boasted of not lacking anything because, as he put it with his inimitable irony, 'I was unhappy in my love; but I simply cannot imagine myself happy unless I were to become a different person altogether.' *Journals*, p. 144.

7 Reflecting on his unhappy love, Kierkegaard wrote: 'So I have chosen the religious. This is closest to me; my faith is in it. So leave loveliness in abeyance; let heaven keep it for her.' 'Guilty? / Not Guilty?' in *Stages on Life's Way*, ed. and tr. by Howard V. Hong and Edna H. Hong (Princeton University Press, 1988), p. 222.

8 Kierkegaard stated explicitly: 'My engagement to her and the break are really my relation to God; they are, if I may say so, divinely speaking, my engagement with God.' *Journals*, p. 224.

9 The 'Seducer's Diary' in *Either/Or*, part I, was part of Kierkegaard's plan to make it easier for Regine to part with him by giving her the idea that in her case

Kierkegaard was a seducer. The diary was, in fact, intended to repel. As Kierkegaard put it in *Fear and Trembling*: 'When the child is to be weaned the mother blackens her breast, for it would be a shame were the breast to look pleasing when the child is not to have it.' *Fear and Trembling*, tr. Alastair Hannay (Penguin, 1985), p. 46.

[10] Kierkegaard's conduct toward Regine met with unanimous condemnation, which gave him the purely intellectual satisfaction of seeing that he had achieved his aim of playing the role of a scoundrel. 'In the unanimous judgement which the town [Copenhagen] has passed on me, I have the proof that I have acted rightly.' Johannes Hohlenberg, *Soren Kierkegaard* (Routledge & Kegan Paul, 1954), p. 110.

[11] Kierkegaard recorded Regine Olsen's reaction when informed of his cruel decision: 'She said, "Forgive me for the pain I have caused you." I answered: "It is for me to ask for forgiveness." She said: "Promise to think of me." I did so. "Kiss me," she said. I did so but without passion. Merciful God.!' *Journals*, p. 73.

[12] *Journals*, p. 217.

[13] In a journal entry of 1851, Kierkegaard had written: 'To die is nothing but the corollary of a man's life. It is not something that happens from outside, but is part of one's life.'

Or as Ibsen's hero Peer Gynt put it, 'One does not die in the middle of the fifth act.' *Peer Gynt*, Act V.

2

Diary
(1910–1911)

O mon âme, le soir est triste sur hier,
O mon âme, le soir est morne sur demain,
O mon âme, le soir est grave sur toi même!
[Oh my soul, the evening weeps for yesterday
Oh my soul, the evening mourns for tomorrow
Oh my soul, the evening grieves even for you]

25 April 1910, at night
. . . How strange and exciting to begin a diary (even in my current state it affects me). There are questions and suggestions: who among my old friends will reappear? What new names will make me fill these terrifying white pages with my blood?

All this sounds childish. I know what will happen – nothing. The whole thing amounted to a moment. Perhaps it was the empty diary that excited me. How beautiful it would be if it contained nothing; if I had died. How little energy I could muster against my sickness; perhaps none. I would go to sleep, that could release my old energies. One thing is certain (discussed it with Ferenc Baumgarten[1] a lot lately): we are waiting for a miracle. I used to be able to conjure up miracles, or just envision miracles? Not any more. Therefore nothing comes and nothing happens, only gradual degeneration and destruction. So ends every song that man sings.

27 April
Things got a bit brighter. At least I am involved in my work. But it appears somewhat haphazard. It might not be a problem. Provided I ignore that by next spring or autumn something definitely must happen, then of course there is no problem. The things I want to do now I will need one day. To reach my goal quickly, who says this is essential?[2] This of course means Budapest. There my drama book[3] would enable me to qualify, while here [Berlin] I need something else. But this must not become the decisive question. For the subsequent dangers are greater than

the gains. I have already shown impatience with [Georg] Simmel,[4] which may have led to a *Haltung*. Most likely it destroyed the whole relationship. (At least that's my impression. Incidentally, not a big problem.) In short, the usual quiet pace and indifference. Something is bound to happen one of these days. A letter from Leo [Popper].[5]

. . . How deep and correct is his insight about me. The Irma affair;[6] how she helps me, and I must not leave her. Have I ever left her? Doesn't this diary, although its mood and perspective differ from what Leo assumes, start with her? And that now (and in Budapest) I believed it was over, what does it prove? And yet, I must dedicate the German essays [*Soul and Form*] to her.

Need patience and humility for work. Right now I lack both. Would like to see something – something tangible, a 'result'. But even when all goes well – it requires years of waiting. To know how to wait, that's what I lack right now.

In the evening, Irma – 'the woman'. I feel she is gone. I don't want her, she neither affects nor appeals to me. One thing remains: 'the woman', the redeemer, the helper, the companion, the mate, the one destined for me. (I doubt I am destined for her.) The problem: I only think of her. She could help me, or, at least, it might help things if I told her about my sorrows. There is nothing else. Everything is going bad. I don't want anyone, for no one can help me, only she. *La bella donna della mia mente* [The beautiful woman of my mind].

28 April
A glimmer of hope. 'The ice age' has begun. I have died, but perhaps works will follow. At least it appears so. I have died, but there is nothing to it. Strangest of all, I have died, but she lives in me, as far as anything can live in me . . .

3 May
. . . Overestimating people, it seems to me, is one of the most frivolous things imaginable in my technique of life (just as my 'compassion' and 'non-interference' are the most brutal and cause the greatest pain). For who can be overestimated and by whom? The question is, should it be done at all? Must we not anxiously examine every 'understanding' for whether it is really an understanding, and every 'love' for whether it is love? And not only this. One must not be loved by one who doesn't deserve to be loved. In other words, only someone special should be overestimated. Only the greatest man is free to do it; who discards thousand of things, for which he has no time or use anyway. Let others find use for it. The distance between him and 'others' is so great that it appears comic when they borrow or copy

something from him. I do not possess such richness and my frivolity is that I make public those things that are also important to me, and abet those who skilfully steal it from me. The problem is not in the fact, but in the possibility that it has happened to me and can happen again. Prodigality denotes distinction. But to let oneself be robbed and cheated: a sucker.

8 May

I felt it, once again at night, Irma is life. I recalled a Margaret Island [on the Danube in Budapest] excursion. Silly little things, plays, guessing-games, who resembles what (fondly recalled that she compared me to a Biedermeier clock, and how silly was my characterization of her). And I remembered this was for the first and last time in my life. How 'serious' things were with Hilda [Bauer],[7] whose 'seriousness' I have never really valued. Unless there is contact, for contact is everything and everything is contact, nothing really happens. The nothingness of 'spiritual community'; and the nothingness of man in 'love'. Herein lies productivity and freedom: to be together . . . All is in vain! Only she exists. Even if I no longer 'love' her, desire her, and no longer want her back. No matter. For recalling an episode with her means more than a life spent with someone else.

11 May

The cause of my débâcle is that I'm weaker as a man than as a 'scholar'. I need something, need human beings, indeed, human warmth. My own 'warmth' is so unyielding (my talk is fluent and achieves superficial intimacy with people) that it is virtually impossible to acquire it. I miss this warmth. It is untrue what I have been saying over the years: that I don't need anyone, and that one can live anywhere. I doubt that I could. In other words, the question is whether my feeling miserable can stimulate my productivity? I am afraid not. With this the final judgement is pronounced. There is one thing I don't understand though, why did I find Baumgarten and Popper being here a burden? Why didn't I feel bad when they left? In fact, deep down, I was glad. As a matter of fact, I miss them. Not any specific human being, but the human warmth. It appears, I am so cynical that it could be anyone. But I lack something required for this someone to appear. It is quite immaterial, not only metaphysically but empirically, where and with whom I live. As things stand right now, metaphysically, I am absolutely faithless, homeless, etc. In reality, I am faithful and earthbound. At this point – for man affects the human context by the metaphysical essence of his being (rightly said: *ens realissimum*) – everybody treats me as if I was faithless. While (in reality!) I am like a faithful and unfortunate lover. It was with Irma that all this became all too evident.

At night

'Everything is in order.' There is lightning. A storm is brewing. What a good science physiology is! Everything is solved now. May was my bad month; the summer heat is never good for me, suffer from headaches, and so on. Nowadays, before the storm breaks, I'm always in a nervous state and have headaches. The storm has arrived. Everything is in order, it will wash away all of my reflections. It would be lovely, if only physiology was not so limited in its explanation. I recall Ignotus's[8] recent remark that in my Novalis essay there is no reference to his tuberculosis. I didn't want to answer him that it is either there or it is not. In a symbolic portrait there are no causes. If Novalis's optimism is that of a man with tuberculosis, then this tuberculosis is part of his '*intelligiblen Ich*', which I have portrayed (in short, as if it was non-existent). It is proper that I should judge myself the same way as I judge Novalis.[9]

The question is whether there isn't some frivolity (an empirical frivolity of laziness caused by transcendental pessimism) in transforming every psychological phenomenon into symbols? After all, there are excesses; and there are 'moods'. But ethics commands[10] us to live (if only potentially) in the highest moral sphere, that is, in the infinitely intensified sphere, irrespective of our 'momentary moods' even if they last for years. Metaphysically, only the moral sphere constitutes the essence of life (*das Ich an sich*), and the mood is merely a phenomenon. This is so even when mere moments constitute our true life. The possibility [of true life] – the unique actualization of a possibility, says Eckhart[11] – means its everlasting reality. Metaphysically, time does not exist. The moment when I am I is truly life, the total life. And yet the 'moods' that permeate the 'whole life' are only 'momentary' . . .

14 May

Is there a greater lie than to 'close' something and is there anything more open and ambivalent than a closed door? Isn't the only 'honest' road of life to let things pass away and then bury the dead? But who is the living and who is the dead? And how often are those who are frequently buried being resurrected?

Once again I find it a weakness the way I have brought things to a 'close' with Irma in Budapest. Weakness because I am still waiting for something (and it won't 'settle' things for her either). What if there was a beautiful 'settlement' and 'parting' of our ways? Very likely it would come to the same. But in the general sense of the term, 'everything is over between us'. Yes, between us. But from me to her: no. And from her to me, who knows?

15 May

Once again, I feel that light is breaking through. Once again, I started to trust myself. But this trust (if I carefully analyse its causes) should give me the greatest mistrust. A very deep one. Why did my mood change? Because I'm writing; because it is going well. Because I've proved to myself that I have talent. However, isn't it a sign of weakness that this needs to be proved? Is it not my deepest human baseness – noted for a long time – that my deeds turn me into something, even before my own eyes. I am the one who did this and that, or thought of this or that. Instead of, this is my deed and therefore it is important because it expresses me perfectly and powerfully. I do not possess a truly self-sufficient and self-evident greatness; it always needs a proof. This is why Leo's feelings toward me and Karli [Karl Polányi][12] are so profoundly right (quite independently of how much he overestimates Karli, and also independent of the reality of his insight). Namely, that Leo believes in Karli, that his faith in Karli is *a priori*; while his faith in me is only *posteriori* faith. In short, while the first needs no effective verification through deeds, the second by contrast does.

23 May

I have come to the cold conclusion – and this coldness is not only subjectively sad, namely, that I will remain cold, but also objectively, for it makes plausible the truth of the statement – that I am regressing. Not only do I hardly show any development, but I am weaker than I ever was. When I think of the great, irresistible momentum I possessed at the time when I met Irma, I feel a strong, profound shame. I have grown weaker. Its key sign is: I need something that is solid, need the appearance of books, I need a doctorate. And the external things are always determined by internal causes. This is precisely why I am denied external success. Until now, my sole power resided in the fact that the people felt I didn't want power. As soon as they discover the truth, and I am afraid such things are quickly discovered, all my external possibilities will cease. And the external and internal things interact in such a complex way that, I am afraid, an external defeat may lead to an internal débâcle . . .

29 May

A bit of inner productivity, it makes me feel good and the need for no one. The statement is important: I need no one. It would be good, if there was someone – but who? Someone who is strong enough to serve as a mirror (and prevent the penetration of sunlight), but remain only a mirror. I see it ever more clearly that very strong and interesting intellectuals (Simmel, Ernst Bloch[13]) offer me almost nothing. I develop not through struggles, but like plants. This is not an evaluation, but a fact. As I am, so must I live.

But something else is important. How did it happen that such compassionate, flexible and agile intellectuals as Irma and Leo (whom I see in this light, and, I think, correctly), who so readily respond to the tone I strike, proved so useful to me? I believe it was because they were strong enough to feel what I thought, but not strong enough, once they started out with me, to strike out in any other direction. On the other hand, their spiritual life is more sensitive and alert than mine. Consequently, they have found things in my sphere of thought, or made me find it, for which – in essence – my asensual, asexual, rationalist experience proved inadequate. This is why everything in our relationship was so productive. And why it was so sterile with others.

It's only now that I understand why my love is so endlessly selfish. For I wanted to protect Irma's personality against *myself*. I desired her as she was. I would have been the loser if she lost her personality by adjusting it to mine. This of course was so unconscious that I only realized it when I declared that I don't need anyone. Of course she could help me if she was here. She could help me because I would talk to her. I could talk to her, but not to others. It is undeniable, I have no need for what the other person says. I only need human beings (and in the light of the above there are few of them) with whom I could talk. In this respect, Paul Ernst[14] is interesting – if indeed we are in the same sphere.

At night, while working
Noticed a strange thing about myself. One of my earlier statements seemed to me quite impossible, and then – almost inaudibly – I muttered to myself: 'yet there must be something in it for I have said it.'

Incidentally, the Ernst essay[15] will also be an Irma essay. Not only because of the '*Begrenzung*' problem in the completed *Brunhild* drama, but because it developed only from my relationship to her; almost from points that had nothing to do with her, points which I would have become aware of through other things. (Curiously enough, these things also become conscious through her.) All this I only realized later on. Interestingly, one evening I started to think of my ambivalent attitude to what she did to me. I feel that, deep down, her deeds have none the less humiliated her. She has besmirched herself, and I too see her as besmirched. But even if we could get together – in 'life' – it would not change anything. The trivial interpretation, to forgive 'and still' love, has no place here. For there is indeed a difference between 'the' life and 'life'. 'The life' washes away everything; the time, the development, the moments. And, despite everything else, 'life' can bring and keep together human beings, who (discounting the discountable) are empirically destined for each other. But 'the' life never 'discounts' anything. It is beyond time and space. There is no forgetting, no forgiveness, no sentiment. In 'the' life essences make contact with essences.

Therefore it is a weakness – but a necessary weakness – on my part to be able to 'forgive' her. Although, I still believe there are strong human beings. As I thought about it, I understood the basic differences between the epic and dramatic forms, around which the Ernst essay will revolve. Hence the whole abstract metaphysics of form will bring me back to the very centre of things: Irma . . . She is the centre of everything, she is the source of everything. Everything had to be what it was, and she had to do what she did, and I have to accept it 'as it is'. I have to see her as a saint in order to value my own life. I have realized all this only now. Earlier I thought: I should condemn her, but was unable to do it. Now the question is whether, strangely enough, an incorrect analysis of an experience became a good, formal analysis, or whether there is, after all, a profounder concept of the world than the dramatic–tragic? Perhaps the religious one? I don't know.

June 1

I still feel that great problems cast their shadows. Perhaps because the last two days I haven't done any decent work. But it hardly matters. After all, what kind of life is that which needs constant and unceasing work-ecstasies in order to 'feel good'. In short, not to think about the real things – to forget everything: what? (I think I have a pretty good idea what.)

I believe that if work can accomplish everything, externally and internally, then? What is accomplished then? Isn't my whole life – in its totality – revolving about its growing purification, its constant elevation, so that one fine day its total emptiness and triviality will stand before me stark naked: the tragedy. I feel it coming. Perhaps never felt it so powerfully as now. (Last year, great pain concealed it. Always had to feel, yes, if these things didn't happen, then perhaps . . .)

Now there is nothing. Most likely, things will get 'better'. I have the feeling that the final reckoning is near. And then? Then I think will shoot myself in the head. I feel it is a sign that I possess the energy to buy a revolver through Otto.[16] (Last year, how often I wanted to buy it through Edith [Hajós][17] or Iván Csorba?[18] (But never said a word to them.) Now this thing [acquiring a revolver], having discussed it, is decided.

But what then? Who knows? It must be terrible to survive a collapse; one really slides downward, irrevocably and totally.

I have a vague feeling that Irma will have something to do with the end. Although, she has nothing to do with the current situation and the climax of the whole thing. Perhaps only this. Because of her, I know there are essential things in the world; and that my world and what I can achieve are not essential. Still, she was but an occasion for me, and such things can never be concealed forever. Sooner or later, it would have burst open when it touched an essential thing. Ultimately, though things turned out this way, I must be grateful to her, and I am, for making me realize it. Otherwise, it is quite conceivable, I might have lived my life 'as a scholar' without ever being aware of it . . .

I think something like this will happen. In the autumn we shall meet in Florence. Or, she will write me one day, and . . .

We shall see. Until then? Work, as if I was at least seventy, as if there was nothing else in the world than to write a few essays, and a few books.

19 June

My coldness has already spread outward. Edith felt it first, and now Hilda. Pretty soon everyone will detach themselves from me, and –? And it makes no difference. Either I endure and do good things; then everything is fine. Or I won't endure, and then everything is fine, too.

The crisis time – of losing real, living human beings – has now arrived. The symptom of the crisis is that I am full of unreal human possibilities. The real human beings have already drifted away from me. I am waiting for some miracle, a miracle to bring me the unreachable, the impossible. That it is connected with Irma – that's almost accidental. With her I still had human experiences, and, among these experiences, she was by far the strongest. Thus she will symbolize my becoming of a value to someone and vice versa . . .

To expect a miracle is always the sign of crisis. As long as there is no difficulty, one can call for a miracle. Then it arrives. But the expected miracle is always impossible.

Then what?

No sooner did I write this down, than I analysed the reasons for my tone; my bad mood almost bordered on the suicidal. This however is only an evaluation of the frame of the mind. Whereas the tone, as one describes it, and the gesture, through which one approaches things, these are the objective reality. The reason therefore for my foul mood is that since yesterday I have been reading a bad book. In the mornings I make corrections, for I lack any incentive for work. Empirically, this would be quite satisfactory. In a few hours I should be done with the book, and then everything would be fine. However, as a symptom it is very dangerous. Herein lies precisely what I tried to explain last winter, here in Berlin, to Baumgarten. Namely, that no great misfortune can befall me. Yet there is no day when my life couldn't overturn a hundred times. I told Baumgarten, one day I will shoot myself on account of a waitress in Jena. Did I exaggerate the external cause?

26 June

The roads are becoming clearer – in scholarship. I see my road. I see that one can progress; that one must progress – and nobody else sees it. I need someone I could talk to! To stutter! Need someone, someone whose silences would lure me into recklessness, whose questions could give strength to my uncertain feelings. Need a human being. I need Irma! For there is nobody else. There are those who could serve as surrogates. Not long ago, wrote to Herbert [Béla Balázs][19] about 'stuttering'. Yes, he would be better than nobody, perhaps Leo, and also Paul Ernst could serve as surrogates. But they are not. And least of all are the 'smart', the excellent and 'talented' people. I would be incapable of saying a single sentence to Simmel, or Bloch or Polányi. The experts are there for those who are ready. Someone else is needed here. This someone, the true one, can only be Irma.

It is ridiculous to talk about 'love' here. I am no longer in 'love' with her. Earlier, and later also, I have loved others more. Something else is involved here. Kassner calls it 'mystical sympathy', and Ernst, talking about Shelley's *Prometheus* and *Asia*, described the whole thing in *Brunhild*. Siegfried is in love with Chriemhild (how lovely is the 'love-potion' there) – and Brunhild is the true one.

However, it is just as ridiculous to talk about 'understanding'. Because I could write down a dozen names here, who understand me better than Irma. How nearly comical are her judgements about my work in her letters. Still, she wrote about the Kassner essay,[20] 'it contains Ravenna, it contains you and myself compressed into a problem'. Without this there would be nothing else. And our conversations. No! How absurd are the philologists who elevate Frau von Stein[21] into a goddess, in order to understand her influence on Goethe! But even more absurd are the psycho-philologists, who subtly demonstrate how she had misunderstood Goethe. Of course she didn't understand him. Friedrich Schlegel understood him, and W. v. Humbolt. From that misunderstanding was born *Iphigenie*. But nothing was born out of understanding. No! We are talking about something mystical: to be able to believe in the miracle of someone; to discern in the subconscious (gradually and naturally) the self-conscious; to give form to her lyrics.

My feeling is that only with such a woman can there be marriage, only such a woman can give one a child. Because then man too can have a child: the objectification of great longing, to gain a form – these are not accidental fruits of an ecstatic moment!

But what does such love mean to a woman? Is it really different from the other, the regular kind of love? Isn't there something manly, after all, in Ernst's *Brunhild*?[22] Or perhaps one day there might be such a woman? Who knows? Nowadays, in my view, it hardly matters. Balázs's poem, 'Woman is only woman . . .', spoken by a woman, could mean the exact opposite.

Therefore one should and must draw the conclusion: I am and will remain lonely. And it must not happen that I give less without her than I would have with her. I owe this much to her memory. One cannot and must not think that I can ever have such an encounter in life.

How strange. I have known her hardly a year and how much time it took me to learn: what she really meant to me.

30 June

It is quite a mystery that, all of a sudden, my productivity is paralysed. I feel pretty good; nothing ails me. But nothing happens. I don't even try to work. I just sit silently, or squander the day in idle thoughts. And I keep waiting. It is inconceivable that in the next moment everything will change suddenly. Of course it doesn't change. The greatest mystery of all is that my feelings about her were different once. My writings appear to me like miracles, as gifts of heaven, as something that 'I', the one who sits here helpless, am no longer capable of. It is incomprehensible that I ever was capable. (Naturally, I do not imply anything about the objective value of my writings.)

3 July

Things are still bad. My life 'stands or falls' on work-ecstasies. Whatever the external reasons might be – Riviera, and now, the headaches – I cannot work, or, at least, not with a strong, hysterical intensity. My life just hangs there – it would be difficult to find an image for it. Once again, anything can happen to me . . .

19 July

It wouldn't surprise me if I turned out to be superstitious. The question is whether I am already. For I wager everything on a single card – work! In the afternoon – just for something to do – I played with my revolver. Messed up something on it, and couldn't fix it. Struggled with it for quite a while, tried everything – in vain! Worked in the evening. Wrote few pages . . .

How strange, my lamp hangs in the wrong place. My hand casts a shadow on the paper. Notice it when I write letters and make these diary entries. But not when I am working. Decided to observe this. May mention the lamp to the landlady . . .

27 July

I feel somewhat embarrassed to note it here. I dislike such anniversaries and this one is truly an anniversary. For weeks I believed that my Irma-emotions were really over. No longer think of her. On my desk, for stylistic reason and because of the Philippe essay[23] there is her picture. Hardly look at it, and it appears so alien when I look at it. She is never on my mind. She has disappeared.

However, I could use a bit of longing and then sadness – on account of the Philippe essay. But such is life. It might have ruined the Ernst essay (pulling it toward the pathetic) that she was always there; even though she didn't organically fit the essay's framework. The essay would be dry without her.

29 July

How strange, and completely groundless are my current suicidal moods. They last for moments, like dizzy-spells. I never dwell on it. And when it passes, I find the whole thing terribly silly. Though there are moments when, stupidly, without any preparation, one just wants to lie down on the bed, tired, as if one wanted to sleep – and then. Then, the great silence. The repose. This is not despair. But what?

31 July

It is quite possible that on account of the Sundays I may, after all, settle down at home [Budapest]. The disgusting, detestable bourgeois, what a primitive lot. What noise they make, jumping and howling! How thin the walls of the pension! One can hear everything! The maids scream and sing . . . It is not in a sentimental sense that someone is kicked out of society, but because he dares, and his nervous system is rudely unaware of it, to lead a different life, because he refuses to conform to their 'cosy and loving' life.

How I sometimes hate 'life'! . . .

29 September
Florence without Irma – and there is something just as important now
as then: Giotto and Michelangelo. It is not as intoxicating now as it
was then. But if I wanted somebody here it would be Leo. It is
undeniable, I can be alone; and I think I am very much that. It doesn't
matter. Those who are close to me 'intellectually' are so far away. A
year ago I could have developed a warm relationship perhaps with
[Lajos] Fülep,[24] or, at least with Baumgarten. Now I notice what
separates me from the people . . . It hardly matters. It doesn't hurt.

Settignano gives a sad impression. It seems things will never be the
same. When I look ahead to the next fifty years, to what is to come, I
see before me a big grey desert. When I think about it, I fear only one
thing: can my fiery productivity survive this icy desert? Will I turn into
a dry pedant? I fear only myself, not my life; only fear for my work,
not for myself. The time has arrived for the final farewell to Irma (and
the reason for the sharpest pain remains: Irma is life) . . .

1 October
Not a single day should pass without reading a few pages from a great
philosopher. I have in my hands Maine de Biran :[25] and the reckoning
of the last few months (without crisis) is complete. I have scattered
myself, I have lived among people and involved myself in petty things.
Must not do it, for the time has not yet arrived. Perhaps, when one
has the total 'grasp' of things. However, the *praktische Vernunft* [prac-
tical reason] can only come after *reine Vernunft* [pure reason]. And I
am still nowhere. Obviously, I must resume last autumn's programme: study hard for years; everything else is secondary – and
hence to be avoided!

11 February 1911
Let's close the diary: the sentimental times are over. Made no entries
in the last four months. I am glad it came to an end, for it was my
weakest period, and it was always out of weakness that I wrote. I have
no regret it turned out this way. I am where I was before – only higher.
I am alone without despair and more richly cold than ever before. One
is no longer where, prior to the diary, one was. Today Irma accepted
my book's dedication. Let it be the last thing I write there. Her name
is the last there, and a simple, serious and profound blessing on her
for what she brought and gave. And if I could have a share in life (that
I don't I know now: it has reason and meaning, and one should rejoice
over this rather than complain about it), it could only be: to help her
life somehow. Embarrassingly enough, I meant little to her. The
question is whether it is embarrassing for me or her? Foolish question.

This is a tragedy – but she could not rise to where I soared. And yet she is the only one and there is no life without her. It is all fine and good, because my only possibility is that:

> Thy face is far from this our war –
>   Our call and counter-cry.
> I may not find Thee breathed and kind,
>   Nor know Thee till I die.
>
> Yet may I look with heart unshook
>   On blow brought home or missed
> Yet may I hear with equal ear
>   The clarions down the list –
>
> Yet set my lance above mischance,
>   And ride the barriere, –
> Oh, hit or miss, how little 'tis,
>   My Lady is not there![26]

... I find it stylistically appropriate that the last Florentine diary entry was already mere 'literature'. It was proper. It shouldn't be otherwise.

24 May
[Editorial note: Irma Seidler, the object of this diary, committed suicide on 18 May 1911.]
No one is so pure, that God cannot still make him purer. I didn't know this. Now I know. Everything is over. Every bond has snapped because she was the bond. There remains but purposeful associations and goals; things, and work. All my thoughts were flowers I have brought her, they were her joy and gave meaning to her life. All hers, and perhaps she noticed and enjoyed them. Once (before the great sadness; long ago) we talked about it. I said to her that, in my view, something must happen if one becomes important to the life of someone else. Namely, something will happen to the one who is important. It is not true. I meant nothing to her . . . And because 'this' [to be important in one's life] couldn't be transfused to the other, so she could receive something of me, it pronounces the death-sentence over my existence. I can never become anything to anyone. And if, by any chance, anyone can mean anything to me, then I must flee. Flee, because I'm inflicted with leprosy, and can infect her. But it can never happen again. All my bonds have snapped. Only work remains – as long as I can.

It is irrelevant now whether she wanted me. Anyone who feels this way about someone must be always and forever ready. He must wait at her doorstep, if perhaps once . . . Only then can he merit the feeling, earn the right to be a man. I have forfeited my right to live.

Actually I forfeited it earlier. I felt then that I could save her from her troubles; although she didn't love me. Perhaps I could have saved her, had I taken her hand and led her. But I didn't do it. From that followed everything. And even if I had taken her hand, even then the same thing would have happened. The judgement would be the same. For only if I had done what could be done, and done it successfully, only then would I have earned the right to the title of 'life'. But now I have lost it.

I still cannot accept her death. I still know she sees it when I suffer. I still know I will tell her everything, and still . . .

And I believe, I will never know it to be otherwise.

NOTES

1 Ferenc Baumgarten (1880–1927), aesthete and critic, born into a rich family, formed a close relationship with Lukács in the 1910s. After completing his education in Budapest, he settled in Germany.

2 Lukács's family, especially his father, put pressure on him to pursue his academic career, preferably in Budapest or in Germany. Lukács however appeared somewhat half-hearted, if not indifferent, about academic life. For instance in 1916, when Lukács expressed interest in studying with Max Weber at Heidelberg, Weber wrote him, 'If the completion of a systematic work is an unbearable pain to you, then I recommend that you forget about qualifications.'

3 Lukács's major work, *History of the Development of Modern Drama*, was completed in 1907 to enter a literary society's competition, and received the first prize. Lukács worked on his drama book until 1909 and had some hopes it might earn him an entry into a German university, although it was not until 1914 that excerpts from the book were published in *Archiv für Sozialwissenschaft und Sozialpolitik*.

4 Georg Simmel (1858–1918) exerted a great influence on Lukács's early writings, most notably on his classic, *History and Class Consciousness*. Lukács himself admired Simmel as teacher and scholar and attended his private seminars.

5 Leo Popper (1886–1911), a prodigy, was Lukács's closest friend, whose early death had a shattering effect on Lukács.

6 Irma Seidler (1883–1911), a painter, was Lukács's immortal beloved and their love affair inspired Lukács's lyrical essays in *Soul and Form*.

7 When Irma Seidler married a fellow artist, Lukács had an affair with Hilda Bauer (1882–1953), the sister of Herbert Bauer, better known as Béla Balázs.

8   Ignotus, original name Hugo Veigelsberg (1869–1949), was editor of the famed *Nyugat* [The West], where some of Lukács's essays in *Soul and Form* originally appeared.

9   Preoccupied with death and suicide because of his tragic love affair with Irma Seidler, Lukács admired Novalis's ability to re-enter life when he had previously been calling for death. Lukács quotes with approval Novalis's statement: 'Disease is certainly a most important subject for humanity . . . We have as yet a very imperfect knowledge of the art of utilizing it.' Lukács, *Soul and Form*, tr. Anna Bostock (Cambridge: The MIT Press, 1974), p. 53.

10   Lukács has in mind Kant's categorical imperative or law of morality which decrees that our conduct should be a model to others. See Kant's *Foundations of the Metaphysics of Morals*.

11   Meister Eckhart (1260–1327), German Dominican and great speculative mystic whose teachings contributed to the future development of protestantism, romanticism, idealism and existentialism. Lukács was drawn to Eckhart's mystical writings and frequently quoted him.

12   Karl Polányi (1886–1964), the noted economist, was Lukács's close friend. Polányi's acclaimed classic, *The Great Transformation* (Beacon Press, 1944), is imbued with the spirit of Lukács.

13   Ernst Bloch (1885–1977), German philosopher, formed a close friendship with Lukács in the 1910s. Lukács's own family disliked Bloch, and it often strained Lukács's already troubled relations with his family, especially his father.

14   Paul Ernst (1866–1933), poet, dramatist and essayist, had a close intellectual and personal friendship with Lukács and helped him in many ways during his years of exile in Vienna and Berlin in the mid-1920s.

15   The Ernst essay, better known as 'The Metaphysics of Tragedy' in *Soul and Form*, centres on the inherent tragedy, as Lukács saw it, of a man who, in quest of greatness, encounters Eros in the shape of Woman.

16   Otto Mandl, a friend of Leo Popper, lived in Dresden and translated some of Lukács's essays into German.

17   Edith Hajós (1888–1976), by training a physician, was Béla Balázs's first wife and belonged to Lukács's inner circle of friends. She lived in London during the war years and when she revisited Hungary in 1949, she was arrested and imprisoned on charges of spying for Britain. She wrote about it in her semi-autobiography, *Seven Years of Solitary*.

18   Iván Csorba belonged to Lukács's circle of friends, but nothing further is is known about him.

19   Béla Balázs (1884–1949) a poet, dramatist, and Béla Bartók's librettist, was Lukács's soul-mate and comrade in arms.

20   Lukács's essay on Rudolf Kassner is entitled 'Platonism, Poetry and Form'. For Kassner, there are two types of men who live in art: the poet and the Platonist. The poet writes in verse, the Platonist in prose, yet both are equally homeless and stand outside life. The poet's lot may be tragic (Baudelaire!), but the Platonist may not even become a hero of tragedy. As Kassner put it, the Platonist is 'a Hamlet bereft even of a murdered father'. Lukács, *Soul and Form*, p. 21.

21 Goethe was twenty-six when he met Frau Charlotte von Stein, who was thirty-three and already the mother of seven children. The love between Goethe and Charlotte developed into what the Germans like to call *Seelenliebe* or love between two souls to the exclusion of the corporal. There is a theory, embraced by Lukács, that Goethe so strongly identified with Charlotte that he transposed her into *Iphigenie*.

22 Paul Ernst's *Brunhild*, admired by Lukács, is a mystery play about love among superior and inferior human beings, about love equal and unequal, about love which elevates and love which debases. Unlike the inferior pair of lovers who, as Schopenhauer put it, indulge in the ignoble passion of sex, the superior pair of lovers, Siegfried and Brunhild, aspire to the privilege of greatness. Indeed, Lukács's essay 'The Metaphysics of Tragedy' invites comparison with Schopenhauer's essay 'On Women' in *Essays and Aphorisms*, tr. R. J. Hollingdale (Penguin, 1970), pp. 80–8.

23 Lukács's essay on 'Longing and Form' concentrates on Charles-Louis Philippe (1874–1909) whose novels, especially *Marie Donadieu*, fascinated Lukács. In the Philippe essay in *Soul and Form*, Lukács places the woman, no other than Irma Seidler, though she is not actually named, between sacred and profane love. Lukács stands for sacred love and Béla Balázs, the Don Juan of Budapest, symbolizes profane love. And when the seducer, Balázs, makes his appearance the woman succumbs and tragedy follows. It is of some interest to note that Lukács's Philippe essay, first published in *Die neue Rundschau* (February 1911), caught Thomas Mann's attention. Indeed, in *Death in Venice*, Mann took issue with Lukács's claim that 'Socrates transformed his longing into a philosophy whose peak was eternally unattainable, the highest goal of all human longing: intellectual contemplation . . . In life [however], longing has to remain love: that is its happiness and its tragedy.' Lukács, *Soul and Form*, p. 94.

24 Lajos Fülep (1885–1970), philosopher and art historian, co-founded with Lukács the journal *A Szellem* [Spirit], edited in Florence, which was dedicated to the proposition that metaphysics is as natural to man as breathing.

25 Maine de Biran (1766–1824), known as Marie-François-Pierre Gonthier de Biran, was one of the most important figures in the history of nineteenth-century French philosophy. As a disciple of Condillac and the ideologues, Biran was known for his independent thinking and for long, deliberate, psychological observations of his innermost personality and the workings of his mind. Most likely the book Lukács refers to is Biran's *Les Perceptions obscures*. It underscores the importance of man as a reflective being whose soul, or ego, resides in the will, who is not formed solely by external circumstances but is free to exercise intellectual and moral choice. Above all, Lukács, during his profound crisis, took solace from Biran that truth lies in the observation and study of one's own hidden soul or ego.

26 Rudyard Kipling, 'To the True Romance' in *Many Inventions* (New York: D. Appleton and Co, 1899), pp. v–viii.

3

On Poverty of Spirit
A Conversation and a Letter

You are right. I was with your son during his last days. Returning home – as you know, I travelled to restore my nerves after my sister's suicide – I found this note from him:

> Martha, don't expect a visit from me. I feel fine, and I am working. Have no need for people. However, I appreciate that you have notified me of your arrival. As always, you are good. In your eyes, I am still 'human'. But you are mistaken there.

The letter upset me, and I went to see him right away.

I found him in his study, sitting at the desk. He didn't look bad. The carelessness in his bearing and in his speech, which had alarmed me so much in the first days after the catastrophe, had almost disappeared. He spoke clearly, quietly and simply, and appeared to be quite composed. I stayed with him for quite a while, and I'll try to describe the essential details of our conversation. I think it might help you understand things a bit better. In my memory his act stands out with terrifying clarity. Frankly, I am somewhat mystified as to why I didn't anticipate it, didn't fear it. In fact, I went away from him almost completely reassured and in a good mood.

He greeted me warmly, and talked at length about my trip to Pisa, Campo Santo, and the composition of the *Last Judgement* with the same passion and conviction as always. At times I had the feeling, as I do now, that he didn't want to speak about himself. And although he knew that he had to be honest with me, he clearly wished to avoid it. Come to think of it, this might be an exaggeration; for we always interpret things in the light of what seems most important to us. I remember that he was talking about the nature of allegorical painting when I interrupted him with the question, how had he dealt with the recent events. He answered, 'I have managed pretty well, thank you.'

I said nothing, and looked at him quietly, questioning.

He repeated: 'very well, thank you'. After a short pause, he said, 'I have existed and exist. Clarity has come over me.'

'Clarity?'

He looked at me sharply, and said calmly, somewhat casually, 'Yes, clarity. I know that I was the cause of her death.'

I jumped up, terrified. 'You? You know, of course, that—'

'Let's just leave that part alone, Martha. Of course, I know it. I know it now after it's all over, and after we have learned everything there is to know. However, I didn't know it then.'

'You couldn't have known it.'

'No. That's just it; I couldn't have.'

I looked at him, puzzled.

He answered calmly, 'Please, be more patient, Martha, and don't assume that I've gone crazy. I'll try to explain everything to you. But please sit down. You have some rough idea what went on between me and her.'

'I know. You were her best friend. Very likely, the only one she had. She often talked about it. I myself have sometimes wondered about your relationship, and how it was possible. You must have suffered a great deal.'

He laughed softly, and said somewhat scornfully, 'You overestimate me – as usual; and what if I did? It most certainly would have been unproductive, blind and pointless.'

I was bewildered. 'Pointless . . .?'

'Who could have helped? Who could have known anything? And you, because you were unaware of things that nobody could have guessed, you reproach yourself with – no, I won't even repeat this nonsense any more.'

I wanted to go on speaking, but his quiet, steady gaze fell on me. I couldn't stand it, stopped talking and kept my eyes on the ground.

'Why are you so afraid of words, Martha? Yes! I bear the guilt of her death. In the eyes of God, definitely. But according to all the precepts of human morality, I am guilty of nothing. On the contrary, I have consciously fulfilled all my duties. (He uttered the last word with great contempt.)[1] I have done everything that I could. We once talked about helping and wanting to help, and she knew that none of her requests would have been in vain. But she made no request, and I neither saw nor heard anything. Her loud, silent cries for help fell on deaf ears, and I preferred the joyous, life-affirming tone of her letters.

'Please don't say that I couldn't have known anything. Perhaps it is true. Still, I should have known. For had I been given the grace of Goodness, her silence would have resounded across the countries that separated us. And if I had been here? Do you believe in clairvoyance,

Martha? Perhaps it would have enabled me to see the agony on her face, and hear the trembling in her voice . . .

'But what would that really have told me . . .? Human knowledge is an interpretation of statements and signs, and who is to know whether they tell the truth or lie. One thing, however, is certain. When we interpret things, we follow our own laws of what is forever unknown to others. Goodness, however, is grace. Do you recall how the private thoughts of others manifested themselves to Francis of Assisi. He was not guessing the thought of others. No! They became manifest to him. His knowledge transcends signs and interpretations. He was good. In moments like these, he was the other . . .

'I hope you still share our old conviction that what was once reality becomes an eternal possibility. Anything anyone has ever accomplished, I must demand of myself – eternally – as an attainable duty, if I don't wish to exclude myself from humanity.'

'But you yourself said, "Goodness is grace!" How can you demand grace? Doesn't your self-reproach amount to a blasphemy, just because God did not single you out for a miracle?'

'You misunderstand me, Martha. The miracle has already occurred, and I have no right to demand another one, or complain about this one. And I am doing neither. What I have said about myself is a judgement, not a complaint. I am only saying: this is the existence that was given to me, and I won't add what I could add to it, and then refuse to accept it. We are talking about life here. However, man can live without life. And often we do. But then one must be fully conscious and clear about it.

'To be sure, most people live without life, without ever being aware of it. Their existence is merely social and interpersonal. These people, you see, are content with their duties and their fulfilment. As a matter of fact, the fulfilment of duties is, for them, the only way to lead an exalted life. Since every ethic is formal, duty is a postulate, a form. The more perfect a form is the more it assumes its own life, and, to that extent, it is the furthest removed from any direct human relationship. Form, then, is like a bridge that separates; a bridge upon which we come and go, only to arrive at ourselves, without ever really meeting anyone else. Such people, moreover, cannot step outside themselves, for their human contact is confined, at best, to psychological sign-interpretation. Only the stern notion of duty can impart to their life, if not a deep inner form, then at least a solid and secure one. The real life is beyond forms, whereas the everyday life lies on this side of forms. Goodness denotes the gift of grace to break through the forms.'

'But isn't your Goodness', I asked him with some alarm, fearing the consequences he would draw from the theory, 'really nothing more than a postulate? Does such Goodness exist at all? I don't believe it', I added, after a short pause.

'You don't believe it, Martha', he said with a soft smile, 'and, you see: you have just broken through the forms. You have seen through my baseness in trying to use your own words to convince myself how untenable my thinking is, largely because I dare not to give it up on my own.'

'But even if that were true . . . I swear to you that only your nervously overwrought state could lead you to think such a thing. Assuming that I am right, it would be the strongest argument against your claim. I wanted to bring you comfort, but what have I achieved? Haven't I merely aroused your mistrust, and made your self-accusation more severe?

'Why should Goodness care about and concern itself with consequences? "Our duty is to do the work, not to try to win its fruits," states a Hindu saying.

'Goodness is useless, for it is without cause and foundation. Consequences reside in the external world of mechanical forces, that are indifferent to us, and the motives of our acts originate from the psyche's sign-world and the soul's periphery. However, Goodness is divine; it is metaphysical. When Goodness manifests itself in us, paradise becomes a reality, and divinity is awakened in us. Do you really believe that if Goodness was effective we would still be human? That this impure and sterile life would continue to exist? Here, indeed, is our boundary, the periphery of our humanity. You may recall my favourite saying: we are human because we can create works of art, and conjure up happy islands in the midst of life's unhappy, restless, polluted streams.

'If art could shape life, and Goodness became a deed, then we would be gods. "Why do you call me good? No one is good except the one God," said Christ. Do you remember Sonya, Prince Myshkin and Alexei Karamazov among Dostoevsky's characters? You wanted to know if there are any good people? Well, here they are. But note: their Goodness is also fruitless, chaotic and futile. It stands out like a great, lonely work of art – incomprehensible and misunderstood. Whom did Prince Myshkin help? Didn't he actually sow tragedy wherever he went? Surely, that was hardly his intention. His world was beyond tragedy, for it was purely ethical, or, if you wish, purely cosmic.

'Prince Myshkin's world is truly beyond tragedy. Like Kierkegaard's Abraham, with his sacrifice, Myshkin had left the world of tragic conflict and heroes, the world of Agamemnon, and his sacrifice. Prince Myshkin and Alyosa are good. But what does it really mean? I can't explain it in any other way than this. Their knowledge became a deed, their thinking left the purely discursive realm of cognition, and their human perspective became intuitive, intellectual. In short, they are Gnostics in the realm of deed. There is no theoretical explanation for this, nor can there be any, because what is theoretically impossible has been actually realized in their deed. Goodness, however, is a knowledge of men that illuminates and makes transparent everything, a knowledge, wherein subject and object collapse into each other. The good man no longer interprets the soul of the other, he reads it as if it was his own; he has become the other . . .

'Goodness then is the miracle, the grace and salvation. The descent of the heavenly realm to the earth. Or, if you like, the authentic life, the living life – no matter whether it ascends from below or descends from above. Goodness is an abandonment of ethic. Indeed, Goodness is not an ethical category. You will not find it in any consistent ethical system. And for very good reason. Ethic is general, binding, and far removed from men. It is the first, and most primitive exaltation of the self out of the chaos of everyday life. Ethic denotes man's moving away from himself, and from his empirical condition. Goodness, however, is the return to authentic life, the true homecoming of man. What do I care, which life you choose to call life? The decisive thing, however, is to distinguish sharply between the two concepts of life.'

'I think I understand you, perhaps better than you understand yourself. You had given free rein to your sophistry, in order to be able to create something positive, some sort of miracle from the very things that you lack. You yourself had conceded that not even your Goodness would have been of any help here . . .'

He interrupted me vehemently: 'No! I didn't say that. I only said that Goodness is no guarantee of one's ability to help. However, it provides verification of the absolute and visionary desire to help. Goodness stands opposite to the duty-born offer to help that is never realized. There is no guarantee! Yet, this much I know. If Goodness had dwelt in me, if I were human, I would have been able to save her. It is certainly no secret to you, that many times everything depended upon a single word.'

'We know that now.'

'But a human being would have known it even then!'

I decided not to push my argument too far. For I saw how each contradiction provoked and excited him. We remained silent for a while, and then I spoke again.

'Let's forget about the specific. I too find the general question more important. In fact, resolving the contradiction seems, for you, a question of life and death.'

'You are right, Martha, but where is the contradiction?'

'I am somewhat apprehensive about bluntly pointing it out. You seem so upset . . .'

'No! Let's have it.'

'It might be difficult to characterize it with complete clarity. Actually, I have something of a moral aversion to your notions. I am fully aware, however, that my feelings fail to make the distinctions that you make. (You always say this is the woman in me.) But my moral sense is aroused even against errors of judgement. My feelings tell me, however, that your Goodness is nothing more than a refined, cunning frivolity, an effortless gift of ecstasy, or – for you! – a cheap renunciation of life. You are fully aware of my suspicion of mysticism as a world view – but Eckhart also displayed it. Surely you recall how he re-interpreted and translated the case of "Martha and Maria"[2] into a practical ethic and a worldly application. I sense a kind of "Zweieinigkeit" [unity of two things] in your Goodness, something that "has its place above the world, yet under God, in the region, first and foremost, of the eternal" [*seine Stelle hat über die Welt, doch unter Gott, am Umkreis erst der Ewigkeit*].

'Granted, this Goodness of yours might be a grace, but in that case one must act out of duty and receive grace, at the same time, as a gift of God. Consequently, everything that you now find so contemptible must be loved with humble submission, for only then can you overcome your contempt. It seems to me that you want to leap over the most important stages to reach the goal – if there is a goal, and if it is attainable – without actually using the road. The expectation of grace is an absolution for everything, in short, it is a personification of frivolity. Your frivolity, however, is not only more refined, but also more self-lacerating. You are an ascetic of frivolity. While you consign the ascetic pleasures to others, you also invent a human type that embodies them. In the meanwhile, you are unhappy, remote from life, and miserable. You evoke the eternal temptation, so that others may partake of eternal sunlight. Whatever the closing words of a book might be, whether they glorify, pass judgement, or condemn, to skip over the pages to reach the end more quickly will remain a frivolous act.'

'You really are stubborn in a womanly way. No matter what, you are determined to save me, not bothering even to ask if I am really in a situation from which you have to save me. As for your accusation of frivolity, it is false and unfair. You pounce on my expressions, as if you didn't know that in explaining things one abstracts in order to make everything conscious. Granted, here I may have unnecessarily exaggerated.

'Yes, Goodness is a grace, a miracle. Not because we wait for it, in a complacent, smug and frivolous manner, but rather because it is a wondrous, unexpected and unpredictable – and, nevertheless, necessary – resolution of an extremely intense paradox. God's claim on us, absolute and unsatisfiable, explodes the bounds of human understanding. Our knowledge of this impossibility is just as absolute as it is unshakeable. But he, to whom the grace of Goodness has been granted, and who is in Goodness, his faith in the "absurd" is just as absolute and unshakeable.

'Goodness is madness; it is neither tamed, refined, nor calm. Goodness is wild and terrifying, blind and adventurous. The soul of a good man is devoid of all psychological content, of causes and consequences. His soul is a pure white slate, upon which fate writes its absurd command. This command is carried out blindly, daringly and mercilessly. The fact that what is impossible turns into deed, blindness into enlightenment, and evil into goodness- that is the miracle, that is the grace.'

'And you? And your . . . sin?'

'You see, Martha, if you want to talk about frivolity – and your intuition is accurate here – you should have charged my old self with frivolity, the one I had when she was still alive. For it was then that I crossed the boundaries and mixed up the categories. I wanted to be good to her. But man is not permitted to be good in relationship to someone else. What is needed is that a man wants to save someone – then he is good. A man wants to save someone, and perhaps he behaves badly, cruelly, tyrannically – all his acts might, in fact, be sinful. But in such cases, not even sin is antithetical to goodness. Indeed, sin is neither more nor less than a necessary dissonance in the harmony.

'The compassion and concern for myself and for others, sensitivity, caution and deliberation – here you have me. Here you have everything that is inhuman, unloving, forsaken by God, and truly sinful. I wanted to live a pure life, and therefore touched everything with careful, immaculately clean hands. This type of living, however, applies false categories to life. The work, which is separate from life, must remain pure. Life, however, cannot and will not be pure. Indeed, everyday life cannot even make sense of purity. In the realm of everyday life, purity is no more than an impotent negation of life. Rather than chart the road from chaos, purity actually perpetuates chaos.

'The great life, the life of Goodness, no longer needs such a purity. It has another purity – a higher one. Purity in life is nothing but a pale ornament, and it can never be an effective motive for action. That I failed to see this constitutes my frivolity. The will to purity, the kind I had, not only negates life, but deprives it of the wild and awe-inspiring "absurd": the ability to remain pure through sin, deception and horror. Herein lies the reason why she was never honest with me. She considered me frivolous, playful and irresolute. Even the tone of her voice, when she spoke to me, was never completely sincere; it had adjusted itself to my insincerity.

'After all, she was a woman. Oh, there may have been a time when I meant something like hope to her. Yes, I wanted to save her, without actually being fully possessed by this desire. Perhaps my desire to save her was but a detour to the Goodness and purity I craved. I have leapt across the road, in order to reach the goal at once. That goal, however, merely led to another road, which I mistook for the goal. But now clarity has come over me. This senselessly absurd, and untragically catastrophic end pronounces a divine judgement on me. I am withdrawing from life. Just as only the genius plays a legitimate role in the philosophy of art, only the man graced with Goodness plays a role in life.'

I jumped up, terrified. The meaning of his words frightened me, although he spoke calmly, and in a tone he used to explain a new theory. I went over to him and took his hand. 'What do you really want? What's on your mind?'

He laughed. 'Don't be frightened, Martha. Suicide is a category of life, and I have died a long time ago. I know that now, and know it more clearly than ever before. When I thought about your coming, I hoped to speak with you about her. At the same time, I also feared it. I feared and hoped – see how childish and confused I was – that I would remain silent and cry. And now we are talking about Goodness. I suppose we could just as well have discussed allegorical painting.

'But tell me, do you find our conversation somewhat brutal? You should know, for you are alive. You will deny it because you are good . . . After all, it is only my conversation; but you, being gracious, have participated in it.'

'You have been crying a lot, and you are still crying. This conversation is your way of crying.'

'You are aware, of course, that you are saying the same thing as I do: this is my crying. The concept of forms got all confused and tangled up in me. My life-forms are not forms of life. I realize it now. This is why her death amounts to a divine judgement on me. She had to die so that my work could be completed – so that nothing remains for me in this world but my work.'

'No! No!'

'Once again you simplify things. Think of the three causalities I have mentioned earlier. Everything has its cause and motives, but also its meaning, and divine judgement resides in the meaning. Let's forget about the external causes and the psychological motives. My question has nothing to do with these things.

'You are familiar with the ancient [Hungarian] legend of Kelemen Kömives and the building of a castle. Every night the wall, which the masons have built during the day, crumbles. Finally, the masons decide that the first wife to arrive, bringing dinner to her husband, will be sacrificed and embalmed in the wall. Mrs Kelemen arrived first. Who could trace all the causes of the fact that she was the first to arrive? There are a number of external causes and psychological motives involved in this. But as long as we approach it from the physical or psychological perspective, it remains an undeniably brutal, senseless coincidence that she was the first to arrive. Think also of Jephthah's daughter.[3] All this of course has meaning – not for Mrs Kelemen or Jephthah, but for the work that grew out of their sacrifice.

'Work grows out of life, but it also outgrows life. And while work originates in things human, it is also inhuman – indeed, anti-human. The cement that binds work to its birth-giving life also divides work and life. However, this cement is made of human blood. Christ said [Luke 14.26]:

> If any man come to me, and hate not his father, and mother, and wife, and children, and brethren, and sisters, yea, and his own life also, he cannot be my disciple.

'I am not thinking at all of the psychological aspects of tragedies. For me, this situation is a simple fact. An inhuman fact, if you will – but we are no longer talking about humanity. I can no longer bear the confusion and dishonesty of everyday life, which desires and receives everything all at once. For such a life desires nothing which is true and therefore real. Everything that is pure is inhuman. So-called 'humanity' is nothing more than the perpetual confusion and blurring of boundaries and spheres. The real life is formless, it is beyond forms, and no form of life can have clarity and purity. As a matter of fact, clarity is the product of chaos,[4] wrenched from it by a force which severs all its earth-bound ties.

'Genuine ethics is also inhuman; think only of Kant! Because she meant everything to me that I could call life, her death – and my inability to help which led to her death – is God's judgement on me. Do not believe for a second that I have contempt for life. Real life is also work, but I was given a different work. Once again, another evasion – another over-simplification!'

'You want to become a monk, but the Reformation can no longer be undone. Is it not your ideal of purity which makes you speak this way? You wanted to achieve a unity between your own self, with all its nervous hypersensitivity towards everything that is cruel, dirty, chaotic – and human life. But having realized that this experiment of yours is a failure, you want to throw away life itself. Doesn't it strike you as being a convenient solution? Isn't your asceticism also somewhat self-serving? And wouldn't your work, the one you want to rescue by cementing it with human blood, become even more bloodless and without foundation?'

'How fortunate you are, Martha, for having no "talent". If you had talent, I would have to worry about you all the time. Never will woman understand, despite all her senses, that "the life" is only a word, and it is only confused thinking that ascribes a uniform reality to it. There is only as much "life" as there is an *a priori* possibility for our actions. For you, life is – just "life". Forgive me, but in my view, you cannot even conceive that something which is truly great wouldn't be the crowning point of life. Undeniably, greatness may come only at the end, perhaps as a result of great suffering, yet it can still crown life with pleasure and ecstasy.

'No woman has ever entered the world beyond pain and pleasure – unless she was deformed, or she had stopped before the gate of life. How wonderfully strong and beautiful is the manifest unity of life, of values and of goals. But only as long as life itself is the goal and purpose of life. Where do you find a place there for creativity? Don't you find it quite remarkable that every talented woman ends up in tragedy or in frivolity? Unable to achieve a unity of life and work, women inevitably destroy either life or work by being frivolous – or they perish. Serious women, who are more than women, are the women of death. Not even Catherine of Siena was a pure and conscious ascetic, for she was the bride of Christ. One cannot simply dismiss the Oriental practice of denying women entry into heaven as something unreasonable and senseless. It may be unfair, it may appear strange; none the less, it is true that women can never achieve poverty of spirit.'

'Poverty of spirit?'

'Don't be so prejudiced against words. I am talking about something very simple, and that's the simplest expression for it. An ordinary and confused person can never be poor in spirit. His life contains countless possibilities, and if one category fails, or he himself fails in it, he simply moves on, happy and content, to another one.

'Poverty of spirit is merely the precondition, the first stage on the way to an authentic life. The Sermon on the Mount promises bliss, and for Fichte life itself spells blissful life. Poverty of spirit means liberating oneself from one's psychological limitations, and thereby delivering oneself to deeper metaphysical and metapsychological necessity.

'Poverty of spirit sacrifices the self for the sake of work; my own work, subjectively speaking, belongs to me only accidentally, but through it I become necessary to myself. We are something like a sheaf in disarray, gathered of longings and fears, of pleasures and pains; something that every moment perishes by its own unreality. What if we had longed for this destruction, would it not negate our insignificance, never to be superseded by another insignificance equally fated to decay? The meaning of our life is forever concealed behind motives, its teleology hidden behind causality, and our fate made invisible by our separate fates.

'We are searching for the meaning of life – the redemption . . . "The good man wants decision, nothing more," said Lao-Tzu. The everyday empirical, however, cannot even offer us a real temptation. We overestimate everyday life if we speak of it in terms of its dissonance. There can be dissonance only in a system of tones, in other words, in a unified world. By itself, confusion, obstacles and chaos do not amount to dissonance. Dissonance is clear and unambiguous. It is antithetical to reality and complements it: it is temptation. We all look for a genuine temptation, something that would shake the very essence of our being, rather than merely stir up and disturb life's periphery. The solution (I could also call it the "process of becoming a form") comprises the great paradox: how to conjoin temptation and the tempted, fate and soul, the devil and man's divinity.

'As you know full well, in the philosophy of art the form arises when the productive, life-awakening paradox of its possibility is discovered, when the terrible boundary bears fruit, and the very act of resignation enriches us. Poverty of spirit makes the soul homogeneous. The homogeneous soul, unresponsive and unmoved by destiny and chance events, is excitable and susceptible to wild temptations.'

'And the work? Your work?'

Martha interrupted him. 'I am afraid', she said, 'that, once again, you want to discuss Goodness, and praise its strange, remote perfection.'

'No, I was speaking purely formally, and only about the prerequisites of moral conduct. I was also talking about Goodness, but not only about that. In essence, I have been talking about some kind of general ethic. An ethic that would embrace everything, rather than confine itself to everyday interpersonal conduct. The fact is that, inasmuch as every one of our activities comprises an act, every act has the same purely formal prerequisites, the same ethic. Therefore this ethic is negative, prohibitive and devoid of content.

'However, if it contains a clearly formulated command, it must be this: do not do what you are not forced to do. The command is negative, it implies a preparation and an intermediate stage. In sum, this is a prerequisite and a path to work, to virtue, to the positive.

'Let me add also: virtue is madness. We do not possess virtue, and we are not virtue. Virtue possesses us. To be poor in spirit means to be ready for our virtue. This is the way we must live. Our life is worthless and without meaning, and thus we should be ready at any moment to consign it to death. In fact, we await at every moment the permission to throw life away. And yet, we must live, live intensely and with all our powers and senses.

'We are no more than a vessel. But the only vessel in which the spirit makes its appearance. The spirit can only pour its wine of manifestation into us. Only in us – through us – can the spirit manifest and transubstantiate itself. We have no right therefore to remove ourselves. The vessel must be kept pure, but this purity is not the purity I spoke earlier; it pertains to the unity and homogeneity of the soul. Threatened by blindness, Edmond de Goncourt wrote:[5]

Il me serait peut-être donné de composer un volume, ou plutôt une série de notes, toutes spiritualistes, toutes philosophiques, et écrites dans l'ombre de la pensée.
[Perhaps it was still given me to produce a volume, or rather, a series of notes, spiritual and philosophical, written in the shadow of thought.]

'He was poor in spirit when he said this, and his aesthetic nature possessed him like a virtue. We must lead the life of the mind, and all our perception and reactive powers must be focused and aligned with the categories of our work. Only then can the depraved, poverty-stricken soul become active, and turn its obsession with work into a terrifying rage that hungers for realization. Poverty of spirit was the prerequisite – the negative principle – of fleeing life's infinite misery, and of forsaking the human world.

'Here a new richness blossoms forth, the richness of unity. As Plotinus put it:[6]

Each and every part comes out of the whole, and yet part and whole always collapse into one another. There is neither variety, nor dissimilarity; everything is indefatigable and inexhaustible. Seeing enlarges itself in perceiving.

'As long as we are stuck in everyday life, we remain but vain caricatures of God. We go on duplicating, in a rather clumsy, fragmentary fashion, the magnificent, fragmentary work of his universal creation. In a work, which is the result of poverty and obsession, the fragmentary is enlarged into a circle, the polyphonic is refined into a single tone in the scale, and the chaotic swirl of the atoms resolves into planets and celestial orbits. What is common to all is the path, one's creative effort, the ethic of virtue. However, every creative effort is distinct from every other work. I don't know whether this path was willed by God, or whether it leads to God. I only know that it is our only road, and without it we are lost in the mire.

Goodness is only one road among many, but this road does lead to God. Because he is the way and in it our whole life loses everything that made it merely lively. Goodness transforms the inhumanity of work into the highest expression of humanity, and disdain of the work for immediacy turns into a genuine contact with reality.'

'If I understand you correctly, you want to re-establish the caste system on a metaphysical basis. In essence, you only recognize one sin: the mixing of castes.'

'You have understood me perfectly. I wasn't sure whether I expressed myself clearly, and feared that you might confuse what I said with the silly, modern individualist notion of the necessary duty to oneself.[7] I am not qualified to determine the number of castes, their various kinds, and their respective duties. But you seem to be as convinced as I am that there are only a specific number of castes. Do you now understand what significance "personal" duty has for virtue?

'Virtue enables us to overcome life's misleading richness and false substance, and they are redeemed in us by that form. The hunger for substance compels the spirit to divide people into castes, to create from the chaotic, unified world the luminous world of the forms. The longing for substance creates forms, and it appears as if the substance, by realizing itself, actually terminates itself. But in reality, only the creative process of the forms and its laws, and the duties of those who do the forming, are different. Every form is but a mirror image of the activity of the spirit. Just as their formal prerequisites were the same, their existence conveys the same meaning: the redemption of substance from falsehood to truth. And redemption has no plural. The forms do not resemble each other: their essence is their uniqueness.

'The virtuous ones, those who fulfilled their duties, ascend to God. As you know, there are only personal duties, and these duties divide people into castes. Here all differences come to an end. Here all doubts grow silent, because there is but one redemption.'

We remained silent for a while. Then quietly, in order to end the conversation, I asked him, 'And your own duty?'

'You know what it is. If I wanted to live, I would transgress my caste. That I loved her and wanted to help was already a transgression. Goodness is the duty and virtue of a caste that is higher than mine.'

Not long thereafter, we took leave of each other, and agreed he would visit me soon. Two days later he shot himself. He left everything he owned to my sister's child. On his desk we found the Bible, open at the Apocalypse, where he had marked the words:

> I know your Works, that you are neither cold nor warm; oh, if only you were cold or warm. Because you are lukewarm, however, and are neither cold nor warm, I will spit you out of my mouth.[8]

NOTES

[1] Lukács's own culpability for Irma's suicide forced him to examine the practical limitations of Kantian ethics based on the necessary or obligatory duty toward others. Lukács felt that Kant's categorical imperative to treat others as an end and never as a means is self-defeating when human conduct is conditioned by social or class differences. To Kant's famous statement, 'The starry heavens above me and the moral law with me,' Lukács replied, 'Kant's starry firmament now illumines only the dark night of pure cognition, it no longer lights any solitary wanderer's path (for to be a man in the new world is to be solitary).' Lukács, *The Theory of the Novel* tr. Anna Bostock (Cambridge: MIT Press 1971), p. 36.

[2] Lukács refers to Meister Eckhart who, to demonstrate that goodness encompasses both contemplation and deeds of virtue, wrote: 'The one [contemplation] is good. The other [deeds of virtue] is necessary. Mary was praised for having chosen the better part but Martha's life was useful, for she waited on Christ and his disciples.' *Meister Eckhart*, tr. Raymond Bernard Blakney (New York: Harper & Brothers, 1941), p. 111.

[3] In the Book of Judges, Jephthah, a great warrior, led Israel to crush Ammon, but not before he made a vow to the Lord: 'If thou wilt deliver the Ammonites into my hands, then the first creature that comes out of the door of my house to meet me when I return from them in peace shall be the Lord's; I will offer that as a whole-offering.' When Jephthah came to his house in Mizpah, who should come out to meet him with tambourines and dances but his daughter, and she his only child; he had no other, neither son nor daughter.

[4] Lukács's notion that clarity originates in chaos owes something to Schlegel who, in *Dialogue on Poetry*, argued that one of the subtlest observations of romantic irony is that the original order of things is chaotic. Hence chaotic order mirrors life and the primeval richness of being, while systematic order is a mere shadow of life.

[5] Edmond de Goncourt (1822–1896) and his brother Jules wrote the famous diary known as *Journal* that reached six volumes. Whether it is considered as a monumental autobiography or as a history of the social

and literary life of Paris in the second half of the nineteenth century, the Goncourt *Journal*, read avidly by Lukács, is a document of absorbing interest and outstanding importance.

6 Plotinus (AD 204–70) was the main exponent of Neoplatonism, his work blended Plato, the Stoics and Aristotle into a new religious formulation. His massive work of synthesis, *The Enneads*, is one of the classics of Western mysticism, frequently cited by Lukács.

7 Kant's categorical imperative states explicitly that every rational being has a 'necessary duty to oneself' to preserve one's own life up to the end of life. The necessary duty to oneself proscribes suicide or self-mutilation.

8 At Kierkegaard's graveside, when the official rites were over, a tall man in black with a Bible in hand stepped forward to the grave. It was Kierkegaard's nephew, Henrik Lund, who read the passage Lukács cites here, saying that it expressed Kierkegaard's views.

4

My Socratic Mask

Letter to Charlotte Ferenczi, January 1909

I just don't know how to justify or make amends for this letter and I feel my heart pound as I consider the great responsibility it entails. Yesterday, everything was so beautiful; we gazed at each other from the distance and saw everything so clearly, looked into each other's eyes with such certainty, though our eyes were but distant bright stars. Why do I then try to get close to you? Why?

I have the feeling that yesterday I understood you and recognized your gesture. Sitting on the sofa close to me, you leaned forward expecting something and, your arms making a wide circle, you were still for a minute – but this stillness was more tense than any of your actions. That very moment could have exploded and yielded anything. What that explosion would have produced depended on who was sitting beside you. Those open arms could have with equal quickness entwined the neck of the other person or shown him the door for good. Everything depended on this man's single word. And I disappeared knowing full well I could never say that word to you, and were you to listen to my words your arms would still remain inactive, resigned. So I disappeared, but I saw you and your friend, who is also my friend, and I understood the world you and he live in. Indeed, neither of you pays much attention to reality and yet both of you live in reality. Though the real world plays no role in your lives,[1] life itself, which holds out myriad possibilities, dances around you and knocks on the door of your soul. You must grant entry to life even though your friend's soul forms a great white circle and yours is like a colourful adventure. Though life's possibilities gain entrance, they have little effect on you or your friend. Once these possibilities depart, your soul resumes its tranquillity and life dances on merrily. Your friend of course is likely to respond to life's possibilities, but you, I am convinced, will remain inactive. These possibilities impart a form to your friend and content to you. And what about me?

All day long I have grappled with the question, and I still don't know whether to send this letter or not.[2] When I left you something cried in me. It cried for intimacy and the need to remove, if only for a moment, the impenetrable mask of my intellect. It cried for someone to notice me, at least for a moment, and say: 'I noticed you, I love you.' Instead of yielding, I pressed the cold, plaster mask against my face until it almost became my flesh. I fully expected it to adhere and become one with my face, so that even in my weak moments I would remain in full command of myself. But unable to wear it any longer, I flung my mask away and it lies shattered in a thousand pieces. Once again, I am alive and am myself. But now, ashamed of my naked face, like Adam and Eve of their nakedness, I search for something to hide my face.

But why do I long for someone who would recognize and love what she sees, and why do I dread that she would glimpse what is behind the mask?

How is it possible that a man like me, who devoted half of his life to keeping his distance and who – do you remember? – was utterly miserable for years over the loss of this distance, longs for absolute closeness and togetherness? Like you, I care nothing for facts, neither mine nor those of others, but life holds no possibilities for me. My life is not colourful like yours nor forms a white circle as in your friend; life for me is neither a placid mountain lake nor a noisy bustle and hustle. So what? Does it really matter? I must find something somewhere that would absorb me and, perhaps like a mirror, reflect my rays, or become a deed in which I could recognize myself. Is this really conceivable? I have no idea, nor do I know what this something might be. All I really know is that I am moving toward something and everything is a stage on life's way. Beauty surrounds me, but it means nothing to me; though already fatigued, I cannot rest even though I know full well that my pilgrim's road leads to empty deserts. As for my accomplishments, they fall from me like so many lonely, overripe fruits from a bare ruined tree whose branches, twisting and mourning in the autumnal wind, no longer believe they once bore fruits or ever will. The fruit tree has its fruits and I have my deeds. And these deeds, this much I know, make me a human being. However, not even my deeds make me human because my deeds cease to be mine the moment they are born. My soul, untouched by life and its possibilities, yearns for things human. But these possibilities bear no connection with my life, and impart neither form nor content to it. The three of us have discussed Platonism a lot of late. You and your friend always talk about Plato, whereas I am fascinated by Socrates' soul. I never see Plato; for he lives so much in my words that I recognize him even before I hear his words. And yet, the closer I get to him the less I understand him. And Socrates? Ah, indeed, the great dialectician. This strong, self-assured man whose words can humble even the most self-assured, who fought a thousand battles and met, with divine calm, his death-in-martyrdom. The soul of Socrates intrigues me. I keep asking myself as I ask you: what was Socrates like when he fell silent? Let me also ask: why did Socrates always talk and talk? Why did his beautiful concepts cut everything in half? In what way did this proud dissembler of ignorance know more than anyone else? Why was he so serene with a mind always on fire, and what enabled him to welcome death?[3] What is the meaning of Socrates' death and what is the meaning of his life? Just what kind of life may have pulsed concealed behind his words?

Why would Socrates never keep quiet? And why didn't he take the hand of the young man[4] he loved or embrace any young men? Why didn't Socrates remain silent when the hymns to Eros [in *Symposium*] came to an end, that led him to discourse on comedy and tragedy until daybreak, only to leave Agathon's place and resume his discussion elsewhere? Why couldn't Socrates ever remain silent? And when he talked it was a real talk. His words were not like yours, Charlotte. Your talk reminds me of windows that open on narrow streets where the whitewashed cottages glow red in the afternoon sun, and the streets lead to beautiful meadows with spectacular sunsets. No, the words Socrates spoke contained everything, his sentences betrayed no chaos in need of form and order. And yet, what was actually concealed behind Socrates' words? That we may never know for he was never speechless. He kept going from one circle of listeners to another, talking incessantly, without actually ever revealing anything. And when his legs were getting cold and numb from the poison, Socrates said: 'Crito, we ought to offer a cock to Asclepius.'

Why did Socrates consider death a redemption? Socrates, above all, who walked through life proud, erect and self-assured? What induced Socrates to welcome death and spurn all offers of escape? Why was he so happy to die?

Could this be the hidden meaning of his discourses? The final recognition of the ultimate futility of life? The great self-discovery that all his strivings came to naught? Could it be that the fleshless veil, which Socrates drew around his nocturnal discourses, merely disguised his cries of longing, and his razor-sharp concepts helped to sever the roots of sentimentality?

Socrates professed ignorance in all things except love. He claimed he recognized a true lover in a pair of lovers, and argued the lover and the beloved are forever alien to each other. He spoke of Eros as being neither beautiful nor good, nor particularly brilliant. Socrates said he admired and worshipped beauty because he possessed none of it. Is this not a more meaningful definition of love than Socrates' later claim that love is neither good nor beautiful? Does this mean the wounds of Philoctetes[5] symbolize Socrates' whole life, and that the magic lance which could have healed his wounds has been lost?

What does it really mean that life is one of desire, need and longing? It could signify: man's life has an empty spot which cannot be filled with anything he possesses. Longings and desires may also imply that something has left us, and, leading a separate life of its own, we want to reclaim and repossess it. Perhaps longing is no more than when two souls, whose hands are joined and whose eyes drink in each other, declare: yes, we became one. This love, filled with longing and desire, was perhaps best captured by Aristophanes in his myth of Eros. According to Aristophanes, Zeus cut the race in half and, as male and female halves, each half now searches and yearns for the other. After Aristophanes claimed that male and female were originally one, Socrates defined love as need and desire for what one does not have. Therefore when we are in love we long for what is alien to us and beyond our reach. And so, those who are born with the Aristophanic power of love readily find each other behind every tree and bush. In the end, however, Socrates proved right after all. The lover and beloved never attain a union. Socrates was the only one who understood the eternal duality of this longing, this love, which no lover can ever fathom. In my view, Socrates' life signifies a life without limits and restraints. He symbolizes what becomes of man's life when he knowingly removes himself completely from his own deeds, and acknowledges the unbridgeable abyss between the lover and the beloved. Plato, too, confronted Eros. Having confronted it, he withdrew into his own self and channelled his desires and longings inward. Plato transposed his soul into a circle, an iridescent white circle from which grew mysterious flowers. These flowers of desires and fulfilments, though joined together by the strength of the form, lacked unity. But neither did Socrates possess the form. His mask was rigid, unyielding. He proved unable to channel his desires and longings inward, they kept breaking through in search of the absolute, to become one with it. But Socrates understood that love never partakes of an eternal oneness because Eros, the child of wealth and poverty, continually chases after beauty, though it can neither take the form of beauty nor attain it,

And so Socrates pressed to his face, like a mask, the impenetrable purity of his words, which never betrayed his own longings and desires, nor made audible the stifled cries of his eternal loneliness. This is why Socrates welcomed death. He knew his soul would gain in death and – who knows? – silence his longings. 'Crito, we ought to offer a cock to Asclepius. See to it, and don't forget,' were Socrates' last words for he expected to be healed.

My own mask lies at my feet shattered in pieces. My longings and desires reach forth like tear-stained emaciated arms. Spread wide, they are waiting. And yet, were anything to approach, my arms would withdraw for fear of opening up old wounds, aware that if love turned to flesh it would become one with it. The lover and beloved must part. The one who departs carries away part of the beloved's flesh, only to increase his loneliness and deepen his wounds.

Plato possessed form but not Socrates. After all, pure dialectics is antithetical to form. Socrates' absolute formlessness comprised a mask which could hide many things. Socrates was a sentimental being – in a true and profound sense – whereas Plato was an artist. There are no greater opposites than form-creating and sentimentality. You have no reason, dear Charlotte, to pity me. Proud of my great problems, I cannot bear the thought of pity. Charlotte, don't ever take my hand into yours even if you feel it would silence my cries momentarily. I don't want to lose you completely, but on my ocean everyone sinks who reaches out for my hand. The hour has struck and I must leave. Where am I going? Who knows? And why do I have to leave? Who knows? I am going alone and one day I, too, may sacrifice a cock to Asclepius when the hour arrives that will silence my longings and desires.

Promise me, Charlotte, you won't be angry with me for my broken mask and send me away having seen my face. Please, let me reassemble my broken mask so I can press it against my face. This time, it may merge with it.

NOTES

[1] Charlotte Ferenczi (1887–1952), the recipient of Lukács's love letter, was a writer, and her friend, Vilmos Szilasi (1889–1966), was a philosopher who succeeded Husserl at Freiburg University in 1928, and served as guest professor under Heidegger from 1918 to 1933.

[2] Lukács did send the letter and she responded.

[3] On Socrates' concept of soul and death, the object of Lukács's analysis, see Plato's two dialogues, *Apology* and *Phaedo*.

[4] Plato, *Phaedrus*, tr. Walter Hamilton (Penguin, 1973). In this dialogue, love is assumed to be a god, whereas in the *Symposium* he is a daemon, a being intermediary between gods and men. Lukács's own concept of love, as one gathers from his love letter, is premised on the notion that love is a link between the sensible world and the world of forms. This thought is also found in *Phaedrus*.

5 Sophocles, *Philoctetes*, tr. David Grene (Chicago: The University of Chicago Press, 1957). Lukács's claim that Philoctetes, this outcast from human sympathy, symbolizes Socrates' whole life is intriguing and wrought with many possibilities, to say the least. My sense of Lukács's intended parallel is that Philoctetes, afflicted by some divine power without having committed a crime, and discarded by others out of disgust with his affliction, none the less refuses and is unwilling to resume normal life itself because, with that life, will come new and unpredictable suffering.

PART II

Drama and Tragedy

Introduction

Drama and Tragedy

The stage is the realm of naked souls and destinies.

Lukács

Lukács's fascination with the theatre dates from his early teens. As an impassioned man of the theatre – one might call him a theatromaniac – Lukács made his first public appearance as a drama critic for the *Magyar Szalon*. As a drama critic, he reviewed some forty plays between 1902 and 1903. Upon graduating with honours from the gymnasium in 1902, he was presented by his father with a railway ticket to Norway and a letter of introduction to Ibsen. Congratulating Lukács on meeting Ibsen, Lukács's childhood friend, Marcell Benedek wrote him, 'I beg you to recount word for word your talk with Ibsen. I am sure you have memorized the conversation.'[1] Lukács's sister Mici was equally impressed with her brother: 'It is my turn to congratulate you. I cannot imagine how you actually managed to speak with Ibsen. I know I would have just stood there, stupefied and speechless.'[2]

Lukács idealized Ibsen the iconoclast who, like a white-maned Samson, toppled the pillars of bourgeois society. 'Old Ibsen should be grateful to you,' Benedek had written to Lukács, adding in wonder, 'just what is your allowance that you can afford to give a copy of Ibsen's books to everyone?' Under Ibsen's spell after his visit in 1902, Lukács literally showered his acquaintances and friends with copies of Ibsen's books.

Ibsen was just recovering from a second stroke he had suffered in 1901, when Lukács, accompanied by his tutor, visited him. Though Ibsen had difficulty walking and though his speech was slightly impaired, his mind was as brilliant as ever. Ibsen's restless daemon, questioning and searching men's hearts, Ibsen the chastiser and visionary, and especially Ibsen's patterns of life and work[3] – all made a lasting impression on Lukács. At seventeen, Lukács looked to Ibsen as an incomparable master who, more even than Shakespeare, had wrestled the secret from life. Above all, Lukács admired Ibsen's absolute indifference to public canons of art, friends and shibboleths. And, like Ibsen, Lukács preferred to walk in the light of his own inward, defiant heroism. For the young Lukács, like Peer Gynt (*Reader* chapter 9), life was a pilgrimage of self-discovery:

> Where was *I*, as myself, as the whole man, the real? Where was *I*, with my forehead stamped with God's seal? (Ibsen, *Peer Gynt* III 421)

To the end of his life, Lukács shared Ibsen's conviction that the dramatist must compel the audience to rethink basic principles which they had never seriously questioned and to challenge social abuses. Hence, for Lukács, reading Ibsen's 'social' plays was like reading Marx. Reacting to Ibsen with his innermost being, Lukács called him the 'loneliest' of all men.

We should also recognize that Ibsen's glorious transition from Norwegian obscurity to European fame struck a responsive chord in Lukács. In the gloomy desert of Hungarian culture, Lukács eagerly identified with Ibsen's self-imposed exile from Norway and his eventual emergence as a dramatist of international status. Indeed, despairing of his milieu, Lukács struck up a fraternal union with Ibsen's protagonists – Brand, Peer Gynt, Rosmer, Hedda Gabler, Rubek – who flounder on the dilemma of what to make of their lives in a society that is half closed.

It was partly due to Ibsen's mesmerizing impact that, in 1904, Lukács co-founded the Thalia Theatre with a repertoire featuring Ibsen, Strindberg and Gerhart Hauptmann. Lukács's obsession with Ibsen, who, as Lukács put it, posed all the questions about human ideals and the problems of life that are important 'to us', upset some of his friends, including his 'Thalia Brothers' (supporters of the Thalia Theatre). As one of Lukács's friends put it, 'I don't want to talk about Ibsen since I hardly know him. He is good. But to place him in the exclusive club that you propose I would have to study him in order to conclude that all his works, like those of Nietzsche, lead to the centre. All right, I will read Ibsen.'[4]

Ibsen's heroes and heroines excited Lukács because, as 'fanatical warriors of idealism' they defied and transformed their age. Lukács not only translated *The Wild Duck*, arguably one of Ibsen's most pessimistic plays, but had it rehearsed some forty-seven times before staging it. Next to Ibsen, Lukács admired Strindberg (*Reader* chapter 7) and despite the Thalia stage director's protest, insisted on staging Strindberg's *The Father*. Lukács's friend Benedek exploded: 'Damn it. Yes, Strindberg's *Father* may be as good as you say it is. But I don't want sequels in the Thalia and, above all, failures within a year. I resent your divine superiority over my alleged stupidity just because I can't stomach Strindberg or Hauptmann.'[5] None the less, the Thalia's production of Strindberg's play *The Father* was premiered in March 1905 in Budapest, but not in Lukács's translation as originally scheduled.

Lukács himself was an aspiring playwright. In his late teens he wrote plays and dramas. Later, having discovered philosophy, Lukács, as though he were acting in accordance with Plato's animadversions, burned his plays. But Lukács also had reservations about the artistic merit of his plays and questioned his ability as a dramatist. Though he gave up writing plays, his love for drama remained undiminished. Lukács's major work, *History of the Development of Modern Drama*, received the prestigious Lukács Krisztina Prize (no relation) of the Kisfaludy Association in 1908. The two volume work, crammed with footnotes and a bibliography of no less than 500 works in English, French, German and other European languages, was published in 1911. To this date, Lukács's *Modern Drama* remains untranslated. This is unfortunate for, in our view, it is by far his most impressive work. Two entries in this section (chapters 10 and 11) are taken from *Modern Drama*.

The Kisfaludy Association invited Lukács to give a talk, based on his *Modern Drama*, on 'Shakespeare and Modern Drama' (*Reader* chapter 5). The date of his lecture was 31 January 1909. The translation is based on the Hungarian Shakespeare Society's publication of Lukács's lecture (volume 4, 1911). Lukács's essay on Ibsen (*Reader* chapter 8) originally appeared in the sociological journal *Huszadik Század* [Twentieth Century] (August 1906). This radical journal, a semaphore for a generation in ferment, was edited by Oszkár Jászi, who was close to the Lukács family. Lukács also published his Strindberg essay (*Reader* chapter 7) in *Huszadik Század* (February 1909). His review of Ibsen's *Peer Gynt* appeared in *Magyar Világ* [Hungarian World] (25 January 1903). The English translations are based on the cited publications.

The noteworthy feature of Lukács's lecture on Shakespeare is that on the much debated question, dating back to Lessing: Sophocles *or* Shakespeare, he answered: Sophocles *and* Shakespeare. Equally noteworthy is Lukács's attempt to underline the social matrix of Shakespearean drama. True, Dr Johnson and Marx set the precedent for this. None the less, for Lukács the interplay between social constraints and dramatic vision, the relation between artist, patron and public are radically social. Hence sociology, as Lukács makes it clear, is as crucial to a reading of Shakespeare as it is to John Ford.

It is also worth mentioning that Lukács's 'Shakespeare and Modern Drama' anticipated George Steiner's classic study, *The Death of Tragedy* (1961). Like Lukács, Steiner intimates a radical split between true tragedy and Shakespearean tragedy. Though Steiner had no prior knowledge of Lukács's essay,[6] he argued, as did Lukács, that Shakespeare's primary impulse was not a tragic one; rather, Shakespeare's vision is that of tragicomedy. I should add here that Lukács relied heavily on Walter Raleigh's *Shakespeare* (1906), which argued that the mixture of tragedy and comedy was a necessity in Elizabethan theatre for the audience wanted to be entertained, to laugh and enjoy itself. The comic actor-clown commanded extraordinary mimetic skill. Not surprisingly, Shakespeare in some of his plays – *The Merchant of Venice, As You Like It, Twelfth Night, King Lear* – gave a magnificent scope to the professional clown. But at the same time, Shakespeare made severe demands on his clowns in many of his plays.

As for Lukács's view of Shaw, there is no doubt that Lukács felt a close kinship with the Shavian world. After all, Lukács, like Shaw, was a puritan in his attitude towards art and drama. Puritan because he resented the ascendancy of sensuous ecstasy over intellectual activity. Above all, Lukács disliked intensely and openly the romanticization of life, of love and emotions. Lukács agreed with Shaw that Strindberg, the only genuine Shakespearean dramatist, shows that the 'female Yahoo, measured by romantic standards, is viler than her male dupe and slave'.[7] Lukács also subscribed to the Shavian edict that there is no new drama without a new philosophy. As for Shakespeare, as the first comer in the Elizabethan epoch, he reaped the whole harvest and reduced contemporaries to the rank of mere gleaners.

The inexorable 'you must be born again' and 'born different' recurs in every generation. But no generation was more insistent and, I may add, strident about changing its life than that of Lukács. Scion of a fabulously rich banker, Lukács, with a developed sense of life, displayed an enormous social appetite and very fastidious personal one.

As Shaw observed,[8] rich men with a developed sense of life – Ruskin, William Morris – and we can add – Lukács, are not content with their villas. They want handsome cities. They are not content with bejewelled wives. Lukács married a Russian terrorist and harlot, Ljena Grabenko, discovered by Balázs in the Bohemian quarter of Paris. This is not as surprising as it may sound, for Lukács, like Ibsen's character Brand (*Reader* chapter 8), demanded all or nothing in all domains of life.

NOTES

[1] Marcell Benedek to Lukács, 20 August 1902, LAK.
[2] Mici to Lukács, n.d., LAK.

[3] On Ibsen's patterns of life and work, see James McFarlane, 'Ibsen's working methods' in *Ibsen*, ed. James McFarlane (Cambridge University Press, 1994), pp. 155–64.

[4] Marcell Hammerschlag to Lukács, 28 August 1904, LAK.

[5] Marcell Benedek to Lukács, 12 July 1904, LAK

[6] George Steiner's personal communication to Arpad Kadarkay, September 1994.

[7] Bernard Shaw, *Three Plays for Puritans*, (Penguin, 1946), p. 30.

[8] Bernard Shaw, *Major Barbara* (Penguin, 1946), p. 20.

5

Shakespeare and Modern Drama

Appearing before you as part of this lecture series, that sang and continues to sing the glory of our great poet, whose stage works are recalled with ecstasy, you may not find – nor do I – my assigned role the most appealing or sympathetic one. [. . .] For it is not Shakespeare's richness, but his boundaries, not his splendours, but his dangers that I wish to address. In fact, my topic is not Shakespeare himself but his influence. The potential of his influence and whether it is good or dangerous.

What does the question mean? What does it mean that that long departed and long gone age can and does influence contemporary art? Let me hasten to add that what I have in mind is neither imitation nor a facile transference of some superficial external features, but whether the essence of any art can be appropriated and developed. Whether the key principles that enable an artist to create his own world, arrange and exclude it from the external world, make it self-enclosed and different from any other created world, whether the key compositional principles – even if their essence is misunderstood – can be appropriated. I have in mind, for instance, the art of Velazquez[1] and Frans Hals[2] that contributed to the development of Impressionist painting, or the way the romantic and humouristic novel, in the late eighteenth and early nineteenth century, discovered the decisive features of its style in Rabelais and Cervantes.

The question I wish to raise, rather than exhaust, is this. What are the essential features of Shakespeare's dramatic composition, and to what degree can they be utilized to create, if need be, a contemporary drama that would hold up a mirror to our life as he did to his own life. Such a modern drama would embody and immortalize our life just as Shakespeare's art embodies his own age.

History gives us the right to raise this question. From the very moment that Shakespeare emerged, so to speak, from the great crowd of his contemporaries, he wielded a dominant influence on the style of the great European drama. (Not to mention the quickly fading popular dramas!) That this is not something unequivocally positive, that we face a real problem here, that Shakespeare's style has its inherent dangers is historically attested by the concealed or open opposition which the greatest thinkers and finest artists, from Voltaire to Tolstoy[3] and Bernard Shaw[4], showed toward the dramatist. I am also thinking of Lessing's shocked discovery that he could not transplant into the praxis of *Sturm und Drang* what he professed and yet guarded against in Shakespeare's art.

There is also Goethe and Schiller's anti-Shakespearean cult of the Greek drama – though they didn't admit it, it is *de facto* – and Byron's open,[5] and Hebbel and Grillparzer's secret[6] opposition to Shakespeare. And just recently, the subtlest exponent of stylized modern art, Paul Ernst, severely criticized Shakespeare's compositions. I am also thinking that where Shakespeare had a total impact (*Sturm und Drang*, the French romantic drama and, in many respects, the German), the movements none the less remained sterile. Let's also remember that the great English poets who, as Swinburne put it, wrote for an imaginary Globe or Blackfriars theatre, never produced a lively, great drama. That those who diligently searched for and grasped Shakespeare's central problem have reached a dead end, just as – to mention the greatest example – did the unfortunate, profound and great artist, Otto Ludwig.[7]

That there is a problem is attested, if by nothing else, by the very question whether Shakespeare's style is really dramatic. We know that Goethe, mature and well versed in great theatrical praxis, had denied this.[8] Many theoretical writers claim that if we really analysed Shakespeare's dramas in depth, and compared it with Greek drama, Shakespeare would prove to be an epic writer. In my view, these polemics are unfair to Shakespeare, but their symptomatic importance is undeniable. If serious people and artists who take their art seriously can question the dramatic nature of Shakespeare's method of composition, then it is legitimate to ask whether it is dramatic in the modern sense of the term. Our question therefore is whether the compositional essence of Shakespeare's dramas is the same as what we demand today from the drama. In short, can modern drama follow in the footsteps of Shakespeare?

How does Shakespeare motivate his characters? Our feeling is that the problem of motivation practically defines the whole problem of drama; that the essence of dramatic structure is the forceful joining of cause and effect. What is Shakespeare's feeling on this? First of all, the territory of motivation is much more confined for him than it is in modern drama. He can dispense with the causal explanation of events, external to the drama and yet integral to it. He never bothers with the causal explanation of historical events. In all Shakespearean dramas, the historical events must be accepted as they are or, more properly, as Shakespeare adopted them from their sources. Think of the introductory part of *King Lear*, in which the chronicle of 'history' – fantastic, fairytale-like, unbelievable and inexplicable – gives rise to a powerful and spellbinding tragedy. That is, of course, provided that we accept the 'history', forego its analysis, and neither demand nor derive conclusions from it that would affect the dramatic character of Lear. Think also of the pre-dramatic events in *The Merchant of Venice* and of *Cymbeline*. (I deliberately choose examples from Shakespeare's different periods.)

Everyone feels a dissonance here. And precisely because one feels it, and feels it with the same intensity in Shakespeare's late period, we attempt to achieve a balance and, subsequently, create a unity where there is no unity. There is no unity because the demand for it, as advanced by us – later we will explain why – was unknown to Shakespeare and his age. They say that Shakespeare's dramas are dramatic tales, and the tale tolerates inconsistency that the drama would not allow. I cannot discuss here whether this is true or not. Namely, to what extent Shakespeare's audience felt that his dramas were tales, and to what extent the audience held, with the same conviction, that they were realistic like, for instance, the dramas of Ibsen. I consider the last proposal plausible. But the requirement of logical structure is, for drama, the requirement of form. The drama is not written to awaken the illusion of reality, for which the drama is inapplicable. Consequently, if we declare drama to be a dramatic tale, all we have really said is that the rigorous system of cause and effect joins various facts and people; that though the content of cause and effect changes, the content has no bearings on the cause and the effect.

Think of Grillparzer's mythological dramas,[9] of Kleist's *Käthchen von Heilbronn*, of Mihaly Vörösmarty's *Csongor és Tünde*, and [Gerhart Hauptmann's] *The Sunken Bell*. In all these works, the source materials and the tale grew from the same world and obey the same laws, the same human beings act in both, and just as nothing is forgotten, nothing is overlooked. Some critics try to inject motives into what is motiveless. They reconstruct Cordelia's whole past in order to make her relationship with Lear necessary. Hebbel had utilized modern theories – like milieu and hereditary transmission – to infuse the actions of Goneril and Regan with relative rights and determinism.

Needless to say, all these attempts have proved futile because they offer arbitrary interpretations, and, as such, are deficient as real explanations. They are deficient because Shakespeare and his age – among his contemporaries, he formulated the motives best – felt no need for motives. We know of an older play ['The True Chronicle History of King Lear, and his Three Daughters, Gonorill, Ragan, and Cordella' (1605)] that inspired Shakespeare's *King Lear*. In the anonymous play there was an attempt, naive and primitive, to provide motives for the actions of Lear, Goneril, Regan and Cordelia. Shakespeare discarded these motives. He also discarded in Cinthio's novel [*Hecatommithi, Parte Prima, Deca Terza, Novella 7*], from which he borrowed the theme of *Othello*, the motives for Iago's intrigues. In Plutarch, he discarded the motives for Cassius' hatred of Caesar. We are dealing here with Shakespeare's intentions, rather than accidents. Specifically, what he kept from his readymade sources, what he developed and what he discarded. We know that Othello, in the original novel, was not a noble hearted tragic hero. Shakespeare made him into that, and it is inconceivable, even if we presuppose a spontaneous, direct but still conscious artistic intention in *Othello*, that it was otherwise in cases where Shakespeare decided to omit certain things.

We also know that in developing the plot of *Othello*, Shakespeare minimizes the role of motive.[10] The most decisive facts and catastrophes are the result of accidents and misunderstandings, rather than the inevitable, logical sequence of events. Shakespeare needs great, pathetic situations that reveal man's whole soul. He is not concerned, just as his age was not concerned, how he arrived at these situations. Let me cite a few examples. Cassius' suicide is the result of accidents and misunderstandings, as is the relationship of Gloucester, Edgar and Edmund. And to cite the greatest example, the tragic end of *Romeo and Juliet* is based on a brutal accident. The tragedy of Othello and Desdemona – where accident has a deep psychological background – resembles an unpredictable game of cards, where the good outcome is just a hairsbreadth away.

How is this possible? Why is Shakespeare so unconcerned with the pragmatic interaction of things, and why is it so important for us? What is Shakespeare's creative objective, what objective decides that he selects some elements and omits others. What was his purpose in composing his tragedies? And what is the purpose of contemporary playwrights? Hebbel – who is as typical a representative of modern drama as Shakespeare was of his own age – reflecting on his own praxis, said that the ultimate goal is to 'plug up every mouse and rat hole', to make the drama self-enclosed and subject to inexorable necessity. It is only from Shakespeare's own works that we can guess his goals, and therefore it is more difficult to formulate, or compress them into a single sentence.

Though fully aware that every formula, by leaving out many things, falsifies reality, I would sum things up as follows. Shakespeare's plays are based on individuals, on characters and on their interplay. The new drama is based on situations, or, more precisely, on men's relation to situations. To put it at its simplest, Shakespeare's conflicts are concrete, those of modern drama are abstract.

What does this mean? It means that Shakespeare's tragic vision pits one individual against another, or others, who are just as real and who, as they are and what they are, can never and nowhere be duplicated. Othello's tragedy is that he is what he is, and Iago and Desdemona are what they are, and these characters have met. Their encounter is a fact, a reality, an event with a history, it is as it is, and beyond dispute. This is what is required for *Othello*, whose tragic essence is precisely that the three characters have come into contact. In a profound sense, we can claim that every tragedy is based on accident – and precisely so from the Shakespearean standpoint.[11] The crossing of the paths of certain individuals can only be accidental, and Shakespeare's profound insight is that he sees life as a series of accidents. In the light of this, it is irrelevant and must remain so that accidents keep piling up (in the first part of *King Lear*), or strongly interact with the tragedy (at the end of *Romeo and Juliet*).

A negative definition can help us to clarify this. We have posed the question: what does Shakespeare's tragic vision contain? And now we ask, what is missing from it. The simple answer is: the abstract. What does this mean? It means that the tragic content of *Julius Caesar* is the strange character of four men, Caesar, Brutus, Cassius and Antonius, whose interaction spells tragedy for Brutus. It means that the play contains nothing from the abstract struggles of that age, a struggle between the declining Roman aristocratic republic and the new Caesarism. It means that in *Coriolanus* it is not the confrontation of aristocrats and plebeians,[12] but the baseness of Sicinius, Brutus and Aufidius, and Volumnia's great nobility that leads to Coriolanus' death. It means, that in the historical struggles portrayed in Shakespeare's dramas of English history it is not English feudalism that collapses, because of the bloody internecine wars, whose outbreak and tenacity were symptomatic of that period of great disintegration. True, the characters display bitter animosities and enact bloody acts. But in the end, Henry VII marks not the triumph of the new over the old, but the success of the noble hero against the monumental villain [*Richard the Second*]. The abstraction was a potential presence in Shakespeare's English history plays. But Shakespeare left it out, deliberately abandoned it, or did not even notice it. He located the problems elsewhere, and saw no problem here.[13]

Consider the opening scenes of *Julius Caesar*, the roles of Flavius and Marullus were readymade for Shakespeare, and yet when the tribunes scold the people for fawning on Caesar, they talk only about the people's ingratitude to Pompey, and not about the struggle against tyranny. Moreover, the essence of Cassius' argument is to question why Caesar should rule, for he is no better than Brutus or Cassius. Brutus of course was a lover of freedom. It is noteworthy that, although not even Brutus is as resolutely and theoretically opposed to the crowning of Caesar as he should have been, freedom and tyranny confront each other here. Brutus is guided and possessed by the fear that kingly power could change Caesar's character. But as Coleridge rightly pointed out, Brutus' fear is historically untenable. Consequently, Brutus' conviction is just as integral to his character (and not to the great historical situation) as is envy to Cassius' character.

The tragic turning point occurs when Brutus, out of noble minded short-sightedness, spares Mark Antony's life and, in fact, allows him to deliver a funeral oration over Caesar's body. The fickle nature of the crowd here is not due to the historical situation (that is to say, abstract). Every crowd in Shakespeare acts this way. But while Antony takes it into account, Brutus does not. And herein lies the key to his tragedy. Recall the episodical treatment of the people's misery (the question of bread), and how much attention is given to the tribunes who, full of hatred, want to deprive Coriolanus of power and destroy him completely. In the same way, in *Antony and Cleopatra* the world's fate depends on – the episodical – Sextus Pompeius' character.

I deliberately choose such illustrations because these dramas, by their very substance, contain the great, historical, abstract necessity. All this could be read without any difficulties into these dramas, once the need and the demand had been made for the drama to express the abstract necessities that reign over life.[14] That this has taken place, I believe hardly needs to be proved by many examples. In the early and mid-nineteenth century, the outstanding German aestheticians, under the pretext of studying Shakespeare, have persisted in their attempt to read into Shakespeare the conflicts of modern life. They tried to reconcile Shakespeare's approach to problems with the actual problems.

The best known case – and the most interesting – is that of Hegel who, in his interpretation of *Macbeth*, traces the conflict to disputes between different systems of hereditary rights. According to Hegel, Macbeth, as the next eldest male relative of Duncan, is therefore strictly heir to the throne. Indeed, Macbeth suffered injustice when Duncan named his own son as his successor. Hegel in fact reproaches Shakespeare for altogether omitting this motive, this justification of

Macbeth, and thus representing him as a criminal. In Hegel's view,[15] Shakespeare's treatment of Macbeth was nothing but a genuflection towards King James. Hegel also criticizes Shakespeare for not letting Macbeth murder Duncan's sons too, but allowing them to escape, while none of the nobles gives them a thought either.

That such a profound philosopher of art, as Hegel, could so misunderstand what is perhaps one of Shakespeare's most wonderfully composed tragedies, demonstrates just how deeply modern drama has already influenced our perceptions. For all practical purposes, what Hegel really described is how Schiller, Grillparzer or Hebbel, or any of the modern playwrights – despite all their differences – would have handled the Macbeth theme if they came across it first in Holinshed's *Chronicles*. We can see what misunderstanding, bordering on the ridiculous, this can lead to when applied to Shakespeare, even on the part of a great thinker like Hegel.

Purely from an artistic standpoint, the essence of Shakespeare's composition is a powerful sequence of great scenes, that depict and portray the tragic feelings of tragic figures. The fundamental elements that connect these scenes reside in the individual, in his character; in the atmosphere which surrounds the individual, his adversaries, and in his interactions with them, rather than in the possibility or necessity of the atmosphere itself. Hebbel saw this clearly and summed it up by saying that, for Shakespeare, the dialectics of drama resides in the character, while for the new drama it resides in the idea, in the abstract.

What holds together every Shakespearean tragic play is that, for instance, the Othello–Iago–Desdemona relationship must lead to tragedy. Tragedy is a necessity, but how it takes place is not a necessity. This question – not being raised as an abstract problem – was a mute question for Shakespeare. He was only interested in how the tragic feelings, based on the relationship of Othello, Iago and Desdemona, manifest themselves. This is the reason why he concentrated on scenes that impart immediacy and force to tragic feelings. It would be unfair to make any other demands on Shakespeare's scenes, expecting them to yield what was not intended in the first place; thus the success or failure of what was not intended cannot be in question.

In Shakespeare's dramas individuals dominate the events. The role of events and circumstances is to provide the individual with an opportunity to express his spiritual feelings, and give these feelings a beautiful, colourful background. Events and circumstances have no life of their own. Abstracted from the life of the individual, in whose life they play a role, events and circumstances are non-existent. (Here let me just add in parenthesis that the great theme that dominates modern drama, variations of which are evident in every great modern writer, is no other than the conflicts and collisions produced by the circumstances, by the separate existence of the external world. So much so, that it would hardly be an exaggeration to say that these conflicts are the central and dominant theme of modern drama.)

Let me remind you of the war in Cyprus in *Othello*, of the Fortinbras episode in *Hamlet* [v ii]; consider that no single circumstance prevents Macbeth's ascension to the throne, and everything is against him when he is doomed. Goethe once remarked that nobody ever designed men's material costumes the same way as did Shakespeare, and perhaps this is more apt than even Goethe thought. For in Shakespeare everything turns into a material costume: place, time, circumstance, action, everything, even spiritual characteristics, which sheds no light on his characters' souls, though large and rich, and the real scene of tragic events.

Apart from some central figures, everyone else merely serves as a background. Characters attain significance in relation to the central figure. This is why it is so futile to analyse in great depth, or by themselves, for instance such characters as Claudius or Polonius. These figures, as [Walter] Raleigh[16] has observed, Shakespeare saw through the eyes of Hamlet, they are no more and no less than what Hamlet sees and needs in them to realize the tragedy of his soul, that gives off light in contact with others. But these figures, unlike those of modern drama, have no separate life of their own. Shakespeare therefore can treat them with absolute arbitrariness. This is how Antigonus disappears in the middle of *The Winter's Tale*, no longer being needed in the drama of principal characters; and this is how Cloten is got rid of in *Cymbeline* IV ii].

But to offer more substantial illustrations, this is how Lepidus and Sextus Pompeius disappear in *Antony and Cleopatra* when Antony and Octavius Caesar fight to decide who will rule the empire. And after the great storm scenes, there is no place for the Fool next to Lear, and he disappears – taking leave of the world in a barely audible sentence – never to be heard of again. Perhaps *The Merchant of Venice* is Shakespeare's only drama in which one character, none other than Shylock, actually outgrows the framework, attains a self-contained life, a life that is independent of the dramatic process. However – as confirmed by conflicting interpretations – Shylock explodes the play, splits it into two plays and, in fact, as far as we are concerned, in essence kills the other play, the genuine one, the Antonio–Bassanio–Portia circular-drama.

In fact, this problem raises the question of the significance of background. In Shakespeare, a few principal characters dominate the

whole play, and nothing else can equal or even approach their importance. However these other things – and I cannot analyse the reasons
for it here – have attained quite different meanings since Shakespeare's time. For no matter how useful Shakespeare's creative
method is, from a purely artistic perspective, it would be useless if one
were to emphasize other than his principal characters. One example
from the fine arts, perhaps, can shed light on this. It is hardly accidental that modern painters whose style is the most consistent, display
the strongest feeling for Giotto's so-called primitivism, and its inde-
scribable and inestimable advantage for his art. That, for instance –
this is merely an example – he borrowed from nature and architecture
exactly what he needed, when he needed it, to compose the background for his human figures, irrespective of their self-centred life and
its visual expression. Virtually everything that is external to the soul
of Shakespeare's principal characters recalls the nature that surrounds
Giotto's figures.[17] But as soon as the intrinsic value of nature is
recognized – in Venice it started with Bellini and Giorgione – new
designs had to be found to accommodate the new perception of
nature in great compositions. And today – in the wake of Impressionism – once more there is a search for new designs. This is also the
situation of new drama in relation to Shakespeare.

Strangely enough, the superficial seems to express the profoundest
things the most vividly. When Goethe criticized Shakespeare's drama,
perhaps he objected to its colourfulness or, most likely, he had in mind
the difficulty of adapting it for the modern stage. For Goethe, Shakespeare's complex actions, based on many short scenes, prove difficult, if
not impossible, for the modern stage, without sacrificing their most
beautiful and appealing features. Undeniably, if the performance of
Shakespeare's plays cannot satisfy us completely, this is all the more true
in other aspects. The reasons for this, in my view, lie deeper than the
theatre's technical ability to overcome the problem of many scenes.

I would summarize this – in a somewhat paradoxical form – by
saying that every literary work, especially drama, is the result of the
mixture of concrete and abstract elements, and that neither the one
nor the other can ever dominate the whole. Thus, in case of Shakespeare, as we saw, the conflict is concrete and, therefore, the place
where the conflict takes place can be abstract. In modern drama, the
conflict is abstract, and this conflict needs a concrete place and time
in which to express itself.

What do I mean when I assert that the locale and time of Shakespeare's dramas are abstract? Among other things, I mean that they
resemble the background in, for instance, the *Mona Lisa*, as distinct from
the background in a Manet landscape, or a figure in Pieter de Hooch's

interiors. [18] I mean that place and time in Shakespeare have no substance, only pictorial quality, and this picturesqueness is the visual,
symbolic projection of the momentary feelings and moods of the characters who dwell in it. From this perspective – apart from the accidental
nature of historical circumstances – Shakespeare's frequent changes of
scene attain a great and deep meaning. Specifically, the background
accompanies his characters everywhere, and everything external merely
serves as a background. But at the same time, this background best
symbolizes what takes place in the character internally.

Think of the court of Macbeth's castle, in Inverness, on the morn-
ing after the murder; think of the churchyard scene in *Hamlet*; think
of the great storm scenes in *King Lear*. You soon realize that these
scenes exert less influence on what is taking place internally, than
does the atmosphere of modern drama. And you also become aware
that no sooner do Shakespeare's characters change their mood, than
the background also changes. The characters, however, receive nothing from their surroundings and, in fact, it only exists inside them.
But, precisely for this reason, location forms such an integral part of
character, it assumes the form of an irretrievable moment, that more
profound, sublime emotion demands a neutral setting. Once the great
feeling becomes manifest, the neutral setting becomes its timeless
symbol, and nothing else. So it is inconceivable that Shakespeare
could have limited his dramas to one act. And it would have a
dissonant effect if we tried to reduce the multiplicity of his symbols to
a single one, or if we tried to transpose his symbolic backgrounds into
something modern.

My limited time prevents me from discussing this issue in greater
depth. Nor have I accomplished what I should have. Namely, to
examine and compare those two great trees, Shakespearean drama
and modern drama, describe their features, the circumstances that
produced them, and what facilitated and what endangered them. The
best I could do is to provide a cross-section of the two tree trunks and,
by comparing them, outline their different natures and tendencies. I
could only draw the respective boundaries of Shakespearean and
modern drama, without addressing the question of why those boundaries exist, and how they manifest themselves.

Of course, I made some critical points about Shakespeare's boundaries – as defined by his age – boundaries that grew from his own
limitations, rather than from his specific and unsurpassed beauties. It
should be obvious that our perception of Shakespeare's boundaries is
informed by the same profound and sympathetic admiration as are his
dithyrambic praises. In fact, our love of Shakespeare may well be a
truer love, because it wants to know what Shakespeare was really like,

what he considered important and what less important. This love of
ours instructed us to approach Shakespeare's dramas from the perspective of his own demands, to see its perfect solutions, without
trying to read into them things he could not even think of, things
without which, outside the context of his intentions, even his best
composition would appear fragmentary.

NOTES

1   Diego de Velazquez (1599–1660) made a deep impression on Edouard
    Manet (1832–83), the leading Impressionist painter.
2   Frans Hals (1580–1666) was, without doubt, one of the greatest portrait-
    ists of all times. Considered a forerunner to the Impressionists in the
    expressiveness of his brushwork, Hals excelled in the clarity and bright-
    ness of his flesh tones and the subtle characterization of his sitters.
3   Tolstoy's diaries contain fascinating, though mostly critical, remarks on Sha-
    kespeare. Tolstoy held that great talents – the Goethes, Shakespeares, Beetho-
    vens, Michelangelos – produced 'side by side with beautiful things not merely
    mediocre ones, but repulsive ones as well'. *Tolstoy's Diaries*, ed. R. F. Christian
    (London: Flamingo, 1994), p. 314.
4   In his devastating attack on Shakespeare, Shaw said: 'With the single
    exception of Homer, there is no eminent writer, not even Sir Walter
    Scott, whom I despise so entirely as I despise Shakespeare when I
    measure my mind against his. The intensity of my impatience with him
    occasionally reaches such a pitch, that it would positively be a relief to
    me to dig him up and throw stones at him, knowing as I do how
    incapable he and his worshippers are of understanding any less obvious
    form of indignity.' Stanley Wells, *Shakespeare* (London: Sinclair-Steven-
    son, 1994), p. 351.
5   Lord Byron (1788–1824) and Percy Bysshe Shelley (1792–1822) engaged
    in a dialogue on *Hamlet*. Byron wondered how one can read *Hamlet* and
    still call Shakespeare a 'thoughtful artist whose whole story, the action,
    after the first prologue and preparation of this ghost, remains stagnant; all
    the rest is stationary, episodical, useless'. Thereupon Shelley read out a
    brilliant defence of *Hamlet*, and when he finished, he found Lord Byron
    fast asleep. *From Sensibility to Romanticism*, eds F. W. Hilles and Harold
    Bloom (New York: Oxford University Press, 1965), pp. 505–8.
6   Franz Grillparzer (1791–1872), Austria's leading poet and dramatist,
    admired Shakespeare's ability to penetrate the depths of human nature
    and to enter the very soul of his characters. Lukács's reference to Grillpar-
    zer's 'secret' opposition to Shakespeare is mystifying, unless it implies
    envy. For Grillparzer's comments on Shakespeare, see *Sämtliche Werke*
    (Munich: Carl Hanser, 1964), vol. iii, pp. 642–59.
7   Otto Ludwig (1813–1865), German novelist and dramatic theorist.
8   In his *Wilhelm Meister's Apprenticeship*, Goethe declared, among other

things, that Shakespeare belongs 'by necessity in the annals of poetry; in the annals of theatre he appears only by accident'.

[9] Lukács refers to Grillparzer's plays that utilize Greek myth and legends. In the tragedy *Sappho*, Grillparzer depicts the Greek poetess Sappho, and in *Medea* he deals with the relationship of Medea and her husband.

[10] In interpreting *Othello*, Lukács appears to subscribe to the Schlegel–Coleridge theory. According to this, Iago's action is not prompted by any plain motive like revenge, jealousy or ambition. It springs from what Coleridge termed 'motiveless malignity' or a disinterested delight in the pain of others. By contrast, Bradley argued that Iago by nature was not malignant, but an evil man. In fact, Iago combines intellect and evil; it is rare, but it exists, and Shakespeare represented it in Iago. A. C. Bradley, *Shakespearean Tragedy*, p. 233.

[11] When Lukács enumerates 'chance' or 'accident' in most of Shakespeare's tragedies, he means any occurrence (not supernatural, of course) which enters the dramatic sequence neither from the agency of a character, nor from the obvious surrounding circumstances. To use Lukács's examples, it is an accident that Romeo never got the Friar's message about the potion [*Romeo and Juliet* v ii]; an accident that Edgar arrived too late to save Cordelia's life [*King Lear* v iii]; an accident that Desdemona dropped her handkerchief at the most fatal of moments [*Othello* III iii].

[12] Lukács dissented from William Hazlitt (1778–1830) who said that anyone who studies *Coriolanus* 'may save himself the trouble of reading Burke's *Reflections*, or Paine's *Rights of Man*, or the Debates of both Houses of Parliament since the French Revolution or our own.' Hazlitt, *On Theater*, ed. William Archer (New York: Hill and Wang, 1957), p. 112.

[13] Lukács implies that in his historical plays, *Henry the Sixth, Part One* and *Part Three*, along with *King John* and *Richard the Second*, Shakespeare treats his source material with characteristic freedom, shaping, omitting, altering and adding.

[14] Lukács's concept of 'necessity' is borrowed from Aristotle's *Poetics* and, applied to Shakespearean tragedy, it implies a power ordaining inevitably the nature of what is, and controlling inevitably the sequence of what becomes.

[15] Hegel, *Aesthetics*, trs. T. M. Knox, 2 vols., (Oxford: At the Clarendon Press, 1975).

[16] Walter Raleigh, *Shakespeare* (London: Macmillan, 1907). This influential book, twice reprinted in 1907, was diligently studied by Lukács.

[17] Giotto (1267–1337) broke sharply with the past in portraying individuals. Representations of the human face in earlier paintings had given it an expressionless stare; he invested it with grief, fear, pity, joy or other emotions to which the viewer could respond with instant understanding. Lukács, who always spoke in superlatives of Giotto, fully subscribed to John Ruskin's statement that Giotto 'painted what no man could look upon without being the better for it'.

[18] Pieter de Hooch (1629–1684) is celebrated for his delightful interiors and use of light. His real contribution to the development of painting lies in his revelation of the atmospheric life of these comfortable interiors.

John Ford

A Modern Dramatic Poet from Shakespeare's Age

It is not in the usual sense of the term that we must define Ford's modernity. My object is not the poet and whether he is still relevant or dated. This question should be raised sooner or later in the context of the whole age, for anyone familiar with the period must feel that the complete neglect of Elizabethan poets in favour of Shakespeare is, after all, a bit unfair. Time itself sided with Shakespeare and took revenge on his contemporaries, who appeared blind to his greatness which overshadowed all others. They considered him as their own kind, not even a *primus inter pares*. In this respect, John Webster's dedication to his tragedy *The White Devil* is very instructive. While he refers to Chapman, Ben Jonson, Beaumont and Fletcher in flattering terms, he mentions Shakespeare in the same breath as Heywood and Dekker, who were hardly more than routine and accomplished masters of that period.

Even in the two poems that Ben Jonson addressed to Shakespeare one senses, despite their passionate and sincere tone, that they are written by a poet who considers himself his equal. Today [1908], however, it seems as if the whole Elizabethan age were dead. All the empty names, which signify nothing to us, merely form a dark background for Shakespeare's luminous presence. It is not the apparent injustice of this judgement that demands close analysis here. In our view, what enables us to talk about Ford as a modern poet is that his works contain many elements that coincide closely with our own feelings. As if our nerves felt it, our eyes saw it, and it was our own art expressing what is uniquely modern – which tomorrow might be dated.

Without doubt Ford was always a lonely man. We know very little about his life: a few meagre details. This seems to be the case with most of the writers of the Elizabethan age. And yet, it appears that Ford's life was quite different from that of his contemporaries. It was the age of geniuses who, maturing early and leading a fast-moving chaotic life, came to an end young. But Ford matured slowly, almost like Flaubert or Ibsen. He started to write when he was twenty, and

was over forty when he found his individual style and shortly thereafter, making his weary farewell to poetry for good,[1] he returned to his
homeland. Of his contemporaries, we hear only exciting incidents and
violent fragments. Anyone who contemplates this age, is bound to
recall the Mermaid Tavern, where the evenings were filled with
passionate and heated debates,[2] and Marlowe's fiery and doomed life.
There are no anecdotes about Ford. A contemporary poem mentions
him, but it speaks of his sadness, loneliness and melancholy.

The very tone of his poems sets him apart. It is more measured and
hesitating, and, at the same time, more subtly tremulous and nuanced
than those of his contemporaries. In short, Ford is an artistic poet,
perhaps an unconscious follower of *l'art pour l'art*. Often one has a
feeling that Ford was not only uncomfortable but troubled by the
colourful conventions of his times. He treats casually the inevitable
episodes and comical scenes required in those days. His buffoons and
clowns are somewhat stiff, mask-like, and identical in every play. The
inexhaustible and flourishing richness of life is absent from his plays,
though it is a more or less common feature of other playwrights.
However, Ford, unlike others, is not a naive naturalist; he is stylized.
This stylization is so powerful and conspicuous that the raw, coarse
elements in Ford strike one as distasteful and distractive. If we want
to enjoy his plays, we must separate from them everything which is
not directly connected with the main action – subtle, in contrast to his
contemporaries, but thin in substance – in order to discover the
tragedies he intended to write. (Maeterlinck demonstrated this quite
neatly when he extracted his play *Annabella* from Ford's tragedy *'Tis
Pity She's a Whore.*)

Let's consider the impression a drama like Ford's *'Tis Pity* would
make today. If we read *Annabella* without knowing its author, we
would be amazed at what dramatic effect the playwright is capable of.
We could easily believe that Maeterlinck wrote it. At any rate, we
would place the author close to Maeterlinck or perhaps Oscar Wilde
himself.

The plays of Ford unfold in a stylized decorative world. Their locale
is Greece or Italy or, in essence, both or neither of them; for it is an
imaginary country with ancient churches and lovely parks. The South
as Northern man envisions it, surrounded with the subdued melancholy of the unattainable. Ford's scenery sometimes recalls the gentle
landscapes of Ludwig von Hofmann,[3] but above all the poetry of
Stefan George. Ford's world is inhabited by men of depth who suffer
in great loneliness. His characters only possess spiritual life, for them
the external world no longer offers or can offer anything. Fame and quest
for glory – so important to the Elizabethan heroes – are non-existent for

Ford's heroes. Most of them are uninterested in fame and glory, and those who attain it discard it as something they do not care for. Ford's characters seem to have a nervous system and feelings, unlike the characters drawn by other playwrights. Ford's characters are quiet, refined, and convey deep spiritual development. Everything about them is calm and subdued.[4] A strong sense of respect prevents his characters' brutal intrusion into each other's secret lives, though each tries – in vain – to sympathize and identify with the spiritual state of the other. Each one feels deeply and painfully his own loneliness. Ford's characters undertake sentimental journeys in order to flee their inner despair; but neither sojourns, religion or philosophy bring any solace.

It is a race doomed to extinction. Undeniably, today we would call it decadent. Ford's characters are a mixture of tough selfishness, sensitive consciousness and delicate feelings. Driven by destructive passions, they are capable of extremes and will attempt anything. None the less, they recoil from the pain they inevitably invoke, and grieve knowing they have inflicted pain on others. The conscience of Ford's characters is solely attached to inner values. In *'Tis Pity*, Giovanni considers his incest with his sister a harsh measure of fate rather than sin.[5] By contrast, in *The Broken Heart*, Penthea, whose brother forced her to marry someone she did not love, feels tainted and impure. She feels – like the heroines of Ibsen later – that she belongs forever to the one she loves; and she complains that, lawful wife of her beloved, she is guilty of infidelity.

Gentle and tough – such is Ford the psychologist. He is, first and foremost, a psychologist, a passionate analyst of the secrets of the soul. He resembles modern writers in being more of an analyst than a drawer of character. He is more interested in the subtle shifts of mood in his characters than in anything else. His characters seem to possess only souls: they are corporeal just to afford decorative possibilities for the soul. No blood courses in their veins. These are not human beings with passion, they are passion itself – at once complex and irrational – which assumes human form. As a result, Ford's female figures lead a much more intense life than his male figures. The elegant stylization of his female figures forms an organic part of their character.

Ford had simplified the masculine soul, and in his repertory of male characters he preferred the exceptional – much more so than with his female figures. He was more attached to his female characters: he knew them better and his portrayal of women is invariably more powerful than that of men. In the English Renaissance – notwithstanding Shakespeare – it is Ford who brought true recognition to women. Some of his female figures (Calantha in *The Broken Heart*, and Bianchia in *Love's Sacrifice*) stand at an intellectual height which none of his fellow dramatists, and few since, have reached, let alone surpassed. In Ford's female figures everything springs spontaneously from their deep, delicate and strong nature. By contrast, his male characters command only knowledge, mostly theoretical and acquired. Men know fate, women sense it.

Ford submits his characters to the test of irreversible fate. For Ford, heroism is never more than heroic passivity. Perhaps it is only in Ford that the word 'fate', the favourite expression of the Elizabethans, is never an empty phrase. His dramas are truly dramas of destiny. His characters are ruled by some unknown, unpredictable, unplanned, irrational and amoral forces. These forces can be portrayed, but not explained or rationalized, and least of all justified. In terms of their inner technique, Ford's dramas are analytical. This is all the more noteworthy because the tendency of the age (think of Shakespeare!) is the exact opposite. In Ford this technique springs from the same inner necessity as, for instance, Ibsen's *Ghosts*, Hebbel's *Maria Magdalene*, or even Sophocles' *Oedipus Rex*. The quintessence of fate is that it is merciless and irrevocable.[6] In the drama itself fate therefore plays no role, because what takes place before our eyes appears as something arbitrary. Dramatic action needs a motive, but everything which is provided with a motive can always be – in our view – otherwise. On the other hand, what has taken place in the past, as an indisputable fact or an isolated situation, is no longer subject to dispute. The perverse passion of the brother and sister, Giovanni and Annabella in *'Tis Pity*, is of long duration; the tragedy of *The Broken Heart* is the consequence of things that have already taken place, and the seeds of Ford's other dramas are also hidden in the past.

Ford pursued fate as far as it can be pursued, and portrays it with unyielding toughness and relentless consistency. It is the concept of fate and its terrifying ordinance[7] that distinguishes Ford from his contemporaries. He lacks the naive aggressiveness of the others. This probably explains why Ford is more consistent intellectually, and reluctant to reach any compromise, to display any sentimentality. We are talking about the bitter, cold-hearted antinomies of necessity. Ford is an observer. His latest editor, Havelock Ellis, rightly compared him to Flaubert.[8] Indeed, Ford often displays the great novelist's impassioned mind.[9] Ford champions neither individuals, nor ideals or view points, let alone plays an adversary as did Shakespeare.

In Ford's scales, the scales of fate, everything is weighed equally; the question is how his characters shoulder or struggle with fate. This is how his somewhat commonplace history (*Perkin Warbeck*) acquires a great human value: the king, the rebels and the pretender, viewed from a higher perspective, all enjoy equal rights. In Ford's dramas everyone, as Hebbel later insisted, is equally right – or equally wrong – for right and wrong are but empty words. In Ford's world of drama there is no sin or moral conflict. He failed to accomplish – though he rarely attempted it – what is so characteristic of his age: to portray genuine and pure villains or even intrigue. Ford's characters are both heroes and villains, at once loveable and loathsome. The necessity of his dramas is beyond all morality. Its necessity resides in the blood's insurgency against the will, in man's eternal loneliness and alienation.

And Ford's characters feel it, and this feeling, though it can hardly appease brutal fate, wraps its soft glow around the catastrophes. In Ford's dramatic world, the characters, having ruined each other, confront each other full of sympathy, understanding and forgiveness. Individuals feel deeply the hand of fate in the deeds of others. But this feeling and sense of understanding is transient, and invariably delayed. Delayed because its strength in character portrayal is precisely that it takes place between alienated beings, and had this feeling presented itself earlier it could not endure.

The human interaction of characters – herein lies Ford's greatest and most enduring creation. These interactions, which sparkle like jewels in the midst of arbitrary, clumsy, unmistakably half-hearted, theatrical stage effects, overshadow everything else. The love poems of Giovanni and Annabella are intoxicating;[10] unforgettable is the rhythm by which couples in *The Broken Heart* enter into loveless marriages, suffer and cause suffering, are destroyed and cause each other's destruction. It is compelling that a young man, in *Love's Sacrifice*, manages to inflame greater passion in the Duke's wife, Biancha, than he himself feels towards her; and it is captivating that Biancha, having at first firmly rejected Fernando's burning proposal, steals from her own boudoir to Fernando's bed.[11]

Ford has found brilliant words to describe the relationship of the Duke and his wife Biancha. But these words have a cold gleam, whose unmistakable purity and intimacy is devoid of any pathos. The gestures and images that accompany the words serve as a symbol for the spiritual content of the words. Calantha's dance in *The Broken Heart* has become justly famous. Calantha dances at the wedding of her friend, where all kinds of misfortune befall her. Different messengers arrive with the news that her beloved friend and then her father have died, and yet she stubbornly dances on, as if she had never heard a single word; she continues her dance until the festivities are over and then, with the same self-control and nobility of gesture, takes possession of the crown she so tragically inherited and earlier danced with. Only at the funeral of her lover – whose death is the last news she receives – does her dignity dissolve.

On the other hand, the incestuous tragic love in *'Tis Pity* is full of primitive, grotesque, perverse and moving images. Giovanni and Annabella, having mutually confessed their love, kneel, face each other, and almost prayer-like repeat their sacred vows of love, which lends the whole scene something of an institutionalized ritual, with rough and primitive edges. It is both grotesque and moving when Giovanni, their incestuous love revealed, stabs his sister, lest she be killed by others. Then he appears at the banquet he has pre-arranged, with Annabella's heart upon his dagger. He carries her heart at the dagger's point as the knight of Arthurian legend carries the white lily in some Pre-Raphaelite painting; as Wilde's Salome holds the vainly tempted Iokannan's head on a silver charger.

NOTES

[1] In the eyes of competent critics, John Ford stands high as a poet. While Charles Lamb placed him in the 'first order of poets', Swinburne described Ford's poetry as 'piercing and intense of sight, steady and sure of stroke, solemn and profound of strain'. Charles Lamb, *Specimens of English Dramatic Poets* (London, 1854), p. 228; Algernon Charles Swinburne, *Essays and Studies* (London, 1875), p. 304.

[2] The leading Shakespeare scholar, A. C. Bradley, whose *Shakespearean Tragedy* (1904) became the most read work of twentieth-century English literary criticism, wrote: 'Who can doubt that at the Mermaid Shakespeare heard from Jonson's lips much more censure of his offences against "art" than Jonson ever confided to Drummond or to paper?' Bradley, *Shakespearean Tragedy* (London: Macmillan, 1951), p. 69.

[3] Ludwig von Hofmann (1861–1945), an impressionistic and expressionist painter, who also experimented with the plastic three-dimensional set and avant-garde stagecraft.

[4] It has been argued that Ford's philosophy of life and approach to tragedy is based on the deterministic philosophy of Robert Burton's *Anatomy of Melancholy*. This famous work, based on the old four humours doctrine of Hippocrates and Galen, emerged in the Renaissance as a corpus of authoritative comment upon the nature of man's body and soul. Ford builds his plot structure upon the four humours doctrine and in so doing presents a mechanistic progress from cause to effect. As one student of Ford put it, 'Ford's heroes and heroines dwell in a world ruled by physical forces which can be considered neither good nor evil. No Macbeth goes to his doom because of overweening ambition; no Othello meets grief because of misguided passion.' G. F. Sensabaugh, *The Tragic Muse of John Ford* (Stanford University Press, 1944), p. 92.

[5] Ford's great play, *'Tis Pity*, whose subject is incest, appears to justify a new code of love, Platonic love, as it permeated court life at the time of Charles

I's Catholic wife, Henrietta Maria. The Platonic drama in court subscribed to the notion that fate rules all lovers. The Platonic idea that
physical beauty postulates a pure soul is the mainspring of Ford's thought
in the play. The incestuous Giovanni, in order to demonstrate that Annabella's beauty mirrors her purity, invokes Platonic casuistry.

> the frame
> And composition of the mind doth follow
> The frame and composition of body
> So, where the body's furniture is beauty,
> The mind must need be virtue; which allow'd,
> virtue itself is reason but refined . . . (III v)

Unrepentant, Giovanni considers incest, like any passion, legitimate:

> O the glory
> Of two united hearts like hers and mine!
> Let poring book-men dream of other worlds;
> My world, and all of happiness is here. (v iii)

This struck directly at the fundamental Puritan philosophy of love and
marriage. When the Queen's coterie began to worship beauty in woman,
to devalue the marital estate, and to defend adultery and incest, many
Puritans angrily attacked coterie members and their rites and beliefs.
Then in September 1642, Parliament decreed, 'that while these sad causes
and set-times of humiliations do continue, public stage-plays will cease
and be forborne.' We do not know whether Ford lived to see that day.

6

The inevitability of fate in Ford's plays arises partly from his own belief in
scientific determinism and partly from his characters' reiteration that fate
governs their lives. Consistent with the Platonic drama, where fate shapes
man's destiny and absolves him from responsible action, in Ford's dramas
no deed, whether of love or of lust, must be queried. 'I dare not ques-
tion/The will of heaven,' says Castanna after Spinella has observed, 'The
courtship's somewhat quick' and has advised her not to 'Reject the use of
fate', to which Malfato adds: 'Unthought of and unlookt for.' *The Lady's
Trial*, ll. 2518–23. And in *The Lover's Melancholy*, Thamasta, after having
changed her affection from Menaphon to Parthenophil, justifies it by
declaring 'in all actions,/Nature yields to Fate,' and argues that 'in vaine
we striue to crosse/The destiny that guides us.' *The Lover's Melancholy*, ll.
1395–401; ll. 1449–50.

7

Ford shows the terrible ordinance of fate in *'Tis Pity*. Early in the action,
Giovanni swears that fate will be his god if he cannot free himself from the
god of vengeance by prayer. And getting no relief from his supplication,
he resigns himself to incestuous love with his sister Annabella. He recognizes that the fates have doomed his death, because

The more I strive, I love; the more I love,
The less I hope: I see my ruin certain.

Giovanni is convinced that it is his 'destiny' to be loved by Annabella, who herself believes that stars have directed their passion, forbidding her to love Soranzo, her husband-to-be:

SORANZO: Have you not will to love?
ANNABELLA: Not you.
SORANZO: Whom then?
ANNABELLA: That's as the fates infer.
GIOVANNI: Of those I'm regent now. (ll. 1172–5)

Lukács is right, the terrifying ordinance of fate could hardly go beyond this.

[8] Havelock Ellis declared Ford the 'most modern of the tribe to whom he belonged'; he went on to say that Ford 'is less nearly related to the men who wrote *Othello*, and *A Woman Killed with Kindness*, and *Valentinian*, than to those poets and artists of the naked human soul, the writer of *Le Rouge et le Noir*, and the yet great writer of *Madame Bovary*.' Havelock Ellis, *John Ford* (London: Vizetelly & Co, 1888), p. xvii.

[9] In his novels, Flaubert ruptured many romantic illusions since his characters, the undoubted ancestors of all the 'unheroic heroes' and 'anti-heroes' of the twentieth century, are mostly unhappy and disillusioned: whether it is Frédéric in *Sentimental Education*, who declared that the happiest moment in a man's life is his first visit to a brothel, or Emma Bovary who 'discovered in adultery all the platitudes of marriage', or Salammbô who, touching the sacred veil of Tanit, 'remained melancholy in the fulfilment of her dreams'.

Flaubert not only exposes the politics of Right and Left, of the twentieth century as much as the nineteenth, with impartial ferocity and disgust, but lays bare the hollowness and fragility of ideals and, above all, presents an insidious devaluation of the power of love.

[10] Saying farewell to their sacred yet incestuous love, and life itself, Giovanni turns to his sister:

GIOVANNI: Kiss me again – forgive me.
ANNABELLA: With my heart.
GIOVANNI: Farewell!
ANNABELLA: Will you be gone?
GIOVANNI: To save thy fame, and kill thee in a kiss.

(*Stabs her*)

Thus die, and die by me, and by my hand!
Revenge is mine; honour doth love command. (*'Tis Pity* v v)

[11] In both *Love's Sacrifice* and *The Broken Heart*, Ford argues openly against the world's ethical order based on the sanctity of marriage. To Ford, and herein lies part of his modernity, tragedy depends not upon Christian notions of justice, or the recognition of the objective ethical law, but upon scientific necessity and individual rights which conflict with the highest ideals of man. As Lukács points out, Ford's tragic muse is closer to Ibsen's *Ghosts* than to Shakespeare's *Macbeth* or *Othello*.

Consider Biancha's argument when, caught by her husband in her lover's bed, she argues that Fernando should be hers because the iron laws of marriage should erect no bars between her and her happiness. She also brazenly points out that the Duke's 'crooked leg', 'scrambling foot' and 'bloodless lip' can hardly hope to compete with Fernando's miracle of flesh and blood, nor is it her fault that the Duke's sheets have never been soiled.

August Strindberg

On his Sixtieth Birthday[1]

It seems there are two representative types of men. One type looks at his own age from the outside, as it were, and at everything that moves or appears to move there. The other type joins every fight and engages in every battle, and yet his life coalesces and revolves around some centre as much – or as little – as does his own age. Thus Michelangelo managed to condense the spirit of the Renaissance on to the vault of Sistine Chapel, and to transmute it into the figures of the Medici tomb. But a clearer and more symbolic expression of this phenomenon can be found in Leonardo da Vinci's disjointed search in the lines he drew leading to his invisible centre. And in the same way, Dante and Shakespeare summed up the essence of their age in their work, and Goethe too provided us with the *summa* of his own complex age. But neither Dante nor Shakespeare had a contemporary whose summary offered a contrary vision. The great synthesizers of the late nineteenth century came from the North. Each was both the representative of his own type and the polar opposite of the other. No wonder that during their lives they ignored each other and would have nothing to do with each other's work: Ibsen and Strindberg.[2]

This phenomenon is quite strange and the readymade explanations open up endless possibilities. But it is exactly the facile proximity of answers which makes one deeply suspicious of the great seekers whose method of search is identical with that of their own age. One would suspect that the life-rhythm of the seekers would provide a quicker, easier and safer access to the life-rhythm of the age than would the great, complete work of the synthesizers. Conversely, we may never fully understand the meaning of history, from the Renaissance to the end of the nineteenth century, until we have defined that technique of Da Vinci, Goethe and Strindberg which enabled them to search for and find new perspectives. Above all, until we have addressed the logic and necessity behind their pauses and progress, the diversity of their vision and its nature, the centripetal and centrifugal forces in their own lives as well as in their concepts of life. And, most important, we must ask why Da Vinci, Goethe and Strindberg considered that the expressive forms available to them were both everything and nothing at the same time.

It would be relatively easy to assert, and would sound quite plausible, that Strindberg's futile searches represent the futility of modern bourgeois, individualistic life; that Strindberg, oscillating between polar opposites, betrays a rudderless existence; that the reason why his life and art have no centre is that our contemporary life no longer inspires ideals, it produces nothing we can believe in, or anything worth struggling for. In our life nothing releases greater storms or has a greater appeal for serious-minded people than the beautiful ecstasies and the headaches of evanescent moments.

As I said, all this may well be true. But one should write it down as the last sentence in a great book (or as the preface to a completed work). It should be the concluding sentence of a book which contained the minutest and most intimate details of Strindberg's life. At this stage [1909], we consider Strindberg's life to be so chaotic, such a pathless jungle, that we cannot even guess what is essential and what is episodic in it. In fact, we don't even know whether everything, or perhaps nothing, is really important in his life. Perhaps one could talk this way about Strindberg at the end of a book, provided that book encompassed our own age, openly or in disguised form, and we saw the threads which – through the mystery of experience – led from our own life to our art, and these threads determined where we are and what we are.

We can only give voice to our own feelings here. Namely that Strindberg's imposingly great and rich oeuvre has no centre. Despite our admiration[3] for his rigorous creative talent and passionate intellectual integrity, we do not believe Strindberg himself is the cause of his being centreless. It is inconceivable that where smaller talents have succeeded, who commanded a vision and shaped it into a transparent whole, there Strindberg would have failed because he was weak. Nor do we believe Strindberg's failure is devoid of symbolic value. We should add here that in Ibsen – Strindberg's great polar opposite – only the centre, around which everything coalesces, is artistic. The fact is that in Ibsen the centreless has gained a form, whereas in Strindberg the centreless remained the content. Let's also note that Da Vinci's lifework is more fragmented than that of Strindberg, and only few of Da Vinci's works are really complete (the completeness and value of some works is a mute issue here), and yet his diverse and divergent efforts comprise an organic whole. All the paths that Da Vinci followed led towards a single point. This is not true of Strindberg or, at least, we see nothing analogous to it here.

We cannot even claim that Strindberg belongs to those types for whom it was not given to formulate what they have felt; a kind of Raphael without hands – that magnificent, sublime and tragic breed of dilettantes. Strindberg – like Da Vinci and Goethe, though of a lesser rank – is a perfect artist, assuming he wants to be one. There is no literary form he failed to dominate with playful virtuoso ease. Except, of course, perfect work can only be perfect by itself, rather than a mere link in the long chain stretching from one end of a life to the other. A work is perfect by itself, rather than symptomatically, or as a manifest expression of an age. Somehow, the profoundest content of Strindberg's work appears as alien to the objective completeness of his perfect plays, as subjective lyricism is alien to his fragmentary products. Strindberg gives the impression of having raced through his lifework. When approached from the perspective of his life, his works appear to be incidental, one cannot help feeling that his plays are but adventures, and his own life merely a path to his dramatic oeuvre.

In the last thirty years or so, Strindberg participated in virtually every literary and non-literary movement. Wherever and whenever he made his appearance and became involved, he played a leading role. And yet, we keep wondering why he got involved in some things and not in others, and even if he had involved himself in these other things the same doubts would assail us. Strindberg is still developing, everyone of his plays and each of his stages of development proved as valuable to him as they are to us, provided we approach them from a higher, symbolic perspective.

Strindberg is still developing, but it appears to lead nowhere. With great detours, his development leads back to the original starting points, only to repeat itself once again at the end of yet another big detour. However, even this description might give a false impression of the unity of his work. After all, we can never know what constitutes the starting point nor, for that matter, what counts as a detour. For instance, obviously what we can achieve in Ibsen is quite impossible to achieve in Strindberg. Namely to establish the sequence of his plays based on their internal features. It is just as impossible to know whether the sixty-year-old Strindberg is completely exhausted,[4] or his life is about to burst into new blossom, for which everything until now was merely a modest preparation.

What then is August Strindberg all about? We can only answer that question with a silent awe. For we know nothing about Strindberg; one of the most subjective of all writers who, next to Rousseau, has written the most transparent and naked confessions.[5]

What then does August Strindberg mean to us? This question is more important than the first one, and perhaps one day the two questions will coincide. And perhaps at some later date, at a proper place and time, the first question will also be answered. For it is our conviction that the greater a man is the more he symbolizes things and, correspondingly, the more his own life serves as a distinct symbol to others. The greatness of every great man appears to grow with each thread that ties his life to the lives of others, and the more adventitious the events of one's life are the more they affect the life of others.

What then does August Strindberg signify for us? There was a time when he signified everything, and there are moments when he still does. There were periods in modern literature when everyone thought the solution to every question lay in the hands of Strindberg. During the great mystical-religious revival of the 1890s[6] it was Strindberg's religious mysticism which best exemplified Europe's misguided God-seeking. There was a period when it seemed – and it may have been the case – that Strindberg, the mystical philosopher of nature, was as far ahead of the natural sciences as had been Goethe and the romantic philosophers of nature in the early part of the century. And it was Strindberg's life and works, armed with the frightening power of truth, that mirrored the great hysterical and monumental struggle of the sexes and captured the erotic basis of intellectual feminism and its manifestations. And no one has captured more poignantly the secret tragedies of the approaching autumn, of old age's unstated and unconfessed signs, than Strindberg.

These are no more than illustrations and I could fill pages with them without ever feeling that all has been said. Even if everything had been said, one would sense that something has been left out. No summary of Strindberg's influence can fully explain his real significance because it has left unanswered what August Strindberg means to us.

This is why we feel, though dare not justify it, that there is something symbolic in Strindberg's secret of being, whose profoundly Sphinx-like life contains the answer. In our view, Strindberg's inexplicable nature is not accidental, for it contains the answer to his centreless existence. We are convinced – this time not only our scholarly conscience but our cowardly nature forbids us to pronounce it as a positive truth – that what is lacking in Strindberg, one of the greatest playwrights, is also lacking in our own life. After all, Strindberg's ultimate fragmentation[7] is our own fragmentation. His life, devoid of purpose, direction and focus, symbolizes our own life.

And so Strindberg is our poet. He is our representative man in life, in poetry, in achievements and in failures. We feel this to be true, but are reluctant, afraid and unwilling to admit it.

NOTES

1　The sixtieth birthday of August Strindberg (1849–1912) fell on 22 January 1909. Lukács's moving and confessional tribute appeared in the *Huszadik Század* (February, 1909) x: 172–5.

2　Ibsen and Strindberg, though both iconoclasts, were opposites in virtually everything. Ibsen was a left-winger all his life, Strindberg had an illiberal streak, including anti-Semitism. Ibsen's efforts as a painter were naturalistic, Strindberg painted in the Impressionist manner. Ibsen had lifted many masks on human nature and modern life, but Strindberg depicted men and women, driven by love and hatred, in that nightmare world where hysteria abuts on madness. Strindberg wrote about sex with a realism, savage and unsparing, which Ibsen never could or dared to match.

3　Lukács was especially taken by Strindberg's *The Father*. Strindberg intended it to be the modern equivalent of Aeschylus' *Agamemnon*, the Swedish captain, like the Greek king, a victim of woman's sexual hatred and lust for power. Lukács, who hated and despised his own mother, was obsessed with *The Father*, whose captain declared:

> I believe all you women are my enemies. My mother did not want me to come into the world because my birth would give her pain. She was my enemy . . . The first woman I took in my arms was my enemy.

The Father in *Six Plays of Strindberg*, tr. Elizabeth Sprigge (Doubleday, 1955), p. 54.

4　A few months after his sixtieth birthday, Strindberg wrote to a friend: 'I don't find it easy to live. But one has to. And one does, with little religion, otherwise it would be impossible. Sometimes I sit like Elijah beneath the Juniper tree and cry; "Enough! Lord, take my soul." Then I get up again and continue. And thus for sixty years!' Michael Meyer, *Strindberg* (New York: Random House, 1985), p. 527.

5　Strindberg's tormented, driven and restless self unfolds with startling honesty in *A Madman's Defence* and *The Inferno*. The first opens with Strindberg's psychological reaction to the conflicts in his dissolving marriage, a reaction that led him towards a tragic vision of life. *The Inferno* entails both a review and revaluation of his entire life. Strindberg's diary, called the *Occult Diary*, which contains entries like, 'Madhouse: God. Caesar (Shakespeare)', must, he said, be 'burned or sealed'.

6　Mainly as a reaction against the ascendancy of positivism and materialism, the decade of the 1890s witnessed rebellions and protests referred to as 'renascent mysticism', including Strindberg's own God-seeking, known as the 'Inferno crisis'. In fact, Strindberg's extraordinarily prolific literary career was interrupted in the mid-1890s by a period of nervous crisis, a season in hell, during which he suffered paranoid delusions and was unable to work. During his breakdown and crisis, he rediscovered his belief in God, and his writings became pronouncedly symbolistic and expressionistic.

   For a masterly study on the decade of the 1890s, see H. Stuart Hughes, *Consciousness and Society* (New York: Vintage Books, 1958).

[7] To Lukács it was axiomatic that the greatest novelists and dramatists have concentrated on one medium at a time, and he could think of no exception to this rule. There have been writers who have succeeded in both, but not at the same time. Indeed, Chekhov, like Shaw and Synge and Beckett, attained greatness as playwrights only when they put narrative fiction aside. As Lukács sees it, Strindberg's diffuse genius, moving not merely between plays and novels, but over numerous other fields, ultimately exacted the price.

8

Thoughts on Henrik Ibsen

Pax vobiscum were the last words of Ibsen's epilogue. Irene (ειρήνη: peace) was his last heroine.[1] It seemed as if his whole life was a harmony. He lived long enough to see his complete triumph, his life's work done, he laid down his pen and said 'enough'. He left behind no incomplete plans nor shattered dreams.

And yet the dominant tone of his work reveals nothing but bitterness, complaint and accusation. What was the origin of this disharmony? If we listen more carefully not to what he denounces and laments, but to why, we soon hear the same refrain echoing everywhere. Others too felt the suffering of great men. The souls of men who knew nothing about each other, and refused to acknowledge any kinship, suffered the same tortures. The same bitterness resounds in Baudelaire's poetry, it is what Flaubert laments – without ever comprehending it – in his letters; this is the concealed tragedy of Grillparzer, and the source of Schopenhauer's pessimism. What a great choir of *poétes maudits*. All these alienated, misunderstood souls in eternal conflict with themselves and their own age.

What is their problem? Very generally, that of being born too late. They lived at a time when romanticism already lay in ruins and had faded away, and rationalism, the romantics' sworn enemy, reigned supreme everywhere.

The golden age of romanticism had a short span everywhere; it exhausted itself in a brief, intense burst of brilliance. There are many external reasons for this which, of course, helps to explain why the romantic movement, despite its impressive beginnings in the early nineteenth century, seemed to come to an end. And where it did continue, it found the ground crumbling under its feet and it turned into a poetry of the *epigonoi*. Let us cite some of the reasons for this. In post-Napoleonic France, silenced and oppressed, a whole generation, growing up with the gleams of unlimited possibilities, suddenly found itself condemned to inaction. (Alfred de Musset describes this in *La Confession d'un enfant du siècle* [Confessions of a Child of the

Century].) Then came the unsuccessful revolutions of 1830 and 1848; to be followed in Germany by the Holy Alliance, and the dashing of revolutionary hopes, and so forth.

But the real cause of the demise of romanticism was, after all, the romantic soul's disposition. What then – and I can only outline the romantic sensibility – is romanticism? First and foremost, it denotes a revolution in human feelings, protesting the fetters placed on man. As a protest movement, romanticism was devoid of any practical direction and, in fact, it spurned any form of rational control. Expansive by nature, the romantics strove to embrace and conquer everything, they wanted to achieve a grand synthesis of feelings comprising science and art, poetry and mathematics. Above all, the romantics proclaimed the supreme importance of art and an aesthetic sensitivity towards everything. But the mysticism of the romantics – reminiscent of the closely cognate Renaissance – proved to be nothing more than an aesthetic, monistic concept of the world. The romantic movement marks the highest triumph of individualism, in whose world objects and reality have no place (see Fichte's philosophy), where all the boundaries have been removed so that the sovereign individual can recreate the world in his own image.

The romantics engaged in an ecstatic, triumphant dance. The romantics discovered things by accident, things which others have yet to explore and areas that were later developed and cultivated by another movement. This – none other than rationalism – followed in the footsteps of romanticism and turned its own weapons against it. However, by then the romantics were fatigued, and the romantic feeling – in its original form – had proved incapable of progress. Resolved to contain and encompass everything, in the hands of the romantics everything turned into fragments. The primacy of feelings, to which the romantics owe their great perspective and grand synthesis, demanded ever new quests and experiences, and consequently the romantics proved unable to execute and complete any single task. The romantics wanted to soar, but it is impossible to soar all the time; they had no goal because their goal was infinity. And so the romantics plummeted. Notice how many died young (Novalis, Hölderlin, Shelley, and so on), while those who lived long enough came to value their youth. Many of the romantics sought consolation in religion (Friedrich Schlegel, Clemens Brentano, Werner, etc.) and came to support reactionary ideas. Some continued what they had started in their youth, even when their youthful fire was long gone, and turned into epigons of their youth. And still others, broken and maimed, sought haven in the grey harbours of the bourgeois.

What then is the position of those who, following the great breakdown of romanticism, nevertheless arrived with romantic feelings? Romanticism has lost its credibility not only with its adversaries but with the younger generation, so sceptical about things romantic. Having lived through a period of disillusion, this generation could never possess the naive courage of the early romantics. What was to become of this younger generation? It hated its own age with the rancour of the crushed who, being powerless, despise their vanquisher. Suspicious of everything, this generation renounced life and, afraid of being disappointed, gave up trying. It reminds us of Ibsen's two characters, Falk and Svanhild, in *Love's Comedy*.[2] This pair of lovers, fearing that their rapture cannot last long, recognize that it is better to go their separate ways. The inflamed lovers lived in a world of ideals, it shaped their passion before they experienced reality, a reality which is never identical with the imagined world. At the same time, Falk and Svanhild's integrity and sense of duty will not allow them to defy the world, and subdue it – as the first romantics did – for which they lacked power.

The emotion of the two lovers swings between extremes, and the more powerful and inclusive their emotion becomes, the more readily it oscillates. Kierkegaard – who is also one of these lovers – wrote somewhere: 'Everywhere, where things are taken seriously, the law is: either–or . . . *Aut-aut; aut Caesar – aut nihil.*' In the romantics, every feeling – seen this way – turns into its opposite. Hence a naive synthesis turns into an all-inclusive scepticism; piety becomes a denial of God; and when the alienated souls erect an altar to an abstract, life-denying art: *l'art pour l'art* is born. The romantics expand art to cover everything and, consequently, being left with no area to conquer, they subordinate everything to art.[3] The romantic artists either ignore or stylize the present which they portray, for the most part, accurately, 'naturally', with the enlarged vision of hatred so as to vindicate themselves over their despised, triumphant age. All romantic feelings have a sense of inclusiveness, even though the feelings move in opposite directions. Romanticism *à rebours* [romanticism of the reverse].

And Ibsen? At first sight, it may seem strange to see him in this company.[4] This Ibsen who, next to Zola, is called the master of modern realism. I can merely outline here the spiritual affinity between Ibsen and, for instance, Flaubert, which may appear all the more striking and important since, to the best of my knowledge, Ibsen and Flaubert were unknown to each other. In their youth, both were romantics. In Rouen, where Flaubert lived, and in Norway, where Ibsen lived, everything arrived late, and both consequently became romantics when it was already out of fashion.

As a young man, Ibsen had imitated Oehlenschläger,[5] read the Nordic legends, as did the Danish–Norwegian romantics, whose style and form invites comparison with his own – as does that of Flaubert. Prejudiced towards Stendhal and Balzac, Flaubert showed great enthusiasm for Chateaubriand and Gautier, and among his literary papers there were discovered novels bearing the influence, for instance, of Hoffmann. Both Flaubert and Ibsen proved rather slow in making the transition from a 'sociological' style in which they attempted to portray the character of the age itself – as can be seen in their respective works – a transition which coincided with their first, bitter disappointments. This may well be a merely fortuitous resemblance in advance of their later move towards realism. The realism of Flaubert and Ibsen has its source in irony (it is perhaps more evident in Ibsen than in Flaubert). It originated in their hatred of the bourgeois. 'Contre les philistins!' is the watchword of romanticism and, in essence, Flaubert and Ibsen's irony is romantic by nature. They ridicule the same things: rationalism, cowardliness, lack of individuality, pettiness, imitation and especially bourgeois narcissism. It is sufficient to recall figures like Flaubert's [Citizen] Regimbart, [Jacques] Arnoux and Homais in *Sentimental Education*; and Ibsen's Hjalmar Ekdal and Peter Stockmann, among others. There is a close kinship between Emma Bovary and Hjalmar Ekdal's self-delusions and comedies. But in Ibsen the irony is more serious, sharper and more spiteful. The other source of romantic irony, self-irony, is also manifest in Flaubert and Ibsen's work.

The self-irony of the romantics is mostly, as Brentano put it, 'an irony that stems from details'. Initially, Ibsen's self-irony is also artistic (for example, *Peer Gynt*, Act v), and, as he becomes more disillusioned, this irony turns completely inward. And then Ibsen begins to persecute his sacred ideals lest anyone should notice or laugh at his own sufferings (Gregers Werle in *The Wild Duck*).

In the same way, Flaubert holds up his great ideal, romantic love to ridicule, in *Madame Bovary*. As for the famous notions of 'impersonality' and 'naturalism', Flaubert has shown they were rooted in hatred of the bourgeois. But neither Flaubert nor Ibsen had to draw a caricature of the bourgeoisie in order to make it odious. On the contrary, they attempted to portray the bourgeoisie in the most authentic and typical light so no one could exclaim: 'it is not me'. Needless to say, this is not the only basis of Flaubert and Ibsen's realism. After all, the romantic self sooner or later found itself in need of additional social support.[6] As we have indicated earlier, religion provided this support. For Ibsen and his kind, objectivity and the scientific spirit served as a mask to conceal from the world their own suspicious, bashful souls. But it also gave them the illusion that they could pass a sentence on their age as judges, rather than as the vanquished full of rancour. In addition, disenchantment and the fear of future disappointments made Flaubert and Ibsen suspect every instinct, inspiration or fantasy. Let us take a good look at Ibsen's characters. Why does he like some and loathe the others? He hates and detests everything petty and bourgeois, and yet seems indifferent towards every so-called sin.

Ibsen passed a harsh judgement on the timid, philistine Torvald Helmer in *A Doll's House*, whereas his wife Nora's act of forging her father's signature on an IOU hardly seems to matter.[7] In *John Gabriel Borkman*, John Gabriel Borkman's sin[8] – what he did to Ella Rentheim – completely overshadows his act of embezzling the bank's money. Undeniably, Ibsen's motives are identical with those of the romantic poets,[9] and he is the furthest removed from those social-critical writers with whom he is usually grouped.

But even Ibsen's late works display an undisguised form of romanticism. Among his characters, in such plays as *The Lady from the Sea*, *The Master Builder* and *Little Eyolf*, there appear some fantastic creatures,[10] just as they do in the novels of Hoffmann and Poe. The lovers in Ibsen's last dramas also remind us of the novelists' romantic lovers, stalked by fate and inescapable nemesis, although Ibsen's lovers are more complete characters and are permeated with his own nihilistic irony.

In other words, Ibsen was a romantic in his late works. Romanticism *à rebours*. The old romantics were adventurers, Ibsen and his brethren are hermits; but the basic feeling is the same in both. [. . .]

Every genuine dramatist aspires to write a tragedy. He searches and searches ever deeper for the sources of conflict, until he finally arrives at a few, truly great questions that no longer contain an answer, and discovers conflicts that defy resolution. Invariably, these conflicts involve the individual and the unknown forces we could call fate, destiny, cosmic order or even deity, but whose true identity we will never know. By its very essence, tragedy always contains some mystical elements.

The reason social drama reached its height rather late is because few writers could or wanted to resist the temptation to locate the essence of human struggle, having disposed of deeper, more permanent motives, in the relative realm of external causes. However, this tendency removed the very possibility of tragedy. The tendency was always rational; it identified the mistakes to be corrected; it instructed, it cautioned. In the social drama, one character is invariably wrong, the other always right. Of course the social drama portrays the same phenomena as does the tendentious drama. Consequently, the tragic element is confined to the treatment of the theme, that is to say, the way the ideas and institutions under scrutiny influence individual actions. Rationalism had assumed that by reforming the institutions, and through the spread of enlightenment, some social conflicts could be avoided. In reality, the rationalist perspective is anti-tragic; it seeks to remove the possibility of tragic conflict. Rationalism appeared blind to the basic source of conflict. Namely that individuals with different spiritual dispositions will, sooner or later, encounter each other at some given points. This remains an immutable fact, at least for the foreseeable future, unless our basic human feelings undergo a complete, qualitative change. When that happens, every single cause of conflict, whose removal depends on the human agent – as does law or our prejudices – could initiate a tragic conflict whose real causes reside in human nature.

The dramas of Ibsen, written before he reached his maturity, contain a curious mixture of destiny, faith, trust, and the conviction that the human order is subject to improvement. The mystic Maximus (in *Emperor and Galilean*)[11] knows that man wills because he must will, and yet Brand shows no mercy where the will is weak. The struggle of King Haakon and Earl Skule [*The Pretenders*] had been decided, for all practical purposes, in the soul of Skule who, just before he dies, says:

> There are men created to live and men created to die. I have never willed to take the path that God has pointed out for me; therefore my way has never been clear to me until now.[12]

Although it was already evident in *Brand* (1861) that Ibsen was something of a fatalist on the question of heredity, none the less his dramas of this period are permeated by a militant, polemical mood.

Ibsen's characters struggle against external and internal forces which stand in the way of the individual. But for this struggle to have any meaning, Ibsen had to assume that the individual is capable of self-realization. In his youth, Bernick [*Pillars of Society*] had bowed to public opinion and popular prejudices, but Lona Hessel had convinced Bernick he must free himself from their oppressive power. Bernick was a coward once, and now he gained courage, and the striving of Falk [*Love's Comedy*], of Dr Stockmann [*An Enemy of the People*] and of Brand are but attempts to instil courage in the individual. But as Gregers Werle [*The Wild Duck*] soon learned, truth and ideals belong to the privileged few. In the play, the character Relling observed:

Take away the life-lie from the average person, and you take his happiness along with it.[13]

Perhaps it is impossible to remove oneself from life-lies. For Gregers truth turns into a lie, and individuality is no more than a pose (Hjalmar Ekdal). The individual therefore must give up the struggle, because few possess the ability to become a personality. The individual becomes the aristocrat.

Nora was right to leave her husband [*A Doll's House*], and Helmer deserved what was coming to him. For a long time, Mrs Alving [*Ghosts*] believed that her relationship with her husband was the same as Nora's relationship with her husband, but later she realized she was as guilty towards her own husband as he was towards her. Mrs Alving's marriage had to end the way it ended. For Mrs Alving to understand what she should have done to prevent the ruin of her marriage, she had to live through everything that followed.[14] Ibsen's portrayal of the deep-rooted causes of failed marriages reach such depths that he no longer engages in polemics, he draws up an indictment of human fate.

After *Rosmersholm* (1886), the indictment is no longer so explicit in Ibsen. In his earlier works, Ibsen had featured two types of character (for example, the two Stockmann brothers [*An Enemy of the People*]), who wage desperate struggles against each other. And yet, despite their differences, this animosity creates a bond between them. This is no longer the case in Ibsen's play *Rosmersholm*.[15] The two character types lead separate lives, and hardly understand each other's speech. The action of one character type is so distorted in the soul-mirror of the other type as to be almost unrecognizable. (Solness and Brovik in *The Master Builder*.) Ibsen gave fullest vent to his scornful sarcasm (romantic irony!) in the character drawing of those plebeian-souled men who, like Mortensgaard [*Rosmersholm*], 'are capable of anything they want, because they want no more than they are capable of. They can live without ideals.' By contrast, the other type[16] is immersed in lyrical moods.

What is the nature of this other type? They are characters who were born for tragedy. The dramatic mood now changes. Earlier, Ibsen accorded tragedy to the forces that restrained the individual and his potential; now tragedy originates in individuals who act upon and experience the opportunities available to them. The opportunities reside in the characters' very souls; there is something demonic about these characters and their ability to achieve great things. At the same time, there are forces which prevail over the characters and impel them in a certain direction. And at the end of the road disaster awaits them. There is Solness climbing up the church spire; there is Rebecca West sending Beata to her death [*Rosmersholm*], and there is Borkman embezzling the bank's money [*John Gabriel Borkman*]. These characters are unable to resist their own selves.[17] Only Hedda Gabler [*Hedda Gabler*] tries to resist – and only out of cowardice.[18] And what is the result? That everything which she wanted to overcome in herself assumes a different, and uglier form. Her tragedy becomes more dissonant than it would otherwise have been; but it was unavoidable.

In other words, Ibsen's characters cannot resist, they cannot stop lest they suffocate, and therefore they press forward to the disaster that awaits them. Is this pessimism? I don't think so. Note how calmly Rosmer and Rebecca await their death; Hedda Gabler's last words [before she shoots herself] are refined and witty, 'Yes, you're looking forward to that, aren't you, Mr Brack? Yourself as the only cock in the yard . . .'[19] When Solness falls from the tower to his death, Hilde's most important point is:

> But he got right to the top. And I heard harps in the air. My . . . my . . . master builder. [20]

'Do the impossible once more!' is what Hilde demands of Solness, who promised her the kingdom of the impossible.

The Ibsenian hero pursues the impossible. His soul dreams of the impossible, he wants to experience it even if for a moment. And after that? 'He who sees the face of God, dies', said Brand. Perhaps Ibsen's heroes no longer want to live any more. I have a feeling that for his heroes, having attempted the impossible, life itself no longer holds any meaning. After all, the impossible moment constituted the true life, and after that the hero's life sinks and declines. Even if the hero continues to live, his life is not a genuine life. Alfred Allmers bids farewell to life when Asta decides to leave [*Little Eyolf*], because he faces a resigned, wretched existence. Ibsen presents a tragic outlook on life. *Amor fati.* Man was born for a tragic fate, whether it is right or wrong I cannot tell, but here on this earth nothing sounds lovelier.

Ibsen's married couples – for him as for all romantics, the ultimate unity is not the individual, but the pair – are also tragic. But tragedies like those of Mrs Alving no longer exist. (It counts even less that Solness and Rubek had wives.) The very character of Ibsen's lovers disposes them to form couples. The lovers are created for each other, for each other's destruction. Hilde had to send Solness climbing the tower, her own love commanded it – and it destroyed both of them. The same irresistible force drew Rebecca toward Rosmer, and the same road which led to her goal had also prevented her from savouring her triumph. It was Rosmer's outlook on life which condemned Rebecca's past, but it was precisely her past that drew her diametrically different soul so strongly towards Rosmer. Consciously or unconsciously, Ibsen's lovers compel each other to draw the final consequences of their own human essence; they drive each other to tragedy.

None the less, Ibsen's married couples desire the same thing. The young Ibsen has fought for the rights of women, in his middle period he treated women as equal partners of men; only to let them go their separate ways in his late works.[21] Man wants one thing, woman another. What is merely an episode for a man is destiny for the woman. The woman loves the man and the concept of maleness – she wants the man to be great. But man also has a job, he is an artist. Deep down in his soul, John Gabriel Borkman is an artist; it dominates him. In quest of his dream, Borkman forsakes Ella Rettheim and shrugs her off to someone else. Professor Arnold Rubek [*When We Dead Awaken*] wants to look at Irene only with the cold, impartial eyes of an artist, in order to protect his sculpture from his emotions. It leads to a life-and-death struggle. Irene is unable to forgive the man who 'murdered' her. She must hate and does hate Rubek; yet he is the only one she has ever loved, and still does . . . Man cannot eschew woman, only in his creative ecstasy is he convinced he can live without her; that those other things – the bank, the sculpture – can fill his soul. But Rubek is unable to forsake his art, for his whole being pulsates with creativity. He must choose, but he is unable to choose.[22] Even if he made a choice, his fate would be still tragic.

Those who are destined for each other, man and woman, art and life, remain forever irreconcilable antagonists.

Art and life . . . An artist must stand outside life in order to portray it. For the artist, the woman is only an outline, a form; the artist's feeling is but a word or rhythm. This is the way it must be, otherwise he cannot create. If the artist looked at his model with the eye of a lover, artistically he would be unable to see anything because it requires cold eyes, unclouded by emotion, to capture nuances and characteristic features. If the artist has feelings, he must suppress them. The artist can have sensations, not feelings. He must not get involved with life, for then his art would loose its perspective. '*Nous sommes faits pour le dire, non pour l'avoir*', said Flaubert [We are born to communicate, not to possess].

Ibsen's heroes live and experience the tragedy of Flaubert. As King Haakon said [*The Pretenders*] about his mother:[23]

She is too dear to me, Earl; . . . a king must not have about him any
who are dear to him; a king must have free hands, must stand alone,
must not be led, must not be tempted.[23]

In the same way, Solness can never have a home of his own because
building homes for others is the price he has to pay. The same fate
holds Borkman and Rubek in its grip.

The Borkmans and Rubeks are ascetics and tyrants. Whatever stands
in their way, they remove it, including their beloved ones. Ibsen is the
first dramatist to give voice to the victims of ascetic tyrants. Flaubert
merely complained about his own fate. In Ibsen, the Ellas and Irenes
stand up and bring an indictment against those who destroyed their
lives. Why are these women brought to ruin? Because a miserable
sculpture [Rubek's masterpiece, 'The Day of Resurrection'] had rele-
gated Irene to the background, a sculpture which ends up in a cemetery,
incomprehensible to everyone, for even the artist had 'progressed
beyond' the original conception of his work. But Irene's life and soul
were victimized by the sculpture. While subsequently the artist merely
inserted his own self, contrite and weighed down with guilt, into the
composition.[24]

The artist's own pain, however, may be even greater. It was Rubek's
icy nature and egocentrism which brought on not only Irene's tragedy, but his own terrible inner struggles. The artist's soul is sensitive
– for he nourishes and trains it to respond to feelings – but the soul is
a tyrant. The artist possesses a weak conscience, and he gives birth to
careless, flighty thoughts, his imagination conjures up unknown
desires and grotesque sins destructive of human lives. The artist's
creative passions, sufferings, struggles and triumphs accomplish nothing, for no one really understands what he has created. And in the
creative process he has destroyed his own life. The pain and suffering
he brought about he feels a hundred times greater, and his every blow
falls on his own flesh. Yet there is nothing he can do; for such is the
life of an artist, such is his fate. 'He who decides to be an artist, no
longer has the right to live like others.' Flaubert wrote this. He was
Ibsen's brother in the great martyrdom of art. But unlike Flaubert,
Ibsen was denied the sad consolation of bewailing his own sufferings
in his work.

NOTES

[1]   Ibsen's play *When We Dead Awaken* (1899) was his last play. Soon after
      completing it, Ibsen was paralysed and wrote no more. The young Lu-

kács, a budding playwright, upon graduating with honours from the gymnasium in 1902, was presented by his father with a railway ticket to Norway and letter of introduction to Ibsen. The meeting with Ibsen had a lasting impact on Lukács. Ibsen subtitled his *When We Dead Awaken* a 'Dramatic Epilogue'. The play forms an epilogue to Ibsen's dramas which start with *A Doll's House* (1879) and end with *When We*. But it is also an epilogue, as fate had it, to Ibsen's life and work.

2 Ibsen's *Love's Comedy* (1862) is in many ways a dramatized version of Kierkegaard's *Either-Or*, especially that work's section on 'The Aesthetic Validity of Marriage', where Kierkegaard has an intriguing explanation of the essence of the relationship between dramatist and dramatized, between poet creator and created poet.

Ibsen's serious message, if a serious message can be attached to such Puckish operetta as *Love's Comedy*, is that to build a marriage merely on romantic rapture is to build on clouds. In Act I, Falk, an aspiring poet, proposes marriageless love to Svanhild, and is rejected. And in Act III, where the businessman Guldstad interposes himself between Falk and Svanhild, and in a loveless marriage claims the girl for himself. Falk wants Svanhild so he can 'grow into a poet'. Hurt and bitter, Svanhild turns on him,

> You prize me as a schoolboy does a reed;
> something to make a flute of . . . for a day.

Ibsen, *Love's Comedy* in *The Oxford Ibsen*, ed. James Walter McFarlane, 8 volumes (Oxford University Press, 1962), vol. 2, p. 134.

3 For the romantic assertions of the supreme importance of art, there are no better examples than Blake's statement, 'Art is the tree of life. Art is Christianity,' or Shelley's 'Poets are the unacknowledged legislators of the world.' For the romantic concept of the poet and the poetic imagination, see Wordsworth, Preface to the *Lyrical Ballads* (1800).

4 Lukács's claim that Ibsen, despite his realism and scepticism, remained a romantic at heart has been seconded by E. M. Forster. His essay, 'Ibsen the Romantic', postdates by some two decades Lukács's essay published in 1906. Both Lukács and Forster dissented from Georges Brandes who said that somewhere in the course of the battle of his life Ibsen had a 'lyric Pegasus killed under him'.

As Forster put it, echoing Lukács whom he obviously never read in Hungarian, in 'Ibsen's extraordinary genius and heart, in that gnarled region, a primeval romanticism lurked.' E. M. Forster, 'Ibsen the Romantic' in *The Wild Duck*, ed. Dounia B. Christiani (New York: W. W. Norton, 1968), pp. 146–7.

5 Adam Gottlob Oehlenschläger (1779–1850), Danish poet and dramatist, friend and disciple of Goethe and Schiller, was a leader of the romantic movement in Denmark. He exerted an influence on Ibsen, Strindberg and Kierkegaard.

6 The romantics, 'servants and fanatics of their own development' as Lukács put it, spoke of the 'I' in defiance of human and social norms.
   Strange as it may sound, the egoism of the romantics is strongly coloured
   with social feelings, because the unfolding of the personality would in the
   end bring human beings closer to one another. Lukács's, 'On the Romantic Philosophy of Life' in *Soul and Form*, pp. 42–54.

7 In Ibsen's *A Doll's House* (1879), Nora, a child-wife, became Helmer's
   possession. Possessiveness is the keynote in bourgeois homes and a
   crisis, like Nora forging the signature of her father on an IOU, merely
   serves to amplify it. As Helmer said to Nora:

> For a man, there's something indescribably moving and very
> satisfying in knowing that he has forgiven his wife – forgiven her,
> completely and genuinely, from the depths of his heart. It's as
> though it made her his property in a double sense: he has, as it
> were, given her a new life, and she becomes in a way both his wife
> and at the same time his child. *A Doll's House*, Act III.

8 In Ibsen's *John Gabriel Borkman* (1896), Borkman is a banker who married for money. In Lukács's early writings one senses the unspoken
   thought that his father has shamefully converted love into commercial
   currency. In fact, young Lukács wrote a drama entitled *John Gabriel*.
   Referred to as a 'family drama', Lukács later burned it. But in Lukács's
   writing there is no denying the terror and contempt at marriage seen in
   terms of commodity. In Ibsen's play, Ella Rentheim, who loved Borkman, speaks of the dark secret that was also the secret of Lukács's
   family.

> ELLA: You have killed love in me . . . Do you understand what that
> means? The Bible speaks of a mysterious sin for which there is no
> forgiveness . . . The great sin for which there is no forgiveness is to
> murder love in a human soul . . . Ibsen, *John Gabriel Borkman* in *The
> Oxford Ibsen*, vol. 8, p. 198.

9 Lukács's own footnote here reads: 'It would be relatively easy to demonstrate this in Ibsen's work. Let me mention one important example. Some
   of his female characters, Nora, Ellida, among others, champion the rights
   of women. It is commonplace knowledge that Hebbel anticipated Ibsen
   here. In Hebbel's *Herodes and Mariamne*, Mariamne declared:

> You, like I, were wounded
> In your sacredness, degraded to things. [Scene iv]

Interestingly enough, this theme also appeared in Ibsen's *The League of
Youth*. Ibsen knew Hebbel. But the relationship of man and woman in
Ibsen's early works, Skule and Ingeborg in *Olaf Liljekrans*, Sigurd and

Hjordis in *The Vikings of Helgeland*, is the same as in his later works. At the most, the emotions of Ibsen's female characters are those of suffering and revenge, rather than of wounded dignity. Most likely, this characterization of women owes something to Hebbel, and beyond that to the romantics.'

10 In *The Lady from the Sea*, where the action takes place in a fjord town in Norway, there appears a stranger whose eyes, like the Ancient Mariner's, were hypnotic. And even ten years later, Ellida, wife of Dr Wangel, could recall his scarf pin with its one large, bluish-white pearl – like a dead fish's eye. The same Ellida appeared in *The Master Builder*. While in *The Lady from the Sea* she was a minor, though highly amusing *enfant terrible*, now she is a troll-princess, a Siren of a very different nature.

The strangest creature is the Ratwife in *Little Eyolf*. This deadly old creature, the Ratwife, is the most vital thing in the play – the most chilling of all Ibsen's symbols – worthy sister of the witches in *Macbeth*.

11 *Emperor and Galilean* (1873), this mega-drama of ten acts, is woven from the Hegelian strands of thesis–antithesis–synthesis. Thus we have Christianity grown dominant, its corruption, which in turn incites a pagan revolt against it, and finally a synthesis, the Third Empire, harmonizing the best of both. And the right man who appears after the synthesis is none other than Maximus the Mystic, who duly swallows up Emperor and Galilean.

This play proves beyond any doubt that Ibsen's real gifts lay, not in Hegelian philosophy or history, but in portraying characters and unmasking their souls in a dramatic situation.

12 Ibsen, *The Pretenders* in *The Oxford Ibsen*, vol. 2, p. 338.

13 Ibsen, *The Wild Duck* (Norton Critical Edition), Act v, p. 64.

14 Ibsen's *Ghosts* (1881), like *A Doll's House*, is a gripping drama of emancipation by ordeal. Both Mrs Alving and Nora slammed the door on their husbands and ran off into the night. But unlike Nora, Mrs Alving returned to her husband; remained loyal to him, though a drunkard, guarding his reputation with selfless devotion at enormous cost to herself and her own happiness. Mrs Alving also had to face the terrible 'ghosts' which, as she says in a memorable passage, 'must be as thick as the sea-sands'. The 'ghosts' are all sorts of old, long-dead ideas, all kinds of old, long-dead beliefs. The 'ghost' is also her son Oswald, a replica of his father – both of them fond of the bottle, and fond of women. The eternal recurrence. And the 'ghosts' proliferate. Relentlessly, Ibsen depicts the 'home' as the source of bigotry, of incest, of blinkered vision; an abode of tyrannical affection and possessiveness.

15 Of all Ibsen's plays, *Rosmersholm* is the most inexhaustible. Lukács is right that the play initiates something new in Ibsen, specifically his overt probing of the uncharted waters of the unconscious mind. The play features Ibsen's most remarkable character, Rebecca West, an intellectual whose passions can find no outlet. Lukács's claim that the two key characters, Rosmer and Rebecca, though lovers as passionate as Romeo

and Juliet, do not establish human contact, is borne out by the play. There is no genuine communication between Rosmer and Rebecca, because of the forces both outside and within them, until the moment when they clasp hands to walk out and drown themselves.

[16] The other type Lukács has in mind is Brand, whose war cry is 'All or nothing':

> Be passion's slave, be pleasure's thrall,
> But be it utterly, all in all;

Undeniably, a personification of romanticism. This Brand, in the poem's first narrative version, had prayed, 'Teach me to will no more than I can'; the Brand whose very name in the Norse ballad means 'fire'. In contrast to Brand, Peter Mortensgaard in *Rosmersholm* never wills more than he can do.

[17] At times Borkman claims, in *John Gabriel Borkman*, that he is acting in obedience to some mysterious force of attraction, a 'pull', an inexplicable and irresistible drawing power. At other moments, he traces his actions and motives to his own unfathomable self: 'People don't understand that I had to do it because I am as I am – because I am John Gabriel Borkman, and not somebody else.' *John Gabriel Borkman* in *The Oxford Ibsen*, vol. 8, p. 207.

[18] Ibsen himself wrote, 'The demonic thing about Hedda is that she wants to exert an influence over another person.' *The Oxford Ibsen*, vol. 7, p. 13.

The demonic in Hedda, a pagan priestess driven by a vision of Dionysian beauty and the thrill of a beautiful death, forces her to intrude into the life of others and control their destiny. But she tries to dominate others to make good some inner deficiency in her own self. She wants to control others, but she cannot control herself.

[19] *Hedda Gabler* in *The Oxford Ibsen*, vol. 7, p. 268. It should be noted that Judge Brack was Hedda's lover, who tried to win sexual domination over her, ruthlessly, by blackmailing her.

[20] *The Master Builder* in *The Oxford Ibsen*, vol. 7, p. 445.

[21] In *Pillars of Society*, Ibsen had drawn two female characters, Lona Hessel and Dina Dorf, with a spirit and mind of their own. In the play, which examines lies in public life, and the tragic struggle of Karsten Bernick to hide his sin and preserve his reputation at the expense of another man's good name, Ibsen gave the last word to Miss Hessel: 'the spirit of truth and the spirit of freedom, they are the pillars of the community.'

But it would be a mistake to imagine that Ibsen himself was necessarily a feminist. True, like Euripides, Shakespeare, and many other dramatists, Ibsen often makes his women characters stronger than his men. Ibsen ridiculed J. S. Mill's claim that Harriet Taylor was his co-equal as author of *On Liberty*, saying: 'Fancy, if you had to read Hegel with the thought that you did not know for certain whether it was Mr or Mrs

Hegel you had before you.' Georg Brandes, *Henrik Ibsen* (New York, 1964), pp. 76–7.

22 Lukács had a personal stake in Ibsen's *When We Dead Awaken*, whose central theme is that the work of art demands human sacrifices. Rubek's creative act had necessitated the exploitation of his model Irene's humanity, had required the draining of her life's essence, had exacted the death of her living soul. Art functions here as a life-destructive force, and the artist, serving as its agent, had left Irene disturbed, deranged, unfulfilled, a shadow of her former self. Rubek has 'murdered' Irene, destroying her death-in-life existence, so he could complete his statue, entitled 'The Day of Resurrection'. Rubek became famous and acclaimed and the model, Irene, who inspired it, a pale ghost, deranged, and thirsting for revenge.

23 *The Pretenders* in *The Oxford Ibsen*, vol. 2, p. 232.

24 Rubek had removed Irene's figure in the sculpture, 'The Day of Resurrection', which portrayed a pure young woman, untainted by the world, waking to light and glory, and made the composition bigger, more complex. Rubek now put himself into the composition. In the foreground, beside a spring, there 'sits a man weighed down with guilt', and full of remorse for a forfeited life. He sits there, racked and tormented by the thought that he will never escape. He must remain forever captive in his hell.

Outraged, Irene hurls one word at Rubek:

IRENE: Poet!
RUBEK: Why poet?
IRENE: Because you are soft and spineless and full of excuses for everything you've done or thought. You killed my soul – then you go and model yourself as a figure of regret and remorse and penitence . . . and you think you've settled your account. (*When We Dead Awaken* Act II)

9

Peer Gynt
Ibsen's Dramatic Poem

'Anyone who does not know *Brand* and *Peer Gynt* cannot know Ibsen', a prestigious German aesthetician once wrote. This is true for the most part. Provided we add *Emperor and Galilean*. I do not wish to suggest – for it would be foolish – that without reading these plays it is impossible to understand Ibsen's later dramas. It would be like pronouncing a death sentence on the major works of the greatest dramatist of our age, because a good dramatic work speaks for itself and achieves its effect without any supportive commentary. Besides, the above suggestion would not even be true. What I want to say is this: though the contours of Henrik Ibsen's character can readily be recognized in his late dramas, which often yield insights into him, it is only in his romantic, philosophical and historical dramas that he can be truly understood, fully comprehended, and we can learn about his outlook on life straight from his own lips. In the same way, we can read *Faust* and *Iphigenie*, *Werther* and *Tasso* and form some idea of Goethe. But in order to know and fully understand Goethe, we must read his *Dichtung und Wahrheit*.

Brand, *Peer Gynt* and *Emperor and Galilean* form a related cycle. This is not a relation of persons, but of thoughts and world views. The questions raised here are none other than: What is man? What is he to be? What is the purpose of life itself? *Faust*. The dramatic poem *Brand* is a great, thundering diatribe, spoken in the voice of Old Testament prophets, against the 'half-men': against those who are somewhat good, somewhat bad, somewhat brave, somewhat cowardly, somewhat moral and somewhat immoral. 'All or Nothing', says Brand–Ibsen,[1] and 'the Lord prefers a "complete" sinner to a "half" innocent.'

It is as if Peer Gynt responded to the first objections levelled against Brand: 'If we obey Brand, we surrender the world to self-interest, unprincipled self-interest.' Ibsen's answer is 'No', and Peer Gynt demonstrates it. 'The ego creates no true self, and true self is the goal (only the true self is a human being); ego is the greatest obstacle to a true self.' This is what Peer Gynt personifies. The selfish man is 'self-sufficient'; the true self is 'faithful unto itself'. The Button-moulder asks Peer Gynt to show the Master's unmistakable intention:

PEER GYNT: But what if a man has never discovered
    What the Master intended?
BUTTONMOULDER: Then he must sense it. (Act v)

And when Gynt discovers what the Master intended, it is too late.

Ibsen grappled with man's role in the history of the world and the freedom or the limits of human will in *Emperor and Galilean*: the mystery of human commitment. It should have been Julian the Apostate's task to revive a debased and decaying Christianity. He failed to do it; he lacked the will. He intended to restore the classical Greek concept of beauty, and persecuted the Christians. And what did he accomplish? The persecution awakened in the Christians their forgotten faith, it destroyed Julian, and Christianity became stronger than ever.

This tragedy mirrors – more precisely it glimmers on the horizon – the world, our world. The goal of mankind: the third empire that would unite all dissonance, the two keys: beauty and truth, Hellas and Christ.

Ibsen is the prophet of individualism; perhaps the greatest of our time, together with Nietzsche. But Nietzsche's kingdom is not of this world; his idol is the superhuman being, the *Übermensch*, who stands in the same relation to man as man to the ape. Ibsen's ten commandments are reduced to one: men, above all, men.

The literary gigolos have embraced the concept of individualism: enjoy life, express your individuality – this is the goal; and the means: pleasure. Thanks to our gilded youth, most serious people neither know nor wish to know the greatest dramatist of our age, the prophet with the loveliest voice. As I say, these splendid people seem to be unaware that the modern 'free' ethics entails more duties and obligations, and offers less tangible good, because the old ethic has already been surpassed.

The old Ibsen wrote a fairytale. True, he was still young. A colourful, luxuriant fantasy; full of the charm of language, of rhyme and lyrics. For *Peer Gynt* is a folk-tale, an old one, like that of *Faust*. Just as Faust is a story-teller, a rogue, the legend of Peer Gynt is about an opportunist day-dreamer. While Goethe's hands moulded the trickster-magician into 'the' man, but not a 'great' one, Peer Gynt represents 'man' in the drama, but in an opposite sense of the term.

The Gynt family has become impoverished. The once rich John

Gynt's widow, Aase, and her son Peer live in poverty. Oblivious to his poverty, Peer inhabits the world of dreams. He is absolutely convinced that, despite all his destitution, misery and humiliation, one day he will be an emperor.

Ingrid, who loved Peer, is marrying the inept Matt Moen, though Peer merely had to stretch out his hand to have her. Uninvited, Peer appears at the wedding, and is mocked and teased by everyone. An immigrant family is also among the guests: the father, mother and their daughters. The oldest is a lovely blonde, gentle and timid, and is called Solveig. Rejected and spurned by the guests, Peer turns to Solveig and asks her to dance with him. Solveig is willing and eager, until she learns his name. In despair, Peer starts to cry, pleads and appeals to her to dance with him. He threatens her. All in vain.

The inept bridegroom turns to Peer for help, because Ingrid has locked her door and won't let him in. Peer can try and open it, for he is a magician – that's what the peasants believe from Peer's made-up tales, which he describes as his own experiences. Once more Peer appeals to Solveig, but she cannot dance with him, her parents will not let her. Thereupon Peer steals the bride Ingrid.

The villagers are after Peer in the mountains, and swear to hang him. Solveig's parents and Aase are also wandering about the mountain plateau, calling and searching for Peer: perhaps they can help him. In the meantime, Peer chases Ingrid away, saying he did what he did out of passion, he was hot for a girl, and now he regrets it. Ingrid pleads and threatens, all in vain. They go their opposite ways.

After an amorous adventure with three shepherd girls, Peer is seduced by the King of the Dovres' daughter. This leads to a great despair in the royal palace of the Dovre King, and the troll courtiers want to have him killed. But the Dovre King will not allow it. On the contrary, he wants Peer to be his son-in-law, and promises him half of the kingdom as a dowry if he renounces his human nature, and becomes a troll. Peer accepts the trolls' motto: 'Troll, to thine own self be all-sufficient.' He eats the trolls' revolting food, and even praises it. He is willing to have a tail tied on to him, because only in this way can he earn the title of 'king'. He even consents to have his eyes plucked out, until he realizes he could never again rejoin the human race. Not even in his compromises is Peer completely his own self; his courage extends only to half-measures.

Having barely managed to escape the trolls, Peer has to struggle with a new monster: an invisible, invincible, mysterious monster – the great Boyg. The Boyg stops Peer getting past him, demanding that Peer go 'around and about'. The great Boyg almost triumphs, when Peer calls out to Solveig:

Solveig, if you mean to save me
Do it quickly! Don't stand staring
Down at the ground. Hurl your prayer-book
With the silver clasp straight at his head . . . (Act II)

and is saved.

In the depths of the pine forest, Peer builds a log cabin, its door secured with a lock to keep out the trolls. But to no avail. Nothing can free Peer from his pestering goblin thoughts. Only Solveig. And she appears because she understands, she senses, that Peer needs her. With Solveig beside him Peer is happy. He believes he has escaped the danger. But hardly is Solveig out of sight when a woman he has seduced appears with her child. She claims her share of love and happiness because it is her due though it is all the result of dream and desire.

Peer is in despair. What is he to do? Not only this woman, but Ingrid and the three shepherd girls come between him and Solveig. The Boyg would say, 'Give up, go round and about'. And Peer yields; he leaves Solveig, asking her only to wait for him.

He lulls his dying mother, Aase, into a deadly sleep with enchanting fairytales and lies:

PEER: In Soria-Moria Castle
   The King and the Prince are feasting.
   Lie back on the sledge cushions;
   I'll drive you there over the moor –
AASE: But, kind son, am I invited?
PEER: Why yes, they've asked us both...(Act III)

and then sets out in search of his kingdom.

In the New World, Peer becomes the Croesus of the slave trade, only to lose everything; he passes himself off as a prophet for an African tribe; rides away with a Bedouin girl, who later rudely deserts the holy prophet:

PEER: That bitch; – she came within an ace
   Of making me lose my head altogether . . .
   Ah well . . .
   Being a prophet is a horrible business!
   Your duty's to wrap yourself in a mist;
   You finish your chances as a prophet
   The moment you start behaving sensibly. (Act IV)

Peer then becomes a scholar and studies the statue of Memnon and the great Sphinx. All this time, Solveig is waiting for him. While he studies the Sphinx, Peer encounters Begriffenfeldt, director of the lunatic asylum in Cairo, who takes charge of him: the 'emperor', who 'invented Reason'. The director informs Peer:

> Absolute Reason
> Dropped dead last night at eleven o'clock.

> PEER: God save us –!
> BEGRIFFENFELDT: Yes, it's most deplorable.
>   And in my position, as you can imagine,
>   Doubly unfortunate; because
>   Up to now this institution
>   Has been what is called a mad-house . . .
>   Here, a man's himself with a vengeance;
>   Himself, and nothing else whatsoever; –
>   The self in full sail, full speed ahead.
>   Each one shut up in the cask of self,
>   Hermetically sealed with the bung of self,
>   The barrel pickled in a bath of self.
>   No one has tears for other men's pain;
>   No one accepts other men's notions.
>   We're ourselves here, thought, word and deed,
>   Ourselves right to the edge of the diving-board, –
>   And so, now we come to elect an Emperor,
>   You are obviously the perfect man. (Act IV)

Peer is introduced to members of the 'Scholars' Club'. He first meets Huhu, who wants to replace language by monkey screams, then Fellah, who thinks he is King Apis, and Hussein, who fancies he is a pen:

> HUSSEIN: Will you do me
>   The honour of dipping me in the ink?
>   (*Bowing deeply*)
>   I am a pen.
> PEER: (*bowing still lower*) And I am simply
>   A crumbled sheet of imperial parchment.
> HUSSEIN: My history, sire, is briefly this:
>   They think I'm a sand-box; I'm really a pen.
> PEER: And mine, Mr Pen, is very soon told:
>   I'm a piece of paper no one has written on.

Peer becomes Emperor of these people. Here everyone is his own 'true self', just as Peer accepts and believes. Such personality is: madness.

Peer returns home. He is old, a man broken by all his adventures. Close by a cottage, he is peeling an onion and calls it 'Peer':

> Here lies Peer Gynt, that decent fellow,
> Emperor? (*He laughs inwardly*)
> You soothsaying jackass!
> You're no Emperor; you're an onion.
> Now I shall peel you, good old Peer!
> It won't help, either, to cry for mercy,

and peels off the layers to the centre to find the heart. But it is all made of layers – there is no heart. He hears a song coming from a hut. Solveig is singing:

> Now all is ready for Whitsun Eve,
> Distant lover, dearest and best:
> Will you come back soon?
> Is the burden so very great?
> Take time to rest.
> I still shall wait
> Here as I promised, under the moon.

Quiet and deathly pale, Peer replies:

> One has remembered – and one has forgotten.
> One has squandered, and one has saved,
> O truth! And time cannot be redeemed!
> O terror! Here's where my empire was! (Act v)

Peer runs away down the forest path. He is tormented by thoughts, thoughts he never thought, deeds that were left undone, songs that he should have sung, and tears he has never let fall. Dead tired, he would welcome death. And it stands before him, but not in a shape he recognizes. He thinks it is the devil, and wants to escape the imminent punishment: he was merely a mild sinner, and took sin lightly, like a splash of mud. However, the Buttonmoulder (who stands before him) informs him that fire and brimstone are not the things for a mud-splashing man; instead he must be melted down and recast.

> PEER: You're not really intending to melt me down
>   With Tom, Dick and Harry into something different?
> BUTTONMOULDER: Yes, that's precisely what I am
>   intending.
> We've done it plenty of times before. (Act v)

Peer is due for the casting-ladle because, neither good nor bad, he was

never his 'own self'. Melted down with other damaged goods, Peer is
to be recast. He protests:

> But this other idea – to be absorbed
> Like a molecule into a foreign body –
> This ladle affair, this Gynt destruction,
> Rouses my innermost soul to revolt . . .

and is determined to prove by witnesses that 'I was myself all through
my life'.

But the first character witness he finds, the King of Dovre tells him
flatly that he never was his 'own true self', only 'all-sufficient to his
own self'. He was not a man, but a mountain troll, an egoist! And the
Buttonmoulder, having explained that 'our sufficiency' gives man
the hallmark of the troll, instructs Peer:

> To be one's self is to kill one's self.
> I doubt if that answer means anything to you.
> So we'll put it this way: to show unmistakably
> The Master's intention whatever you're doing.

But what if a man has never discovered what the Master intended?
Then he must sense it.

Now Peer seeks escape by professing to be a tremendous sinner. But
hell won't admit gutless nonentities. So Peer has come to the second
crossroads (his final meeting with the Buttonmoulder will be at the
third crossroads), when he sees Solveig's hut. Now – for the first time
in his life – he does not hesitate:

> Round and about, said the Boyg!
>   (*Hears a song in the hut*)
> No; this time
> Straight to it, however narrow the path is!

He asks Solveig for the list of his sins. She has none, because Peer
made her life a cause for singing:

> Bless you, for coming back at last!

He hides his face in her lap as Solveig sings the cradle song:

> Sleep, my boy, my precious dear.
> I will rock you, you my care.

BUTTONMOULDER: (*behind the house*) We shall meet at the last cross-roads, Peer;
And *then* we'll see whether –; I say no more.

SOLVEIG: (*singing more loudly in the growing light*) I will rock you, you my care;
Sleep, and dream, my home-returner.

NOTES

[1] In his later life, Ibsen admitted, 'Brand is myself in my best moments, just as I also derived many features of Peer Gynt . . . from self-dissection.' Henrik Ibsen, *Peer Gynt*, tr. Christopher Fry and Johan Fillinger (Oxford University Press, 1989), p. ix.

In his *The Western Canon*, Harold Bloom wrote: 'Clearly, *Peer Gynt* is Ibsen's *Hamlet* and his *Faust*, the play or dramatic poem in which the full range of an imagination is exposed. With *Brand* as its prelude and *Emperor and Galilean* as its huge epilogue, *Peer Gynt* is the center of Ibsen, containing everything he had, everything he quarried for the prose plays of his supposedly major phase.' Harold Bloom, *The Western Canon* (New York: Harcourt Brace & Co, 1994), pp. 366–7.

10

Oscar Wilde

Oscar Wilde was not a true dramatist. In his only drama that can be seriously considered here, *Salome*, he was interested in and fascinated by beautiful rhythm and decorative effect, rather than dramatic conflicts. His first play, *The Duchess of Padua*,[1] is an imitation of the Elizabethan drama. His so-called social dramas are, in essence, melodramas, full of spicy Dumas-fils reminiscences, Sardou's sentimental hokum,[2] and Wilde's own witty, aphoristic sayings gleaned from his own works.[3] His drawing-room comedy, *The Importance of Being Earnest*, is an entertaining self-parody, but insignificant. From the personal notes of Wilde's Parisian friends we know that he was drawn to the decorative potentials of Salome's life. Her story, human figure, and character evolved from day to day, depending on the paintings Wilde saw or the books he read, which engendered different pictorial poses and tableaux.[4]

The character drawing in *Salome* is Maeterlinckian. Like Maeterlinck, Wilde sketched only those features of his characters that were absolutely essential for their fate. However, Wilde went a step further than Maeterlinck. Maeterlinck has tried to express and unite the complex spiritual nature of his characters with a decorative simplicity, whereas Wilde sought to express the primitive nature of his characters for pictorial reasons. Each one of his characters – with the possible exception of Herod – displays one single quality, though it is exceptionally powerful and unique. As a result, the intensity of Wilde's characters exceeds that of Maeterlinck, which in itself creates the illusion of drama. His characters appear on the stage readymade and therefore, given their primitive, disembodied nature, cannot undergo any development, other than meeting their fate. This enabled Wilde to condense the whole drama of Salome into a fast-paced scene. The language of *Salome* is quite often Maeterlinckian, not so much in detail as in texture and tone: the quality of the language is borrowed from music, and the cognitive meaning of the words is subordinated to their decorative effect. At the same time, some things derive directly from Maeterlinck. For instance, the way characters, who neither understand nor wish to understand each other, speak to each other. But while in Maeterlinck the interweaving monologues were designed to convey loneliness, in Wilde they denote the struggle of wills, they are melodies that try to out-do each other (for example, Salome and the prophet Iokanaan, Salome and Herod).

The language of Wilde is more rhythmic, passionate and encompassing than that of Maeterlinck. This difference arises partly in relation to character portrayal and partly from their different starting point. As a disciple of the Parisian *vers libre* school, Maeterlinck's professed aim was analysis and to achieve direct effect. Whereas Wilde was influenced by the more tradition-bound, archaic and eclectic English Pre-Raphaelites, especially Swinburne.[5] Not surprisingly, the language of Wilde and his sense of rhythm are much more remote from any possibility of realism than is the case in Maeterlinck. On the other hand, Wilde's language is more robust, spirited and emotional. The direct and sensual nature of Wilde's images however, made his language even more distant from the abstract language of the epigons than from the language of naturalism; even though there was a greater danger for Wilde than Maeterlinck of sliding back into naturalism.

Every one of Wilde's scenes is much more dramatic than any of Maeterlinck's plays, and yet Wilde on the whole is far removed from a genuine drama. Everything that we have said about Maeterlinck, concerning the difference between the drama and ballad, applies even more to Wilde's *Salome*. There an 'episode' remains more emphatically an episode; so much so that it does not even become general in nature. Next to Wilde's technique of character portrayal, the spiritual motives of an extraordinary episode exert such a dominant influence on characters that some, like the prophet Iokonaan, behave as monomaniacs. The same technique creates the perspective that lends such a perverse appearance to Salome and Herod.[6]

Images and music:[7] this is the basis of *Salome*'s impact, and its potential value for the future development of drama. These images (by which I mean, both in Wilde and Maeterlinck, the unity of words and situation) are often very dramatic, and encompass the whole tragedy of man. Just as Salome's seductive smile and the melody of her spoken words encompass the whole tragedy of the young Syrian.[8] Or consider Herod's melancholic response to the situation:

It is not wise to find symbols in everything that one sees. It makes life too full of terrors. It were better to say that stains of blood are as lovely as rose-petals. It were better far to say that . . .[9]

Herod's words and gestures, his longings, fears and despair are expressed in powerful images. The dramatic, picturesque images of Wilde are much more intense than those of the young Maeterlinck, even though Wilde was less selective in framing them. For not all of Wilde's images are as perfect as those in *Salome*. In fact, some of his images attain dominance quite independently of the drama. And his images with a purely literary appeal appear empty and insignificant from a dramatic perspective, or merely help to strengthen the nondramatic decorative effect. The decorative element receives a direct expression in Wilde's dialogues. While in Maeterlinck the dialogues merely mirror things, and we only see their shadows and reflections, in Wilde's dialogues everything appears to imply a full and intense life.

Wilde made full use of his mentor Swinburne, and Swinburne's mentors, the Parnassian poets' most important decorative method – the impressionistic description. In place of the substantive, detailed description of things, Wilde introduced a frenzied succession of images – images that appear to chase each other – that capture the character's excited state of mind and what preoccupies him at any given moment. Sometimes this produces a strong dramatic effect. For instance, when Herod enumerates his rarest treasures, offering them to Salome if she will no longer demand the prophet's head. Or when, in response to Herod's escalating offers of riches and treasures, Salome intones her monotone and stubborn demand.[10] But this procedure is not always effective. Since the succession of images is introduced for decorative effect, it often stands in the way of dramatic progress: it risks drowning the drama itself in beautiful words.

NOTES

[1] Actually, Wilde's first play, *Vera, or the Nihilist* (1880) was his first published work. Only three copies of this edition are known. The heroine Vera plans to kill the Czar, but instead saves his life, as if she had suddenly been made aware of her contradictory impulses and decided not to resist them. Wilde's interest in Russian revolutionary nihilists may have been sparked by Prince Peter Kropotkin (1842–1921), whom he considered, next to Verlaine, the most perfect being he had ever come across. Oscar Wilde, *De Profundis and Other Writings* (Penguin, 1986), p. 180.

[2] Victorien Sardou (1831–1908), French dramatist, whose best known play is probably *Madame Sans-Géne* (1893) and *La Tosca*, later used by Puccini for his opera *Tosca*. Bernard Shaw, who loathed Sardou and his plays, coined the word Sardoodledom to describe his 'well-made' plays.

[3] Wilde's three plays, *Lady Windermere's Fan* (1892), *A Woman of No*

Importance (1893) and *The Importance of Being Earnest* (1895), are grafted on to and relate to the French tradition. While the unmotherly mother in *Lady Windermere's Fan* recalls Alexandre Dumas's *La Dame aux camélias*, the *Woman of No Importance*, where the father is confronted with a bastard son who spurns his offer of legitimacy, owes a lot to Dumas's *Le Fils naturel* (1858). Essentially, Lukács's point is that Wilde imported a specialized French drama, refurbished it with English atmosphere and characters, while restating what Dumas and others had already said.

4 Wilde was fascinated by two paintings of Salome by Gustave Moreau. In one painting, the aged Herod is being stirred by Salome's lascivious but indifferent dance; in the other, titled *Salome at Column*, the *femme fatale*, preying upon men, is holding a large dish containing John the Baptist's severed head. Wilde also profited from the German poet Heinrich Heine's retelling of the story of Salome in *Atta Troll* (1847). Heine daringly shifted the story away from its sacred context towards a meaning that would be further diverted by succeeding artists. In *The Romantic Agony* (1966), Mario Praz wrote: 'The *Salomes* of Flaubert, of Moreau, Lafargue and Mallarmé are known only to the students of literature and connoisseurs, but the *Salome* of the genial comedian Wilde is known to all the world.' (p. 337)

5 Wilde admired Swinburne's passion, rhythm and vocabulary. In the poem 'The Garden of Eros', Wilde says of Swinburne:

> And he hath kissed the lips of Proserpine
>   And sung the Galilean's requiem,
> That wounded forehead dashed with blood and wine
>   He hath discrowned . . .

6 Wilde's *Salome* was fully consonant with his idea of tragedy, which he said he liked 'to walk in purple and to be remote', adding that the public is a monster of 'strange appetites: it swallows, so it seems to me, honeycake and hellebore, with avidity.' Not surprisingly, *Salome* dwells on incest and necrophilia, among other things, for it is, as Wilde noted, 'only the shudder that counts'. Richard Ellmann, *Oscar Wilde* (New York: Knopf, 1988), pp. 340–1.

7 Wilde himself spoke of the 'refrains whose recurring motifs make *Salome* so like a piece of music and bind it together as a ballad.' *The Letters of Oscar Wilde*, ed. Rupert Hart-Davis (New York: Harcourt, Brace and World, 1962), p. 475.

Richard Strauss said that Wilde's *Salome* was 'simply crying out for music'. It is not without irony that Strauss's *Salome* (1905), with Wilde's text as the libretto, became more famous than the play which inspired it.

8 When Salome orders the soldiers to bring out the prophet from the cistern in which he is imprisoned, Narraboth, a young Syrian captain of the guard, pleads with her that Herod has formally forbidden that any man should raise the cover of this well. Flashing her seductive smile at the young Syrian,

Salome intones, 'Look at me, Narraboth, look at me. Ah! thou knowest that thou will do what I ask of thee. Thou knowest it . . . I know that thou will do this thing.' The young Syrian, aflame with passionate love for Salome, orders the prophet to come forth from the cistern, and then kills himself and falls at her feet.

9 Oscar Wilde, *The Complete Works* (New York: Wm. H. Wise, 1927), vol. 9, pp. 163–4.

10 After Salome dances the dance of seven veils, the enraptured Herod tells her she can have whatsoever she desires. When she asks for the head of the prophet on a silver charger, Herod, horror stricken, tries to dissuade her with gold, treasures and kingdoms. To every desperate plea of Herod, Salome's monotone answer is, 'Give me the head of Iokanaan!'

11

Bernard Shaw

Bernard Shaw introduced a new voice to the history of drama, for his dramas can hardly boast any predecessors. Though his outlook shows some kinship with Anzengruber, it is inconceivable that he could have influenced Shaw. One of the first to proclaim the greatness of Ibsen in England, Shaw was already well established when he got to know Ibsen. The few Ibsen reminiscences that we can find in Shaw can hardly be taken seriously.[1] They both shared one thing, but then, almost all modern writers possess it: an unmasking vision.

But Shaw is the most radical unmasker in the whole of modern literature. Much more so than Ibsen, or anyone else who retained any contact with romanticism. Though all his illusions were dispelled, Ibsen retained – even if in new form – a faith in the hero, the tragic man. This is the exact object of Shaw's polemics; he is an open adversary of all romanticism, professes to be a puritan (in the English sense of course), and believes neither in heroism nor in tragedy. This is no more than a literary, a psychological way of saying that Shaw is a socialist.

Basically the romantic individualism of the nineteenth century was fundamentally bourgeois as were, in essence, the strident anti-romantic struggles and the profound disillusions with romanticism. The anti-romantic polemics of Schopenhauer, Flaubert and Ibsen hardly shook the foundation of romanticism. Indeed, it took no time for everyone to realize that the anti-romantic struggles were fraternal struggles, and soon the sense of compromise had altogether obliterated the differences.

Shaw stands quite apart from every aspect of romanticism; herein lies his affinity with Anzengruber. But what is merely intuitive here becomes conscious in Shaw, based on political and social convictions. The primary objective of Shaw's plays is to strip away the mask from all seductive posturing and heroism, which for Shaw meant one and the same. The world he drew appears in a cold, sharp light. The characters and conflicts Shaw portrayed are not different from those of other dramatists,[2] but for Shaw great sufferings and genuine struggles rarely, if ever, end in a tragic failure. A Shavian character, who dares to defy his circumstances, may keel over or receive a slap in the face, but afterwards, hobbling or with a swollen face, he goes on his way without further ado.

This is why Shaw's notion of the grotesque differs from that of other dramatists. Shaw surveys and portrays the same situations as they do, but his irony makes them much colder and less painful. And in Shaw, where everything merges into satire, the collapse of old values no longer means the collapse of the world. Even if nothing positive is opposed to the collapsed values (which is inconceivable today), the individuals, in their various ways, survive these destructions. When in *Man and Superman* the issue is the inscription over the gate of hell, Shaw talks about the great joy inherent in Dante's lines; namely, what a great joy it is to live without any hope and without any fear.[3]

The removal of tragedy from life and art: this is the primary aim of Shaw's activities. Not that he sees life as something beautiful, good and harmonious. On the contrary, life is full of trouble, suffering and bitterness. In one of his clowning scenes, a young man, about to get married, asks a more experienced and smarter man whether it is wise to get married. The answer is, 'No, every marriage is silly. Our birth is silly, our marriage is silly, our life is silly and it is wise to die.' At the end of his first comedy, *The Philanderer*, some people are quite moved by the girl's deep and real sufferings.[4] And Caesar, during a discussion about death, when others have said they would like to live and that they fear death, admitted he was tired and ready to die when his time came.

Death always casts its shadow even on Shaw's liveliest scenes. Why is there then no tragedy anywhere? Why is tragedy by definition excluded from the Shavian world? In Shaw, new character types make their appearance next to the old character types and, beside the old powers, new powers interfere with man's fate. The coming together and interaction of these two powers give rise to a strange, non-optimistic, non-tragic world, which none the less contains all the troubles of life.

Although metaphysics is not the ultimate cause of every action and event in Shavian dramas, as is the case with Hebbel, Ibsen or Maeterlinck (in the final analysis, this is also true of Wedekind's eroticism), Shaw is not content with mere psychological or simple social causalities. For Shaw, the ulterior cause of human conduct is the economic situation. Inasmuch as all his dramas take place in the modern period (in the conceptual if not the historical sense) this implies the existence of capitalist society based on money, private property and class conflict. At first sight, this hardly seems to make Shaw unique among modern dramatists. After all, anyone who aspires to draw a true portrait of modern life must recognize, whether he likes it or not, that economic relations form one of the motives for human actions and interactions.

But what is novel in Shaw is that economic relations, which for other dramatists denote their own complacent view of what has taken place, consciously occupy the central place among his motives. It is from the perspective of economic relations that he explains things, and explains them with undisguised, consciously polemical intent. Herein lies the true explanation for the novelty of the grotesque Shavian effect. Inherent in the incongruity of events, which produces the grotesque effect, is their temporal nature. Wedekind, for instance, considered these incongruities as timeless dissonances, which of course magnified the serious and tragic propensity of his characterization. By contrast, Shaw draws attention to the social determinants of what appears to be the weightiest, the eternally relevant, and 'generally human' characteristics. This adds correctness and clarity to his comic effects, partly because it sharpens the emotional conflict between the purely social motive and the profoundly spiritual action, and partly because it helps Shaw to suppress the very possibility of tragedy.

Sociologically speaking, we could say that Shaw writes the comedy of '*Überbau*' [superstructure]; he offers a socialist, Marxist perspective on history and its causes, and the dissonance between human visions and the disenchanted world men create and inhabit. The contrast between the imagined motive of alienation and the real motive of human actions becomes more pronounced, but it is precisely for this reason that conflict and the possibility of tragedy disappear. In addition, tragedy disappears because the powers which dominate life prove so powerful that they preclude any struggle against them, and these powers also form the very basis of human existence. Consequently when men oppose these powers they actually oppose their own existence which, even when it takes a serious form, leads to tragi-comic effect.

Hence Shavian characters either lack any image of the world or their idealism – which fails to correspond to reality – or, if it does, has all the appearance of a comic pose. Shaw's characters are the slaves of their circumstances.[5] This is all the more so because in Shaw circumstances are not depicted as hostile forces, bent on subjugating and enslaving men, as is the case in Ibsen or Hauptmann. The circumstances attack the mass of men like a slowly spreading cancerous

growth, and people recognize the symptoms when they are already
infected, and then it is too late; and many never even recognize them.
Insisting on the social conformity of individual actions, society is
indifferent to what the individual says, thinks or feels. In fact, society
assumes that the individual's lovely phrases and platitudes, more or
less true, express his sacred convictions – the exact opposite of what
really happens.

Happy is that man who commands strong feelings, while his eyes
and brains are not sharp enough to recognize the contradictions. And
happier the man whose conscious determination or unconscious instincts instilled in him illusions that mask the real motives of his
actions, so that no disappointment can ever lift the scales from his
eyes (one hears in the distance the faint echoes of the life-affirming lie
motive in *The Wild Duck*). But unfortunate is the man who is smart
and honest enough to confront the truth, provided he is resolved to
confront it. In most cases, there is nothing he can do; he must
continue to lead a life based on a lie, except that until now he had
self-esteem, but no longer. It is impossible to remain pure in this life.
Money, the foundation of everything, the source of splendid human
possibilities, is inextricably tainted and polluted, because it derives
from the exploitation of the weak by the strong.

Given the anonymous nature of capitalism, everyone is implicated
in its iniquity, without of course bearing any individual responsibility.
After all, man does not and cannot know that his money, which
enabled him to grow up in comfort, lead a life without worries and
dedicated to the pursuit of ideals, has been tainted by ruined lives and
broken human existence, by the curses and woes of bought women,
and the tears of widows and orphans. Inevitably, the refined aristocrat, Dr Harry Trench in *Widowers' Houses*,[6] has no choice but to
profess a collective identity with the rich, unscrupulous slum landlord, Sartorius. All his wealth, on which his whole life is based and
organized, is derived from extortion and usury. It is engraved on the
homes Sartorius owns; if he skins the poor, he does so because, in the
first place, he must pay seven per cent interest on loans.

In *Mrs Warren's Profession*, Vivie Warren recognizes that she has no
right to condemn her mother, whose prosperity came from keeping a
brothel. In essence, Vivie's ability to pass judgement on her mother is
the result of her college education.[7] For had Mrs Warren lived a life
other than the one she lived, Vivie would not have received her
education. She would be working fourteen hours a day to pay for her
room and board and save four shillings a week, instead of winning a
prize at Cambridge University. And the wealthy arms manufacturer
Undershaft's daughter in *Major Barbara* also discovered that the

noblest of things – the Salvation Army – cannot exist without the money of leading capitalists. And yet her father's money is directly tainted with blood, while those of others is tainted indirectly.[8]

But Barbara, who proudly spurned poor Bill Walker's pound note who wished to redeem his sin, because salvation is not for sale, accepts Undershaft's money. She has no choice but to acquiesce, because without money she cannot make a single step. In one comical scene in *Man and Superman*, Shaw gives the clearest symbolic expression of his view of the role of money. An American millionaire invests part of his fortune in the Mendoza company's stocks, without – as is mostly the case when buying stocks – knowing anything about the company. This company happens to be a large-scale robbery, which operates on the Spanish border and robs and loots the rich tourists in their automobiles – including, among others, the millionaire's son and his wife.

In modern circumstances, most people are unaware of who or what sets them in motion and makes them act, and it is a rude awakening when circumstances force them to face this. Not surprisingly, most people – one could say that the survival instinct inoculates them – surround themselves with beautiful lies, which they defend stubbornly and desperately as their sole weapon against the brutality of life. But there are a few men – Shaw's new human type – who hate and condemn these beautiful lies and empty romanticism. These characters are fully cognizant of the true source of their own actions as well as those of others, whose opinions are judged paradoxical, and who are regarded as eccentrics and cynics.

The Shavian new human type, with its acerbic remarks and by its very existence, exposes the beautiful poses of others. Shaw's characters are not cynics, at least not in the ordinary sense of the term. In essence, they represent the bourgeois man, who knows the true value of things, for whom every illusion is an illusion, dream is not reality, and the facts are brutal. But since these characters cannot find a place – much as they want to – where life might be different, they accept things as they are.[9] A strange aura of poetry surrounds this human type – it does not seem quite bourgeois. The way these characters walk conveys resolve and a sense of rhythm, and their physical appearance is made attractive by regular sport and exercise; their voices are clear and pure; altogether there is something radiant, appealing about these characters. When they come in contact with others, they appear like a shaft of light in a dark cave, or like a burst of fresh air in a stuffy room with closed windows.

The disillusion this human type creates for others is not the disillusion of the disenchanted romantics: it is a cure. This kind of disillusion destroys only those human beings whose loss is hardly a loss at all, and has no effect only on those who no longer merit any concern. The Shavian new human type comprises characters who are strong and active; energetic, quick, mobile, always doing something and always conscious, without their conscious state of mind impeding their activity. Their viewpoints and activities form an organic whole which exudes the poetry of the metropolis; no wonder it was first produced by an Englishman.

It is instinct which enables Shaw's female figures to feel and act the way they do, whereas the men act as they think. This may well explain why there are more women than men who act instinctively; for women's instincts are stronger and expressing their opinions is of less importance to them than to men. By contrast men, who reach the emotional level of women, appear more valuable than the women.[10] Vivie Warren is the first of this female type. But she is still quite doctrinaire, too much of a one-sided intellectual, and must sacrifice many of her pleasures in order to attain her goal, to lead a useful, independent, working life. Candida already possesses that female geniality which enables her to sense instantly, behind every male pose and beautiful speech, the truth.[11]

But Candida senses not only this but also what she herself and the man who is important to her, really want at any given moment, and she manages to reconcile these different interests directly, effectively and, in fact, poetically. Shaw's heroines always achieve what they want; they play cat and mouse with men, who warble poetry about women. In their own way, the women are very practical and rather prosaic, while their poetic image is confined to the men. This is how the servant Louka manages to marry the proud Major Sergius Saranoff in *Arms and the Man*; this is how Violet Robinson in *Man and Superman*, after a short conversation, terrorizes her father-in-law, the self-made American millionaire, not to mention her own husband; this is how Ann Whitefield plays a game with two men and catches the one she wants.

But Lady Cicely, in *Captain Brassbound's Conversion*, is without any malice or aggressiveness – she refuses to marry even the men who are in love with her; and yet everything goes her way. All she has to do is talk to people, to start a conversation with them in her lovely, quiet, appealing manner, and everything goes her way. She always makes demands, as a mother demands something of her child, and it never occurs to anyone that things could be done any other way.[12] Lady Cicely's mere presence cancels out bloody revenge and violent murders; it would be ridiculous even to think of such schemes in her presence. In many ways, Jennifer [Mrs Dubedat] in *The Doctor's*

Dilemma[13] closely resembles her. And there are some young girls, Sylvia Craven in *The Philanderer*, Dolly Clandon in *You Never Can Tell*, who make their appearance in Shaw's plays, whose lively, naive, childishly straightforward jokes deflate every pose and pretence.[14]

For the most part, Shaw's male figures are more prone to posture, and even the most impressive of his male characters is less prosaic (in Shaw's sense of the term) than his female figures. But some of his male figures, precisely because they are conscious, surpass all the females who resemble them; though they seem less secure. One thinks, first of all, of Captain Bluntschli in *Arms and the Man*, son of a Swiss hotelier who became a professional soldier. Bluntschli has no illusions about his profession, he knows full well what decides the outcome of a battle. He learned early that for him as an artillery officer it hardly mattered whether his pistol was loaded or not, for the battle was already lost if he had to fire his pistol. So, instead of cartridges, he always carries chocolate in his pocket. During an engagement with the enemy, with things looking bad, Bluntschli, trembling with fear and totally exhausted after being in the firing line for three days, takes refuge in a lady's bedchamber in a small town in Bulgaria – which was on the enemy side – and duly seduces her. Bluntschli strips away Raina Petkoff's illusions while the Serbian guns crackle outside her window.

But the greatest of the non-heroic human types are Julius Caesar and the waiter in *You Never Can Tell*.[15] The waiter is totally devoid of any posturing; he is plain, gentle and charming, and is full of deep human understanding (like Shakespeare – Dolly Clandon calls him 'William'). He resolves critical situations by his casual remarks and, like a psychologist, administers to human needs by serving food and cleaning the table; he is always there where he is needed, whether by situations or people. But Caesar is posturing and he knows it. He is not cross when one of his subordinates cautions him against preaching his favourite sermon about life and death.

Caesar strikes poses both public and before his subordinates, and he confesses why. Magnanimously, he frees his Egyptian prisoners – for he is short of soldiers and every prisoner requires two guards. He appears unmoved when the library of Alexandria is in flames for it allows him to capture a strategic point.[16] He is permissive and indulgent toward his subordinates, in order to get to know them, and treats them well; he is good to everyone, just as a man is usually good to his animals. No one is close to Caesar's heart, he lives in a great, all-understanding loneliness, impregnable to every cunning, evil and intrigue. In his lonely reflection on his youth, Caesar is ashamed of the time when he put Vercingetorix to death,[17] he despises the assassins of Pompey;[18] and now he achieves his ends with small sacrifices. None the less, he wears an oak wreath to conceal his baldness, and gets angry when people remind him of his age.

Shaw's other anti-heroes strike poses, for the most part unconsciously. They utter beautiful words and make impressive moves; their thoughts and feelings have a great appeal. This intoxicates them as it intoxicates others, because it all makes life so beautiful, blinding man to everything else so that, intoxicated by beauty, he no longer needs to think. As Shaw shows it, every human action has its absolution, but in most cases there is no need for it. For a beautiful sentence or an idea conceals what the individual actually does. There are characters like Major Saranoff, the operetta soldier who stupidly, and acting without orders, led a cavalry charge against live cannon. A single cannon shot could have wiped out the whole unit. Fortunately, the enemy's artillery ran out of ammunition, everyone escaped, the battle was lost, and Saranoff thereafter regarded himself as a national hero.

Shaw's opposition to the pose here springs from social analysis. Ibsen's character Hjalmar – at least for Ibsen the poet – was an average human type. In Shaw, the pose, the sentimentality and romanticism are bourgeois traits, the characteristics of the middle class. They are the consequences of an anarchy of feeling, of not knowing the world, of greatly overestimating petty individual emotions. As a result, Shaw's strong character types transcend the middle class, they no longer take seriously its narrow-minded, anarchistic individualism, and its blind, eccentric, sentimental romanticism.

When Shaw wants to inflict on the devil his severest irony in *Man and Superman*, he turns him into a sentimental, romantic, bourgeois amateur and aesthete. Needless to say, there are also consciously posturing characters, like General Bonapart in *The Man of Destiny* who acquiesces, in the interest of future plans, to be dispatched as a general to Italy, lest he disturb the idyll of Josephine and Barras, who enact a brilliant comedy for Bonapart's benefit. Many of the Shavian characters are smart, they see clearly the poses of others and their ephemeral ideals, without ever thinking, even for a moment, about their own.

But life does not spare such people. Those who are fully conscious, like Napoleon, manage to escape, whereas the naive are mercilessly unmasked. What gives meaning to Captain Brassbound's life is a romantic notion of revenge. He is about to achieve his aim when Lady Cicely's casual remarks undermine his whole scheme. Life itself unmasks Saranoff and his admirers' heroism, just as it lifts the mask on Morrell's socialist gospel (*Candida*), full of beautiful but empty words; life itself destroyed Mrs Warren, because she talked and thought differently from the way she lived; and the curtain rises on the stupid lies of English militarism in *The Devil's Disciple*, and so on.

All this reveals Shaw's deliberate attempt to educate. According to Shaw, only those survive who are prepared to take life as it is, no matter where or how. Vivie Warren is alienated from her mother, not because she has discovered her mother's past, but because, as Vivie puts it:

> If I had been you, mother, I might have done as you did; but I should not have lived one life and believed in another. You are a conventional woman at heart. That is why I am bidding you goodbye now.[19]

However, if life was this simple for Shaw, one could only admire (or hate) his ethics. Indeed, from an artistic standpoint, the Shavian outlook on life would amount to little; for it would be merely a modern variant of the old, bourgeois-philistine concept of life.

Undeniably, for Shaw life is much more complex. What is certain is that the poses of men are unmasked, but the nature of reason remains very questionable. Bluntschli, Lady Cicely and Candida attain what they want, whereas Gloria Clandon's feminist phrases, in *You Never Can Tell*, prove ineffective against the passions of Valentine; it matters not that John Tanner knows Ann Whitefield well, that he is familiar with her intentions, that he flees from her in an automobile. He cannot escape his fate – he must marry her. It avails General Burgoyne nothing, in *The Devil's Disciple*,[20] that he sees how badly the English fight the war. He can only tell bad jokes while others burst out in stupid, helpless rage; but in the end Burgoyne is just as helpless as the others.

In *John Bull's Other Island*, Larry Doyle [an Irishman] calculates everything and sees what is coming, but all the things he wants to do, will be done by his friend Tom Broadbent [an Englishman], whose manners are ridiculous and who recites stupid sermons. Occasionally, a smart man can assume a sovereignty over life, and yet not be its sovereign. Not only will man never reach his goal, but once he really reaches it, the goal takes over and dominates him. Undershaft the millionaire rose from poverty, because he wanted to be independent. As a millionaire, he is less independent then when he was poor: now his company rules over him.

Of all the human qualities, smartness counts the most, but even that amounts to little. For Shaw this is hardly tragic, on the contrary, it is the key to overcoming every tragedy. This is the first instance in modern drama of the glorification of the dominance of material things over man. This is the positive side of the struggle against bourgeois romanticism. It denotes the social, anti-individualistic vision of man, whose social feelings determine the rhythm of his life. This magnifies to the highest degree, to the point of heroism, that which Ibsen's Brand dismissed with such contempt, namely that a human being can achieve everything he desires so long as he does not want more than what he is capable of.

In Ibsen, who located the ego at the centre of an individual's existence, the ego became a grey, petit-bourgeois egotism, in contrast to the radiant egotism of the 'heroes'. In Shaw, the irreducible soul enables the fulfilment of life-chances, at every possible stage and in every direction. It allows man's total commitment when he stands in defiance of circumstances and, in the service of his commitment, expresses his own personality, instead of merely undertaking quixotic fights against oppressive forces.

In this way, there is no Shavian tragedy to be found anywhere. Fate is helpless against Lady Cicely, whose mere presence cancels out tragedy, and if the cannons were actually fired, it would have turned Saranoff's cavalry charge into a comedy; nor is the young artist's death, in *The Doctor's Dilemma*, tragic.[21] But Caesar . . . , we know, was murdered in Rome. However, though it casts light on the to-ing and fro-ing of Caesar's life, we would never be able to understand the tragic Roman hero from Shaw's Caesar drama – which of course concentrates on the Egyptian episode. Shaw should have made us feel that Caesar, having talked to Brutus and Cassius, convinced them of the futility of their fateful conspiracy. Caesar should have exposed the high-minded Republican pose of the conspirators, which led to his death.

Shaw, on the other hand, consciously avoids the tragedy; rather than reshaping for us an actual historical tragedy, he evades it.[22] This evasion is quite obvious in *The Devil's Disciple*. Here we have the only instance in which Shaw's hero is a tragic figure; Dick Dudgeon's instincts, at a decisive moment, command him to sacrifice himself for an unknown, apathetic man. The tragic hero's power of conviction is so passionate and so strong, so simple and unaffected, that no internal irony, no matter how cunning, can undermine it. The hero's act of self-sacrifice and the comical consequences of the improbable plot are irrelevant here. With a genuine stage effect, Shaw the poet rescues his hero from the gallows,[23] and this otherwise external, strictly theatrical end betrays Shaw's own inner hesitation; it demonstrates that this play cannot be internally deprived of its tragic aspect.

As a brilliant polemicist, Shaw always equivocates when he confronts the primary object of his polemics. His integrity and honesty will not allow him to ignore that there are tragedies, but his whole concept of life refutes the notion that tragedies signify and symbolize life. He refuses to see in tragedies anything more than a single occurrence. Consequently, the logical and technical expression of Shaw's conviction is the happy ending, the escape from a tragic situation. After all, the tragic situation defies a solution only as long as its world view remains insoluble. Short of this, the merely technical, the inadvertently achieved solution is symptomatic of the non-tragic vision, and has no effect on the fundamental problem of the drama.

However, this has bearing on only a few of Shaw's plays. A more serious problem is the formless nature of his plays. From a technical point of view, his dramatic structure is loose, casual, and seems to be composed somewhat carelessly; as if the prime importance was the refined, witty and fluent dialogue. Shaw's loose dramatic structure brings him unconsciously close to naturalism. His form of dialogue – despite its sparkling wit – also shows an affinity with naturalism. But what makes his humorous passages so appealing is chiefly the characters who carry the narrative, and the situations in which they appear, rather than his witty style. This said, it is only Shaw's loose dramatic construction that is close to naturalism; for the probable nature of reality – like all humorists – concerns him very little.

The lack of composition in his dramas is the consequence of their formless nature. Shaw's vision is undramatic, in fact, it is anti-dramatic, and yet his feelings receive a dramatic form. The sharp and insoluble nature of his dissonances cannot lead to anything but dissonance. That this is indeed the case is attested by Shaw's first dramas which, from a technical standpoint, are very good. On the other hand, his own development as a dramatist, his mature and rich vision have undermined the dramatic form. There was a period of transition, roughly from *Candida* to the Caesar comedy, when the rich life of his characters somewhat compensated for the lack of dramatic construction. Later on, the formless construction reached such depths that it adversely affected his characters' credibility. It yielded Shavian dramas that became a kind of theoretical discourse, featuring characters as spokesmen for the life force.

As we have seen, the most positive side of Shaw's acute vision is the undramatic, non-tragic man. Not only can he never be tragic, but his mere presence negates the tragic fate of others. The Shavian non-tragic man recalls Maeterlinck's 'sage'. But Shaw, being more consistent and realistic than Maeterlinck, placed this new man, in quite a radical way, at the very centre of his drama. What is the consequence of this? That on more than one occasion, the Shavian drama reaches a powerful dramatic climax, in order that, at the last moment, the presence of the new man reverses the tragic situation. This not only blunts the sharpness of dramatic events but, by overcoming their tragic nature, it makes these events seem episodic.

The result is that what appeared to signify man's whole life now loses its significance; his life, both in a subjective and objective sense, becomes but an episode. The Shavian characters seem to take a stroll through the drama in search of new adventures, which in turn become mere episodes. The drama itself assumes an epic form: containing one or few adventures full of interest and excitement. It is enhanced by Shaw's tendency to intellectualize things. But a tragic event can only be expressed through emotions, through the dynamic conflict of opposing wills. What negates the tragic in Shaw is the power of his convictions, his superior and condescending intellect, whose luminous light, focused on the limitations of the potentially tragic, dispels it altogether. An enlightened, insightful and rational mind's triumph over the dull and irrational will – herein lies reason's paralysing effect on tragedy.

But all this comes at the cost of over-intellectualizing, at the cost that Shaw's dramatic dialogues assume the form of polemics, a conflict of viewpoints. In these polemics it is less significant whether they represent individuals, wills or philosophical concepts. This intellectual approach and tendency to convert dramatic conflicts into theoretical disputes, shifts our attention away from Shaw's characters and forces us to concentrate on their opinions. The Shavian tendency to generalize, rather than endowing his characters with symbolic importance, makes their true human essence superfluous.

Shaw's development as a dramatist, characterized by the progressive displacement of drama as the dialectic of wills with a drama of viewpoints, seems to draw ever closer to a Platonic dialogue. At first, before his new concept of life found a satisfactory form, his transitions were abrupt, and created grotesque effects. As the Shavian drama achieved a more conscious and higher expression, the more it dispensed with every form of sensual expression of man's fate. At first, the drama disappeared from the Shavian drama, and then, step by step, the characters also disappeared. They disappeared because, from a dramatic perspective, neither theory nor intellect can impart life to anyone. Brought to its logical conclusion, the Shavian philosophy of life dissolves the dramatic form.

Shaw's last dramas have already reached this stage, and their strong contemporary stage appeal hardly disproves our claim. Today, the Shavian views are very topical, enjoy great popular currency, and exert wide influence. But Shaw's influence will cease as soon as their topicality ceases. Shaw's dramatic vision cannot assume a form, for its adequate expression in drama leads to formlessness, the very negation of form.

NOTES

[1] Shaw, 'The Quintessence of Ibsenism' in *Major Critical Essays* (Penguin, 1986), pp. 23–173. Lukács's chief objection to Shaw's interpretation of Ibsen is that he turned him into an unheroic Fabian, and thereby ignored the poet and dramatist.

[2] With his characteristic candour, Shaw admitted, 'But my stories are the old stories; my characters are the familiar harlequin and columbine, clown and pantaloon (note the harlequin's leap in the third act of *Caesar and Cleopatra*); my stage tricks and suspenses and thrills and jests are the ones in vogue when I was a boy, by which time my grandfather was tired of them.' Shaw, *Three Plays for Puritans*, ed. Dan H. Laurence (Penguin, 1946), p. 37.

[3] Shaw's Don Juan cheerfully inverts Dante's hell by proclaiming:

> there is justice in Hell . . . Hell is the home of honour, duty, justice and the rest of the seven deadly virtues. All the wickedness on earth is done in their name: where else but in Hell should they have their reward? Have I not told you that the truly damned are those who are happy in Hell? Shaw, *Man and Superman* (Penguin 1946), Act III, p. 127.

[4] When Charteris thanks Julia for 'revealing' his manhood to him and blesses her for it, she explodes in disgust: 'Don't say that: I hate it. It sounds as if I were a mere animal.' Charteris consoles her by saying there is nothing wrong with animal qualities, for 'it is hardly moral qualities man seeks or admires in woman.'

Julia articulates fully the plight of Victorian women when she protests, 'Must I stand to be bargained for by two men – passed from one to the other like a slave in the market, and not say a word in my own defence?' (Shaw, *The Philanderer* Act III)

[5] On character and circumstances, Shaw wrote:

> In short, though character is independent of circumstances, conduct is not; and our moral judgements of character are not: both are circumstantial. Take any condition of life in which the circumstances are for a mass of men practically alike: felony, the House of Lords, the factory, the stables, the gipsy encampment or where you please! In spite of diversity of character and temperament, the conduct and morals of individuals in each group are as predictable and as alike in the main as if they were a flock of sheep, morals being mostly only social habits and circumstantial necessities. Shaw, *Major Barbara*, pp. 35–6.

6   The slum landlord Sartorius, who pretends to be a gentleman of consid-
     erable wealth, has a daughter, Blanche, to be married to Dr Harry
     Trench, who is too proud to take money from Sartorius, or to marry for
     money. Sartorius collects his rents by all sorts of bullying and tyranny
     while children go hungry in the tenement houses. In due course, Dr
     Trench discovers that he holds a mortgage in Sartorius's slum empire and
     derives his income from the misery of others. In typical Shavian fashion,
     Trench's idealism and 'stage socialism' is exposed as a sham.

7   When Mrs Warren informed her daughter Vivie that she too would have
     gone to college and become a lady if 'I'd had the chance,' Vivie re-
     sponded: 'Everybody has some choice, mother. The poorest girl alive may
     not be able to choose between being Queen of England or Principal of
     Newnam; but she can choose between ragpicking and flowerselling, ac-
     cording to her taste. People always blame their circumstances for what
     they are. I don't believe in circumstances.' (Shaw, *Mrs Warren's Profes-
     sion*, Act II)

8   Undershaft's terrifying discovery in *Major Barbara*, which Shaw himself
     also discovered when he read Henry George's *Progress and Poverty* and
     followed it by Marx's *Capital*, is that poverty is the 'greatest of evils and
     the worst of crimes, and that our first duty – a duty to which every other
     consideration should be sacrificed – is not to be poor.' Or as Undershaft,
     the English Machiavelli, put it: 'Poverty blights whole cities; spreads
     horrible pestilences; strikes dead the very souls of all who come within
     sight, sound, or smell of it . . . Only fools fear crime: we all fear poverty.'
     (Shaw, *Major Barbara*, Act III)

9   The hero of *Major Barbara*, Undershaft exclaimed impatiently to the
     Plato-quoting Cusins: 'Ought! ought! ought! ought! ought! Are you going
     to spend your life saying ought, like the rest of our moralists! Turn your
     oughts into shalls, man. Come and make explosives with me. Whatever
     can blow men up can blow society up.' (Act III)

10   In Shaw's sexual world, man is woman's instrument for fulfilling nature's
     plan, and marriage – that most licentious of human institutions – is the
     means for trapping him so that he carries out nature's bidding. In the
     Shavian sex war, woman is invariably the pursuer and man the pursued.
     And Shaw, like Lukács, saw little possibility that women could combine
     motherhood and creative work.

11   Candida, the wife of Reverend James Morell, a Christian socialist clergyman,
     is the object of the young poet Marchbanks's romantic passion and worship.
     The husband and the poet, representing realism and idealism, contend for
     Candida's love and she has to choose, for she must belong to one or the other.
     She asserts her own independence from both the poet and husband and asks
     them to bid for her. Candida says she will give herself to the weaker of the two
     – and she chooses her husband. As she reveals her intention he falls to his
     knees. Candida kisses the poet's forehead. She then turns to her husband,
     holding out her arms to him, 'Ah, James!' (*Candida*, Act III)

12   *Captain Brassbound's Conversion* represents an advance in optimism on
     Caesar and Cleopatra in the sense that whereas Caesar changes no one's

mind in Egypt, Lady Cicely Waynflete does convert Brassbound in Morocco. Robbed of his determination to revenge what he imagined his uncle Sir Howard had done to his mother, the idealistic Brassbound says to Lady Cicely: 'Now everything is gone. You have taken the old meaning out of my life; but you have put no new meaning into it . . . You've lamed me by showing me that I take life the wrong way when I'm left to myself.' (*Captain Brassbound's Conversion*, Act III)

In order to fill his empty life with meaning, he asks Cicely to be his wife. But Brassbound's love is rejected as a solution, as it had been earlier by Caesar and by Shaw himself in *The Perfect Wagnerite*. Besides, being a wife would alter Lady Cicely's romantic ideal of being sweet and indulgent to all men. She preferred the adoration of men to the dutiful attentions of a husband.

[13] Shaw's original intention was to call the heroine of *The Doctor's Dilemma* (subtitled 'A Tragedy'), Andromeda; but Mrs Andromeda Dubedat sounded strange to English ears. The play portrays the dishonourable man of genius, Dubedat, a slave to his art, whose wife, Jennifer, embodies romanticism. Jennifer dreams of saving Dubedat, she wants to bring some charm and happiness to his driven and tragic life, framed in poverty and idealism. It is of some interest that the model for Dubedat was Edward Aveling, the notorious deceiver idolized by Marx's daughter Eleanor, whose promising life ended in suicide.

[14] Dolly Clandon is the daughter of Mrs Clandon, a veteran of the Old Guard of the Women's Rights Movement which had for its Bible J. S. Mill's treatise on *The Subjection of Women*. When her mother preaches mutual respect and privacy for members of the family, Dolly replies, jokingly, 'See Twentieth Century Parents, chapter *On Liberty*, passim.' (Shaw, *You Never Can Tell*, Act I)

[15] The waiter William in *You Never Can Tell* is a sickly old man. White haired and delicate looking, but so cheerful and contented that in his encouraging presence ambition stands rebuked as vulgarity, and imagination as treason to the abounding sufficiency and intention of the actual. Dolly Clandon tells him, 'Remember William: we come to this hotel on your account, having heard what a perfect waiter you are.' And she remarks, 'You really are like Shakespeare, William!' (*You Never Can Tell*, Act II)

[16] When informed that the library of Alexandria is in flames and Caesar should order some of his legions to extinguish it, Caesar replies: 'Theodotus: I am an author myself; and I tell you it is better that the Egyptians should live their lives than dream them away with the help of books.' When reminded that what is burning is the memory of mankind, Caesar remarks, 'Let it burn . . . a few sheepskins scrawled with errors.' (Shaw, *Caesar and Cleopatra* Act II)

[17] Vercingetorix, an Arvernian, commander-in-chief in the revolt of 52 BC in Gaul, which Caesar put down. In his *The Conquest of Gaul*, Caesar pays a fine tribute to the qualities of leadership which enabled Vercingetorix to strengthen his hold upon his followers and re-animate them in the hour of

defeat (VII 29–30). But Caesar either could not or would not protect Vercingetorix from the fate which Roman custom demanded of a vanquished barbarian. Six years after his capture Vercingetorix was exhibited at Rome in Caesar's triumph and then executed. On Vercingetorix and his revolt against Rome, see Caesar, *The Conquest of Gaul*, tr. S. A. Handford *(Penguin Books, 1982)*, VII 4, 8, 9, 12–21, 26–89.

[18] Pompey (Gnaeus Pompeius Magnus), consul 70 BC, 55 BC, 52 BC,; member with Caesar of the 'first triumvirate'; after his defeat by Caesar at Pharsalus in the Civil War (48 BC), he withdrew to Egypt, where he was murdered. Plutarch left a moving portrait of Pompey's end. The assassins cut off Pompey's head and threw the rest of his body naked out of the boat, leaving it there as a spectacle for those who desired to see such a sight. When Caesar arrived in Egypt, one of the Egyptians brought him Pompey's head. Caesar turned away from him with loathing, as from an assassin; and when he received Pompey's signet ring on which was engraved a lion holding a sword in his paws, he burst into tears. Plutarch, *Fall of the Roman Republic*, tr. Rex Warner (Penguin Books, 1958), pp. 241–2.

[19] *Mrs. Warren's Profession*, Act IV.

[20] The play takes place in 1777 when passions were roused in England by the separation of the American colonies from England. Idealism and pride reigned supreme on both sides: on the American side the high minded ideals of the Rights of Man, on the English side the ideals of an empire and its prestige. General Burgoyne was an imperialist, yet he sympathized with the colonists.

[21] Shaw wrote his play, *The Doctor's Dilemma*, in response to William Archer's article entitled 'Death and Mr Bernard Shaw'. Archer argued that Shaw's comic genius and impish sense of humour prevented him from writing a convincing death scene. In short, Shavian humour kills tragedy. Shaw's *Doctor's Dilemma* is tragic comedy with death conducting the orchestra. However, Dubedat's death takes place in the presence of a newspaper reporter – so death and comedy do indeed come together in the Shavian tragic world.

[22] Shaw said explicitly that he offered his Caesar to the public as an improvement on Shakespeare's. While Shakespeare knew human weakness, he never knew human strength of the Caesarian type. Shakespeare's Caesar, said Shaw, is an admitted failure. Hence Shaw sets forth Caesar in a 'modern light'.

[23] The question which preoccupied Lukács, as it does other commentators on *The Devil's Disciple*, is why would the atheist Richard Dudgeon, the devil's disciple, sacrifice his life for the parson Anthony Anderson, a fleshy incarnation of a Presbyterian divine. One plausible answer is that since Dudgeon personifies the Shavian life force, a variant of Wagnerian resurrection, he chooses death rather than let death choose him. For Shaw, the decision to live or die is the last glorified act of free will.

Part III

Art and Literature

Introduction

Art and Literature

In December 1909 a Hungarian avant-garde group, known as The Eight, or the Seekers as they were first called, mounted its first exhibition in Budapest. This radical group of eight artists broke with Impressionism and marched under the banner of Cézanne and Gauguin. The leader of the group, Károly Kernstok (1873–1940), attended the Académie Julien in Paris and came under the influence of Cézanne, Gauguin, Van Gogh, Matisse and Picasso, and issued a daring manifesto entitled 'Art as Exploration' which appeared in the *Nyugat* (January 1910). Lukács's essay, 'The Parting of the Ways', was a response to the Eight's first exhibition, which sparked an incredible public and press reaction, was reprinted in the *Nyugat* (February 1910). Our translation is based on this source.

Lukács's seminal essay, 'Aesthetic Culture', was originally published in the journal *Renaissance* (25 May 1910), the source for this English translation, and later published in a small book entitled *Aesthetic Culture* (1913). This contained some of his commentaries on Thomas Mann and Arthur Schnitzler, plus his reflections on Strindberg, a brilliant study of the Hungarian poet Endre Ady, and his daring manifesto on art, 'The Parting of the Ways'.

Here we already see that it was Cézanne's break with Impressionism that literally sanctified him as the patron saint of the Lukács circle, which included such now renowned figures in the world of art as Charles Tolnay, Arnold Hauser, Antal Frigyes and Lajos Fülep, the teacher of Tolnay. Arnold Bennett, a friend of Fülep, confided to his diary that 'He [Fülep] said that Cézanne was as great as Titian, and put Monet and Degas with him, and he had a special affection for Renoir and especially Matisse.'[1] Lukács agreed with Fülep on the importance of Cézanne and Gauguin. There can be little doubt that Gauguin, who left his comfortable life and became an artist, as if driven by fate to make the tough choice of solitude, made a great impact on Lukács. His essay on Gauguin, published in the *Huszadik Század* (June 1907), the source of this English translation, glows with admiration. Drawing up the philosophical manifesto of the Lukács circle, Karl Mannheim listed its patron saints and ideals as follows: Dostoevsky's concept of life, Kierkegaard's ethical convictions, Cézanne's instinctive classicism, Bartók's folk music and Endre Ady's poetry.[2]

Fine arts, especially painting, played an important role in Lukács's early writings. He makes frequent references to artists, and leading members of The Eight were close to the Lukács family, whose villa contained many paintings by them. In 1911, Lukács declared categorically, 'Today there is only French painting. And those who do not want to learn directly from Giotto or the Greeks can only attend Cézanne's school.'[3]

Lukács's 'Integrated Civilizations' is reprinted from his classic work, *The Theory of the Novel* (1920). This work, written in the winter of 1914–15, has a curious history. Following Irma Seidler's suicide, Lukács, full of guilt and craving redemption, sought solace in Dostoevsky, who taught him that the 'great life, the life of goodness' no longer presupposes purity. In Dostoevsky's works, 'interesting sinners' (see 'Stavrogin's Confession', *Reader* chapter 15), seem to have a secure passage to 'goodness'. As his personal crisis deepened and the 'death-drunken and death-yearning world' of 1914 plunged into the bloody chaos of war, Lukács worked at feverish pace on his book on Dostoevsky. But ultimately, partly under the urging of Max Weber, he gave up on Dostoevsky, and instead, from his notes on Dostoevsky grew *The Theory of the Novel*, which expresses Lukács's own '*recherche du temps perdu*'. The opening sentence (*Reader* chapter 16), 'Happy are those ages when the starry sky is the map of all possible paths – ages whose paths are illuminated by the light of the stars', summed up Lukács's gloom and horror at the sight of European civilization torn by war.

But whether Lukács analyses art, civilization or literature as he does in 'The Ideology of Modernism', reprinted from his *Realism in Our Time* (1964), his judgement and perception is that of a radical moralist. No one summed up Lukács, the literary critic, better than George Steiner:[4]

> Like Victorian critics, Lukács tends to condemn art whose themes he finds unsavoury, or in which man is shown in the light of obsession or weakness. Hence his insensitivity to Dostoevsky and his failure to grasp the real scope of Proust. The luxuriance and perversities of which Proust builds his tragic vision outrage Lukács's ascetic, optimistic morality. He does not see that in Proust the classic energies of the French novel come to their natural unfolding, or that Proust's irony gives as severe an indictment of his society as does that of Mann. Similar motives are at work in his rejection of Joyce. To Lukács, the saga of Bloom is merely *petit-bourgeois* narcissism run mad. In this great Marxist, there is an old-style puritan.

At the same time, the puritan element in Lukács lends a sense of urgency, supreme seriousness and lofty humanism to his vision and judgement. As Lukács put it (*Reader*, p. 45):

> We are human because we can create works of art, and conjure up happy islands in the midst of life's unhappy, restless, polluted streams.

If art could shape life, and Goodness became a deed, then we would be gods.

NOTES

[1] Arnold Bennett, *The Journals* (New York: Penguin, 1971), p. 302.

[2] Karl Mannheim, *Lélek és Kultúra* [Soul and Culture] (Budapest, 1918), p. 7.

[3] Lukács, 'The Gallic Danger' in *Ifjukori müvek (1901–1918)* [Early works], ed. Arpád Timár (Budapest: Magvetö, 1977), p. 562.

[4] See George Steiner's 'A Preface' to Lukács's *Realism in Our Time* (New York: Harper and Row, 1964), p. 15.

12

Aesthetic Culture

The world is full of armies,
But that is not what will kill us.

Béla Balázs

If there is culture today, it can only be an aesthetic culture. If one wants to raise seriously the question whether there is a centre to man's self-alienation and egocentrism, that question should be raised here. If one is critically disposed towards modern life, one must critique the aesthete in the same way that the Sophist[1] would have done in Socrates' Athens, as the Pope and the robber knights in the bright days of medieval times, the warbling troubadour and the mystic in the waning Middle Ages, as the petty tyrant and militant philosopher in the eighteenth century.

There are or course those who hold a different view – but their talk merely confirms our own perception. There are those who, when the topic turns to culture, prefer to talk about aeroplanes and railways, the speed and efficiency of telegraphs. They discuss the rise of literacy in modern 'democracy' (as if modern man's soul really craved to read) and point out the number of people whose rights are denied in a democracy (even if they phrase it differently). But let us never forget one thing: all these manifestations – even in the best of circumstances – are merely roads to a culture; they merely provide an opportunity, enhance the potential, and lend substance to the formative power of culture.

But culture can impart substance to anything, provided it possesses the innate power of creativity. Culture: the unifier of life; a unity strong enough to intensify and enrich life. And yet, can we claim that travel means more to us just because we reach our destination in a day, rather than a month? Have our letters gained in depth and become more soulful on account of a faster mail service? Did human responses to life become stronger and more homogeneous only because a larger number of people get closer to things and to more things?

Indisputably, modern culture has produced two pure types: the expert and the aesthete. They are incompatible and mutually exclusive – and yet each needs the other to complement himself. The life of the expert: the sacrifice of one's whole life so that one segment of 'the' life becomes more manageable; the external aspects of life define its inner content, where means turn into ends. And the life of the aesthete? What else, but exclusively an inner life? What else, but the complete disappearance of all 'secondary' things from a genuine and real life? What else, but life in the realms of the soul, confined, as Maeterlinck put it, exclusively there?

It is by no means pure chance that placed the expert and aesthete side by side as mutually exclusive. For I could just as easily describe their respective essences as follows. The expert embraces the *l'art pour l'art* of professionalism; the goodness of 'accomplishing' things as man's primary goal, irrespective of what is being said or accomplished. The aesthete embraces sensation as an occupation, a profession. But a sensation which conceals from man life itself. Therefore, the deep solidarity of the two types (which lends real content to their seemingly formal contrast) is that their respective roads, whose meaning and significance lies in the goals to which they lead, become self-serving. In both, their respective purity as types is the result of inner impoverishment. The unity of the two types is due to their one-sided lives, and the one-dimensionality of their soul. The souls of aesthete and expert are devoid of that richness and strength that can relate everything to the centre of one's being, because it knows everything does in fact relate to it.

The aesthetic culture. Everyone knows what it has brought about. For in the past decade hardly a week has passed without someone not singing in brilliant words the glories of aesthetic culture. At first, the proponents of aesthetic culture wanted to conquer life for art alone, to remove from life without a trace everything innate to it and alien to art. Everything was considered to be art and everything equally artistic. 'There was no value difference between a well painted bowl of porridge and a well painted Madonna.' This of course would still only comprise an 'art' (often very good art), but not culture.

The greatest of the old aesthetes could proclaim, '*L'homme n'est rien; l'oeuvre est tout*' [Man is nothing, work is everything]; this aesthete had art in mind. Aesthetic art, which saw all life as a form of expression, tolerated no differences other than those of potential moods and their aesthetic expression. Life itself resided somewhere else; far away, beyond what was important and interesting.

Every culture denotes the conquest of life. Culture signifies a powerful unity of all aspects of life (this is never a conceptual unity of course), so that no matter what perspective we choose on life, we see essentially the same thing everywhere. In an authentic culture everything is symbolic, because everything expresses – and expresses it equally – what is of paramount importance: how the individual reacts to life, how his whole being responds to and confronts life as a whole.

The centre of aesthetic culture is: the mood [its artistic aspects are analysed in 'The Parting of the Ways', *Reader* chapter 14]. The mood is the most common mediator (though hardly the most important or profound) of an artwork. The essence of mood is its accidental, non-analysable nature and, in fact, its conscious distance from the non-analytical approach is due to the transient relation which obtains between the observer and the object of observation. Aesthetic culture owes its birth to the very moment when man's spiritual activity expands and encompasses the whole of life, in other words, the moment when life itself is seen as an endless sequence of transient moods. It was born when objects ceased to exist, because everything was merely an occasion for the mood; when all that was permanent disappeared from life, because the mood proved intolerant of what was permanent and recurrent. It was born when life was stripped of all values, and it now values the products of moods, that is to say, the products of fortuitous circumstances devoid of any necessary correlation with values.

In a sense the unity of aesthetic culture does exist: as a lack of unity. Aesthetic culture has a central tenet: the peripheral nature of all things. This culture also has a symbol for everything: namely that nothing is symbolic, that everything is what it appears to be in the very moment we experience it, nor is there anything anywhere that amounts to more than this. What enables aesthetic culture to transcend the purely individual (for man's heritage forms an essential part of culture) is that only the particular individual moods are regarded as transcendent. Aesthetic culture also has its own concept of human relations: the total loneliness of man,[2] the complete negation of human contacts.

Aesthetic culture becomes the art of life; the elevation of life into an art. In the hands of the sovereign artist everything becomes a substance. It matters not whether he paints, composes a sonnet, or just lives.

But we now know better. It was a lie that the art of life is a genuine art for, in essence, it merely imposed the dominant powers and directions of art on life itself. No. The art of life is merely the enjoyment of life; not artistic creativity. The art of life in reality applied the theories of artistic gratification (more correctly: some theories) against life itself.

The fundamental lie of aesthetic culture or (in some of its serious representatives) its tragic paradox is that it has proscribed all real spiritual activity, and equated all manifestations of life with an affectionate surrender to transient moments. And precisely because everything comes from within, nothing really comes from without. It is only the external world and its objects that induce moods, and if someone elects to enjoy the manifestation of his soul as a beautiful moment, even then he remains a passive observer of something that chance brought in his way. For absolute freedom is the most terrifying of unfreedoms. 'Everything is only a mood', even the beautiful, majestic freedom of the soul, whose sovereignty lies in its ability to absorb all that exists in the dynamic, active soul. 'Everything is only a mood': so nothing counts more than mood, the most confining form of slavery, the most horrifying self-mutilation of the soul. Complete passivity can never constitute the principle of life (only in the formal sense that death and life,[3] health and sickness can be one – in a definition), nor can anarchy be the cornerstone of its foundation.

The 'aesthetic culture', the 'art of life' glorifies the soul's debasement, its inability to create and to act, and pronounces the soul's surrender to moods as the very principle of life. Aesthetic culture amounts to an admission, conscious or unconscious, compounded by a lie, of its own inability to know how to live (to rule over life or form it). The 'art of life': it amounts to no more than dilettantism in life; to being stone-blind about true creativity and its real essence.

But dilettantism has rebounded on art itself. The unity of life and art that aesthetic culture aimed at, instead of lifting life to the sublime, transcendent realm of art by giving form to its contingencies and necessity to its trivialities, actually imbued art with its own dilettante hedonism. In sum, aesthetic culture pulled art down to its own level, the petty, ramshackle realm of perpetual indecision.

The mood is merely a work of art's creative, transient contact with the soul of the beholder. If the endless succession of moods is caused by something else, then its effect is more valuable and quite different from the sum total of the random, chaotic, endless succession of moods. This something, present nowhere and yet apparent everywhere, makes art an art. This art is dynamic, organic, cosmic, and symbolizes in the world what in itself appears dead and trivial. It is precisely this, the dynamic nature of art, which had perished under the onslaught of 'aesthetic culture'. The advocates of 'form' have killed the form; the high priests of *l'art pour l'art* have paralysed art.

The form these people introduced was but an attractive collage of surfaces, rather than an innate, organic unity, with its own growth and an inner, purposeful teleology. The concept of form, a genuine form, signifies the sovereign mastery of things, but it is a mastery over things. All things are subservient to the concept of form, but what is being conquered springs to life, in the same way that what is sovereign takes on life. Herein lies the form's life-affirming power, which also comprises its ethic. The form's self-evident strength and mystery resides in its very essence; it imparts depth and unequivocal meaning to the ultimate relations of life.

In order for the form to reign, there must be resistance, which in turn presupposes certain things. Because power without resistance is dysfunctional. No world view can ever realize itself if it ignores the resistance of reality, the inherent power of the self and its opposition. But how is the self to know it possesses real power, unless a wise foresight instructs it to avoid an obviously hopeless struggle? The aesthetes' world view is oblivious of the disharmony of things and their embittered struggles. The aesthete is condemned to an existence of enjoyment, of collecting the beautiful moments, and then – at best – weaving them with blissful interludes into a wreath.

Aesthetic culture confines the potential effect of art to the surface. It regards any artwork which is monumental as obsolete. It declares tragedy irrelevant, unfit for modern man, and assumes that since we 'understand' and 'empathize' with everything, there are no longer any irreconcilable conflicts. Modern man considers every thought super-ficial and burdensome, for what is really important is 'good writing'. Besides, thoughts are without meaning for they are but concocted lies, and all thoughts are equal lies, whose sole difference is in their formulation. Conversely, modern man refers to all systems as an organized lie, since with each passing moment we think differently, and it is both futile and self-defeating to search for roots and relations when our values are the values of evanescent moods. There is no need to compose and to build; no need to live fully or to have profound thoughts: this is the joyful hymn of aesthetic culture. Wherever it makes its appearance, there is no architecture, no tragedy, no philos-ophy, no monumental painting, nothing truly epic. But there is a perfectly polished technique, and a cunningly intricate psychology; witty aphorisms and gossamer-like moods. Perhaps these are the ingredients of a genuine art – provided such art really needed what was being created.

This mood-inspired, mood-adhering aesthetic culture has lost all contact with life. Perhaps at no time was there a culture which meant less for so many people of importance. There is something very professional about modern art's influence: writers write for writers, painters paint for painters, or, at best, for writers and painters whose career has come to an end. Today, artists have hardly anything to 'say' (indeed, proudly boast of it), their values are mostly appreciated by the experts, while their main impact is confined to the garrets. After all, general cultural development, which uses man for one purpose only and never touches his whole personality, subdues and subverts the 'human' element in man, and thereby his obscure and debilitated spiritual needs are unable to make contact with any art.

The masses readily believe there is no need for such contact (how much of this is due to bourgeois smugness, and how much to aesthetic hedonism?) or, at most, need leisure time in order to kill time, to stimulate and soothe the weary nerves. Whereas the most serious minded people are full of contempt for all art; most of them 'enjoy' it with deep apathy, or grow accustomed to it as part of being 'culturally educated'.

Unfortunately, this apathy and contempt is not strong enough. The proletariat and socialism seem to hold out the only hope. The hope that the barbarians are coming and with callous hands will tear apart all delicate, refined things; that the persecuted might have a redeeming value beyond refinement. And perhaps, just as Ibsen believed that Russian tyranny is the best educator of freedom, art will grow and flourish in a period that opposes and hates culture. Of course this would hardly be the most decisive factor: merely a residual and contingent consideration. On the other hand one could rightly expect that the revolutionary spirit, whose power had 'unmasked' all ideologies and identified the real historical forces, will show vision and understanding here. And the revolutionary spirit, having swept aside all things peripheral, will return once again, after the long hiatus of anti-artistic feelings, to what is essential in art. However, what we have seen so far provides little ground for hope. It appears that socialism does not possess the soul-expanding, religious strength of early primitive Christianity. It took early Christianity's anti-artistic stand to give birth to the art of Giotto and Dante, of Meister Eckhart and Wolfram von Eschenbach. Christianity produced the Bible whose rich offerings inspired art and artists throughout the centuries. Being a true religion, whose power created the Bible, Christianity had no need for art; it neither desired nor tolerated it. Christianity aspired to the absolute mastery of man's soul for it possessed the power to reign supreme. Socialism lacks this power and consequently it cannot become the real adversary of bourgeois aestheticism, as it wants to be and knows it ought to be.

Partly for this reason, socialism's conscious aim is to create a proletarian art in the midst of bourgeois culture. The result is a weak and gross caricature of bourgeois art; just as fragile and superficial, but without the seductive charm of bourgeois art. In some measure, the socialists are aesthetes too. They enjoy the same things, and, like the bourgeoisie, know full well that 'expression' is all that counts, and the theme signifies nothing. For the socialists, no less than for the bourgeoisie, everything involves the question of taste, of a viewpoint and of moods. In socialism, as in bourgeois society, things are confined to the surface without ever making contact with the centre of life. In fact, it is much more so in socialism where human life is framed in purpose and anchored to a centre. And yet, the masses are unable to see that this has nothing to do with them, for purpose and centre merely hang on them like a loose garment. But what do they care, it feels pleasant and comfortable and, besides, it indicates they have overcome prejudice and attained superiority.

There are of course those who see the situation clearly, and describe it in sharp, tough words. One with a resonant voice, full of vision and noble feelings, wrote:

> When I see that art leads to a regular worship of sensualism, then I must declare that the best programme would be to blow up all the churches, with organs, pictures and everything, no matter the woes raised by all the critics and advocates of art.

But its author – Bernard Shaw – was one of the most passionate apostles of Wagner.

In the absence of a healthy persecution of art and any serious contact with it, total apathy and privileged dominance characterizes art's polarized relation to life. It would hardly be an exaggeration to say that reality only recognizes these extremes, and ignores the transition between them. There is art because there are people who, being born with an unfortunate physical-spiritual disposition, are incapable of anything in this great wide world other than art. Thomas Mann once defined, in a serious and bitter tone, the modern artist as follows. The artist: the useless man; the artistic culture: to create a style out of one's useless, good-for-nothing existence.

Put this way, the situation appears tragic, and the greatest, the really serious artists and human beings, (the Keats, Flauberts, Ibsens) did indeed lead a life framed in tragedies. But it is inconceivable that other artists have not also felt the tragic paradox in some form. An artist must feel his own rootless existence, and be aware of his inability to relate to others and establish human contact. Especially an artist who cannot but feel the unbearable burden of being trapped in his own life, a life whose only genuine content can come from communication and a profound sense of community with others.

From this perspective, the life of an aesthete – whether it is confessed or concealed, consciously heroic or wrapped in a lie – inescapably unfolds within the atmosphere of tragedy. And what in most aesthetes' writing is so strongly felt and so genuinely inspiring is invariably rooted in tragedy. Tragedy forms the human background of Wilde's hard-beaten aphorisms; the sadly-proud concealment of tragedy illuminates Hofmannsthal's turgid poems, and tragedy surrounds with light airiness Thomas Mann's images drawn with dry, sharp objectivity.

But in the life of aesthetes – as in every tragic paradox – also coincide and converge virtues and powers, sins and weaknesses. The very tragedy of the aesthetes' life is the one thing which somehow lends sacred unity and strength to their oeuvre. It is the *a priori* tragedy of their art which makes their life so frivolous and empty. It all reminds me of Ferencz Herceg's [Hungarian novelist 1863–1954] most astute observation. His character, Captain Gyurkovics, is fully resolved that the moment society deems his conduct to be incorrect, he will shoot himself in the head. Meanwhile, of course, the good captain does what he likes, or what suits his self-interest. In short, his conduct, ethically speaking, is incorrect. His heroic resolve to commit suicide, rather than preventing his improper behaviour, actually encourages it. If this or that happens, Gyurkovics says, I will kill myself anyway. Needless to say, he never shoots himself.

The permanent tragedy – and this is the essence of Herceg's brilliant observation – is the greatest of all frivolities. It is the greatest because, while one awaits the great reckoning (which never comes), everything becomes permissible. After all, on the day of judgement everything will be found trivial – and where, in the real processes of life, resides the difference between the light and serious? And since both life and art are tragic, it hardly matters what weight and seriousness we attach to its parts. 'It makes no difference': one is allowed to say this – perhaps – only at the very end of the tragedy. And even then one must not say it, or believe it to be the essence of life. This then is the eternal melody of the philosophy of life. 'It is all the same': only the intensity of various sensations is different: the sense of permanent tragedy absolves all indolence.

What is to come? What must come? One thing is certain: it is not the pious dreamers' utopian deliverance of the world. Today, the best of those who were born for art look back full of longing on those happier times when art was different. When art created and shaped culture, or, at least, it believed this to be its mission in life.

Art believed in its mission. This explains the real flaw in every art-inspired cultural prophecy. Art was always only a consequence of cultures; often serving as their far advanced herald, and, at other times, as their tough-minded, honest and unsparing judge. But art's rhythm of words was invariably set by the rhythm of cultural progress. And because it is easier to sense cultural progress, which helps us to understand and recognize art, many people continue to believe in the creative priority of culture. There were periods when people genuinely believed this, and had every right to their faith: the power which grew from it and the fruits it bore have legitimized this faith.

Today we would have to close our eyes to attain such a faith, aided by ignorance or self-delusion. This is why faith like this today is devoid of all pathos, and this is why – in the best cases – the Gregers Werle's[4] pathetic glory surrounds the militant advocates of art's world-redeeming and culture-creating power. Any knowledge which was once imposed on us can never again be eradicated from our life, even if our previous state of ignorance turned out to be more productive, richer and brighter. If Herder and Schiller, if Goethe and the romantics believed in the soul's world-creating power, their mistake would have been a tragic mistake at best, provided they acknowledged it. Today, knowing what we know, it would be comic if we tried to realize an illusion that once appeared plausible.

Thus we face reality: it was made that way by necessities that are greater than we are, and these necessities, riding roughshod over us, achieve their ends driven by an inner inevitability. If it is really true that in the whole complex of culture there are primary forces which set things in motion (and motion does not originate in the incalculable complexity of interactions), then people who take account of these forces and are convinced their own life-work can actually have an impact, do perhaps command the power to change culture. Perhaps. But those who live for and around art never command such a power.

However, the acknowledgement of determinism produces fatalism only in the weak; only in those for whom the metaphysical inability of the will serves as an excuse to confirm their own ineptitude. Whereas the born activist learns from the same knowledge that his own inner drives also constitute a necessity, and if by chance his actions produce no external results, he knows equally well that what he did was just as necessary. Only the direction of action changes once the illusionary nature of an illusion is revealed; it merely forces us to choose different roads to attain the same ideals. For no understanding of the external relation of things can bring about a change in the will's intensity or in the soul's innate power. Where this appears to be otherwise, it merely covers up the lack of inner intensity in man.

The external situation is given. And no genius can undermine its iron necessity; no individualistic culture can produce the social, and what is inner can never become outer. And yet, the inner is just as much a necessary reality. This is why it is an inner débâcle to escape into socialism. What a pleasant-sounding motto: 'serve progress, and subordinate your individual aspirations and needs to it.' But it is nothing but a motto, nothing but a proclaimed or assumed motive for action. If the born aesthetes of culture talk this way then their talk conceals just as much despair as that of the quietist prophets of determinism. However, the aesthetes' despair unmasks their inability to bear the tragic loneliness for which their deepest spiritual powers predestined them. Unable to bear it, they indulge in escapism and renounce their highest values, in order to find solace somewhere. Repose and security, anywhere and at any price. Anatole France's 'conversion' to socialism is as sad an example of a broken life as was Friedrich Schlegel or Clemens Brentano's escape into the beatified silence of faith. For what difference does it make that here the clash of arms is a cradle song to soothe all pains? (Let us not mention Bernard Shaw and his kind in this context, for they were always socialists; born agitators.)

The situation is given, the internal as well as the external: therefore we cannot ask whether anything else could happen, nor can we ask whether it should happen or, for that matter, what ought to happen. All we can do is watch: is there any other way to resolve the dissonances? And if so: what is common to the solutions? Solutions that transcend every vision and state of consciousness are based on identical experiences and struggles. The fact is, each individual struggles inside his own self and by himself. And communities owe their existence to the truly great men whose understanding of their own problems and the problem of life in general reaches such a depth, that everything assumes a symbolic importance and all distinctions between human beings, in terms of their 'personality', virtually disappear.

For what is truly individualistic, in the innermost depth of one's soul, is that which transcends the purely individual: perhaps with this I have summed up all that needs to be said. The greatest lie of modern science (though somewhat receding) is that there are only quantitative differences between things; that events in identical circumstances bear a true resemblance: except that one event is more meaningful, lovelier, or greater than the other. But the profoundest lie is: there is no basic, qualitative distinction between an event that 'almost' occurred and an event which actually transpired, even though the starting point of these two events was the same. The notion of 'almost' is so deeply ingrained in man that, compared to it, the difference between two events that have taken place (or 'almost') appears almost negligible.

And no wonder. We are witnessing a new type of 'aesthete' in the making. But no man can change things as they are. Namely, the rootless artist who not only personifies art but for whom art comprises his true reality and shapes his relationship to life. That artist's whole life unfolds in the sphere of the soul; all things become of equal value in the soul's sovereign, life-forming power. But this raises the question: why must all this lead to spiritual emptiness and anarchy, and become the source of weakness and sterility, and induce futile laments and melancholic pride? Why not build the fortresses of the soul from the same rock-hard foundations, in place of the ephemeral castles founded on moods? Just because everything relates to and forms part of the soul, why must this by necessity enervate the souls of others? Just because we comprehend all and perceive the transparency of things, must this bury and lay to rest all our struggles? And because we want and can build something from our own sufferings,[5] why should this be construed to mean that nothing exists? Are there no differences in values just because we were forced to relocate them? And why should the necessary loneliness of man spell anarchy, and life's impregnable tragedy invite frivolous and cynical pessimism?

As we have said: seen from the perspective of life, an aesthete is one who imposes the laws of his art on life. Were we to condense into a single sentence our strictures on the aesthete as a type, we would have to say: those who professed to be aesthetes were not aesthetes in a sufficient, deep and rigorous sense of the term. With this we have already said why not: the aesthetes failed to apply the essence of art to life (and art). And being superficial and indolent at the outset of their careers, the few serious minded aesthetes are now unable to rectify this.

The essence of art is to formulate things, to overcome resistance, to bring under yoke the hostile forces, to forge a unity out of the diverse and divergent. To create form: to pronounce the last judgement on things; this last judgement redeems what is redeemable, and its near-divine power dispenses grace.

The form: the maximum expression of potential forces in a given situation; this constitutes the true ethic of forms. The form sets the outward boundary, and inwardly it creates infinity. What is inexpressible is non-existent, declared an old aesthete, and he was right more than he may have realized. There is no 'possibility' within the life of forms, for what is unrealizable cannot exist, and what is realizable will be realized. There is, however, one transgression: not to be born; but what has been born is already destined to live forever.

In the systems of the old philosophers, the form symbolized the world and its order, it was the only human medium that in some way conveyed the cosmic harmony. Today, all we can hope for is our own harmony, and so the forms only speak about our own metaphysical reality, not that of the world.

Yes, it all transpires in the sphere of the soul. But this, rather than being debilitating, actually gives depth to and internalizes the struggles and sufferings bound up with the paradoxes of human existence. The very fact that everything is ours and belongs to the soul where every tragic event takes place, means we feel each dissonance much more strongly and sharply, especially as the dissonances are internalized and can no longer be shifted anywhere else or transposed to others. Since absolution is bestowed – via the redemptive power of form – only at the end of the roads we travel and the pains we suffer, absolution hinges upon an unempirical and unprovable act of faith that the soul's divergent roads ultimately converge. They must converge because they radiate from the same centre. The form is the sole proof of this faith, for the form is more realizable than life itself.

To reiterate: the aesthete applies the concept of form to life; aesthetic culture forms the soul. This means, not the ornamentation of the soul, but its actual formation; this formation does not fix its stages, but retrieves and delineates its purest essence from the chaos of events and experiences. The soul is the road, not the result, an endless road where fully formed lives serve as signposts. How is the soul formed? The soul lies dormant in that chaos we usually associate with the spiritual life of man, that we casually refer to as the soul. The dormant soul is real and always alive, but only for those with discerning vision. The soul has to be divined and brought to life, in the same way as Michelangelo divined his statues in the block of marble that entombed them. But it required his superhuman efforts to breathe life into his statues, chiselling and chipping away the formless chaos that embraced them. The human span may prove too short to express and realize what is pure and sublime in us. And yet, even if at the end of one's spiritual life the soul resembles Rodin's incomplete statue, rising but still imprisoned in the marble, even then the true reality, the tragic, metaphysical reality can be no other than the statue, which always lived submerged in the marble. The soul of man, not unlike Michelangelo's statue, can be discerned and brought to life only through interminable struggle and suffering – the only true and real life.

This kind of life is an exemplary life, it is a symbolic life – and every symbol bears a kinship to others. This kind of life is a symbolic life in a profound and true sense, it is a genuinely individual life. It is the soul in the marble which turns into a statue. Although in the process the soul parts with its marble brothers, it finds its brothers in other statues. This then is the soul's road: to chip away all that is not truly its own; this is the forming of the soul, making it genuinely individualistic, though what has been formed transcends the purely individual. This is why this kind of life is exemplary. It is exemplary because the realization of one man's life signifies the same possibility for others. As Eckhart put it:

> Where a clod falls, there falls a piece of the earth; thus we see that the earth is the resting place of all earth. When a spark flies upward, it means that heaven is its true resting place. Now we have such a spark sent to us in Jesus Christ's soul. The soul shows that our resting place is in heaven and nowhere else.[6]

This is why the aesthete's tragic life and tragic isolation is no longer tragic. True, the tragedy of loneliness is also an *a priori* of life, but here this loneliness precipitates a great heroic act, that of forming the self. In the same way as original sin prompted a desire for the possibility, and reality of redemption.

It is irrelevant whether the example is followed by others, or who they are and how many there are. For man can achieve salvation only for himself, and nothing can intensify the grace of the one who is saved. Even if one's triumphant struggle to attain salvation clears the road for others in the jungle of life, man must journey alone, and hope for deliverance only at the end of his road.

Such men create no culture, nor do they want to; what lends sanctity to their lives is the absence of all illusions. They create no culture, but live almost as if they lived in culture. They create no culture, but lead a life that would merit it. The whole atmosphere of their life is best described by Kant's insightful category, the 'as if', the *als ob*. It is this unassuming heroism which gives sanctity to their lives. It surrounds the life of Hans von Meree, Stefan George, Paul Ernst and Charles Louis Philippe with the glory of pure air, which today is perhaps visible only around their heads.

And in fear and trembling, I write down here – as the only possible final chords after what has been said – the name of the greatest one of all, who was in my mind while I wrote this, our most sublime epic poet, the sacred name of Dostoevsky.

NOTES

1 Lukács seems to forget that Plato's *Protagoras* features Socrates and the Sophist Protagoras debating the merits of two opposing schools of

thought. Although Socrates cautions his young friend not to entrust the care of his soul to a Sophist, the result is not what one would expect from Plato, namely Protagoras' complete defeat. Far from that, he is shown to have the better reason a number of times, and Socrates appears more than once as the weaker of the two. In this sense Lukács is right that the Sophist should have been criticized more rigorously.

2   Lukács had in mind the kind of loneliness to which Byron refers when he says:

> To feel me in the solitude of kings,
> Without the power that makes them bear a crown.

> *The Prophecy of Dante*, canto i, l. 166

3   In Plato's *Phaedo*, Socrates, discoursing on the immortality of the soul, pronounces death as a rebirth and the beginning of a new life. Hence Socrates, having drunk the poison, was recovering, not dying. He was entering not into death, but into life, 'life more abundantly'. And in *Apology* (25d-e), Socrates offers the famous reflection, 'Death is one of two things. Either it is annihilation, and the dead have no consciousness of anything, or, as we are told, it is really a change – a migration of the soul from this place to another.'

4   In Ibsen's *The Wild Duck*, Gregers Werle, like Parson Brand, is a man with a mission. But he is an idealist even more fatally doomed to run to seed than Brand's distorted character. In the pursuit of his ideals, Gregers spreads turmoil and disaster to others.

5   For Lukács, aesthetic enjoyment proceeds from suffering which is positive and, in fact, willed. Reminiscent of Schopenhauer, Lukács believed that once a pure will-less knowledge is attained, the self vanishes and, with it, the possibility of suffering is abolished.

For theoretical background, see Schopenhauer, *The World as World and Representation*, vol. 2, chapter xxx.

6   I was unable to trace and identify Lukács's quote from Meister Eckhart.

13

Paul Gauguin

In my view, many people overestimate the importance of Gauguin[1]
when they see him as the high point of modern art and, at the same
time, underestimate his real importance. Gauguin provides an answer
to a very general question which many people have without actually
being conscious of it, and which ruined the lives of quite a few artists
who thought deeply. It is an answer to that very general question:
what is the relationship between the modern artist and Life? Only the
question is general, the answer is so individualistic in nature that it
ceases to have any exemplary, or symbolic meaning. It suggests the
possibility of a harmonious solution to a tragic situation; but in
essence the solution depends so much on individual feelings as to
leave the tragic conflict unresolved.

The whole development of modern painting (like that of art in
general) was such that it had to confront this problem. We can merely
refer to the situation itself, whose real causes have yet to be studied
and, to the extent that the causes are known, they require deeper
analysis than they have so far received. Meanwhile, complete anarchy
and vacuity prevails everywhere. The situation is felt to be intolerable
by every artist who, as poor Vincent van Gogh said of himself, 'likes
order and harmony, and yet has to lead an isolated life, and suffer in
order to introduce style to all his artistic endeavours.'

The art of painting had liberated itself from its former employments
(the church, interior decoration, etc.), broken its bondage to intellectual content and symbols, freed itself of the arbitrary tyranny of
patrons, and attained complete independence.[2] Step by step, the
artists felt the full consequences of their newly-gained freedom. Subsequently, the old forms and contents that endured over time, due to
laziness and poverty of thought, even when they proved completely
useless, were now abandoned.

An altogether new concept of the picturesque came into being; an
absolute painting, completely independent of everything that, after a
long period and through many struggles, created its own uniquely

new aesthetics. Earlier, the function of a painting was predetermined even before it was completed, but now the artist determined everything about his work. This had brought about a great *Umwertung* [re-evaluation]; good painters were seldom original thinkers.[3] Because creating ideas is hardly their role and because ideas were no longer given them readymade as earlier, the subject matter came to lose all its significance in painting. For the medieval painter, the Madonna was not a conceptual problem for she was already conceptualized and she therefore presented only an artistic problem. But any artist who wanted to paint the Madonna today would have to conceptualize – for himself – his own relationship with the Bible; and this relationship would constitute the substance of his artistic process.

However, this is not the only reason why Biblical themes no longer form the object of modern paintings; there is no audience which has the same emotional and intellectual nexus with any object as does the artist, even if he happens to find a theme. The very moment when the relation between the object, the artist and the public ceases to be conventional, and becomes the product of individual thought, at that moment the pictorial rendition of thought becomes problematic. In the end, everything that forms no exclusive part of the *monde visible* becomes no longer a subject for art.[4] For the time being, the primary goal of modern art is to express in ever more perfect form the external world.

Nor could modern art have any other goal; for its decorative value is to furnish architecture with ornaments, and modern paintings have no place here. Indeed, the whole development of the architectural style of public buildings and private homes has made no allowance for the organic necessity of paintings. As a result, painting has become separate from every 'functional' art. There is no longer a culture where the same instinct determines the shape and form of one's home, one's style of furniture, the fashion of one's clothes and one's artistic taste; total anarchy reigns.

Thus the public find it hard to follow the autonomous development of painting which is the result of interaction among artists. Gradually the public gets 'used' to paintings which at first caused an outrage, later the same works become 'fashionable', only to go 'out of fashion' once again. More than ever, artists grow distinct and separate, they all work for the market and each strives to create something original and new. Not only because every artist wants to gain public attention, but because in modern art only originality counts as art; and where there is no culture, everything conventional is deemed anti-artistic.

Fortunately for the art of painting, only a few people – and they rather late in the day – became conscious of its problematic nature. It

was fortunate because the paradoxical development in fine arts produced so many new, unknown beauties that any of us, though fully
aware of the unique nature of the situation, could forget about it while
viewing a particular work of art. Naturally enough, for the painters it
was always more important to resolve the problem of art through
struggle, than to despair and agonize over a situation they had nothing
to do with, and which defied solution.

Until the triumph of Impressionism, which discovered and conquered a whole new world for painting, every artist was preoccupied
with this problem. After Impressionism won its decisive victories,
when all the means were available for a great art, the artists – precisely
those with the profoundest feelings – made the painful discovery that
great art was now out of the question. Impressionism could merely
serve as decoration in a great building, but where could this building
be? Vincent van Gogh's whole life was consumed in a wild, ceaseless
and tragic search for great art. He sensed the causes behind it: the
anarchy, the absence of culture, the isolation of art and artists in life.

But Cézanne, full of resignation, stood remote and transposed his
feelings, heroically imposing, primitive, brutally magnificent and yet
so complex, into the very objects that happened to be in front of him;
the random arrangement of some bottles and glasses, of an apple and
tablecloth. At times, Cézanne's still lifes convey an oceanic calm, at
others they betray a violent, almost animal-like frenzy, or a piercing
cry of pain. Cézanne stood remote.[5] He painted for himself and those
select few who, like himself, gave up everything to devote themselves
exclusively to art (to write, or compose) because it was part of their
character and they could do nothing else.

Gauguin was softer and more lyrical than Cézanne, but also more
conscious and spiritually complex (or at least more literary, or, let's
say much more of an intellect). Gauguin's starting point was Cézanne
and Impressionism. But it didn't take Gauguin long to realize the
relative significance and problematic aspect of working from nature.
His early years are marked by a tense, desperate search for a style. He
visited the island of Martinique [1887], and then returned to Paris
with some exotic, stylized Impressionistic paintings; behind the luxuriant tropical vegetation we glimpse the cobalt blue sea; trees painted
in blue stretch out nervously from the sun-scorched yellow foreground.

Gauguin returned to Europe. He worked with Van Gogh at Arles,[6]
and set up an artists' colony at Pont-Aven. Gauguin already saw the
goal: '*Cherchez l'harmonie et non l'opposition, l'accord et non le heurt*'; he
had the method, or, at least he thought he had found it. One must
paint from memory; it is fine to have a model but one must not look

at it while painting, so as to achieve a sufficient distance. Unlike the then fashionable neo-Impressionism – which, in order to emphasize the atmosphere, left out all contours, and decomposed every colour – Gauguin strove for simplicity and the synthesis of sensations.

In Brittany[7] he painted some beautiful pictures that captured the rhythm of human figures at work. On pink ground, women dressed in blue under light blue sky, an endless row of workers (yet in the pictures no more than five or six appear), and on a glowing red hill two bending figures, against an ever sizzling yellow sky.[8] And yet, these pictures are merely experiments, just as were the paintings of the Impressionists Gauguin tried to go beyond. That was precisely his aim: to go beyond Impressionism.

For Gauguin, Tahiti was not an escape as many believed, but the reaching of his goal, the end of his experimentations. They said he was disgusted with our European culture, and took refuge among the savages.[9] First of all, there were no savages in Tahiti, and we have no culture here in Europe. It was only our civilization that Gauguin forcefully shed when he went to Tahiti, he only gave up comfort and material things in order to receive, in exchange, peace and quiet[10] among the natives with a thousand-year-old culture (even though the culture was rather primitive and already dying).

But above all Tahiti restored Gauguin as a human being. He had found his place in society, no longer an exotic, luxury item in the hands of amateur collectors, nor a restless anarchist who threatened public safety. A primitive man pointed out to him – for the first time in his life – that he could produce what no one else could, that he was a useful human being. Gauguin felt he was useful, they loved him and he was happy.[11] This intense sense of happiness and peace of mind permeates his last paintings.[12]

At first, he sought harmony in the realm of art; now he found it in his own life. All he had to do was to forget; a few technical skills, tricks that merely served to make his paintings interesting. He no longer wanted to be interesting, for now beauty surrounded and dwelt in him. In every respect, Gauguin progressed beyond *l'art pour l'art*.[13] He became attentive to old legends, drawn to the primitive symbols of the natives who believed in them, and to the life of the Tahitians. He did not recoil – as many other painters did – from nude female figures in order to achieve a symbolic effect. In one of his letters to Strindberg, Gauguin wrote, 'The Eve I painted (she alone) can, logically, go naked before our eyes.' This Eve [The Tahitian Eve][14] is not stripped naked just to serve as a model.

In his paintings, Gauguin achieved an ever greater harmony and tranquillity. More and more the details, reality itself disappeared from his pictures; there remained but a symphony of lovely surfaces and dazzling colours; the harmony of undulating horizontal lines and planes. What we have here is not so much painting, as a decorative art.

Gauguin had reached his goal; this is what he searched for all his life. He is the only modern artist who did reach his goal. The others, though still alive mid-way through their lives, had either resigned themselves and stepped aside, or, in the end perished tragically.

From his own perspective, Gauguin's life is not tragic. But it is tragic for us. It is tragic because his solution to the problem which deeply concerns all of us – for in the final analysis, it involves the relationship of art and life – remained as it was – tragic. Every artist searches for his own Tahiti, and, other than Gauguin, none have found it, nor are they likely to find it, unless things change so radically that anyone can anywhere conjure up his imaginary Tahiti.

Until then, Gauguin's life remains an isolated case; a lovely dream; a beautiful possibility; a marvellous illusion. After all, Gauguin's paintings for us here [Hungary] are just as problematic as those of the others. Perfect decorative frescoes as Gauguin's paintings are, there is no architecture that could accommodate his art.

NOTES

[1]   Paul Gauguin (1848–1903) was a gifted and innovative artist. He not only painted, but produced a number of woodcuts, sculptures, revived stoneware techniques under the influence of Japanese ceramics, and invented synthesism and cloisonnism.

[2]   What Lukács tries to emphasize is that for centuries, choosing to be an artist was simply a matter of imitation. A painter-to-be carried on a tradition handed down from father to son. Apprenticeship was a family affair, and the artist's first studio was under the family roof. Then in the romantic era, to be an artist was an act of rebellion, an endless, highly personal struggle for identity and independence. This was the case with Cézanne and Gauguin – admired by Lukács and his generation.

[3]   Gauguin has said that what the philosophers rationalize, the artists are able to sense. As he put it:

The Raphaels and others were people in whom sensation was formulated long before thought, which allowed them, even while they were studying, to help keep that sensation forever intact and to remain artists. As I see it, a great artist is the most intelligent of formulators; he receives the most delicate and, consequently, most visible feelings or translations of the mind. Françoise Cachin, *Gauguin: The Quest for Paradise* (New York: Harry N. Abrams, n.d.), pp. 134–5.

4 For Lukács, as a neo-Platonist, the natural and ultimate goal of painting – indeed, of all the arts – cannot be the direct representation of objects. Its end is to express ideas by translating them into a special language. According to Lukács, in the artist's eyes, only the essential entities (ideas) are significant; they are letters, as it were, in an immense alphabet that only a man of genius knows how to spell out and give a form.

5 Writing to his friend Emile Schuffenecker, Gauguin compared Cézanne to Virgil, adding: 'A man of the Midi, he spends entire days on mountaintops reading Virgil and gazing at the sky. Thus, his horizons are very high, his blues very intense, his reds stunningly vibrant. Like Virgil, who has more than one meaning and can be interpreted as one likes, the literature of his paintings has a parabolic, twofold meaning.' Cachin, *Gauguin*, p. 135.

6 Gauguin's famous two-month stay in 1888 with Van Gogh at Arles, an explosive, disaster-ridden friendship between the two heroes of modern painting, is fully chronicled. As Gauguin put it, 'Between two such beings as he and I, the one a perfect volcano, the other boiling too, inwardly, a sort of struggle was simmering.' Gauguin, *Intimate Journals*, tr. Van Wyck Brooks (New York: Liveright, 1921), p. 31.

7 Starting with the romantic era, no region in France displayed more resistance to new ideas than Brittany. Here paganism and its myths and legends lurked behind the thin veneer of Christianity. In their *Voyage en Bretagne*, Flaubert and Maxime du Camp wrote that they found in Brittany the 'human form in its pristine freedom, as on the first day of Creation'.

8 Lukács appears to be describing Gauguin's painting, *Grape Gathering: Human Misery*, that conveys weariness and dejection. Gauguin said of his painting, 'Purple vines forming triangles against an upper area of chrome yellow. On the left, a Breton woman of Le Pouldu in black with a grey apron. Two Breton women bending over in light blue-green dresses with black bodices . . . It's a study of some vineyards I saw at Arles.'

9 Like Rousseau, whom he admired, Gauguin always yearned for paradise, a peaceful and carefree communal life as lived before the Fall, before the lust for power and possessions. And like Rousseau, Gauguin presupposed that the natives of Tahiti embodied humanity in its natural state of liberty, free of social compulsion. Gauguin summed up his inborn opposition to civilization in Rousseauesque fashion, 'When a man says to me, "You must", I rebel.' Gauguin, *Intimate Journals*, p. 241.

10 Gauguin wrote to the wife he left behind in Copenhagen: 'As I write to you it is evening. The stillness of night in Tahiti is the strangest thing of all. It exists nowhere but here, without so much as a birdcall to disturb one's nest. Here and there a large dry leaf falls but without making the slightest sound. It is more like the rustling of a spirit. The islanders often move about at night, but barefoot and silently. Always this silence.' Cachin, *Gauguin*, pp. 72–3.

11 Far from being happy and content in his Garden of Eden, Gauguin was just as miserable and full of discontent in Tahiti as in Paris or in Copen-

hagen. Gauguin himself said, 'Living among the savages is all very well, but there is such a thing as homesickness.' *Intimate Journals*, p. 222.

12 A year before he died (1903), Gauguin took stock of his life's work in various writings and through a poignant self-portrait. He wrote: 'I feel I have been right about art . . . and if my works do not endure, there will remain the memory of an artist who set painting free.' Cachin, *Gauguin*, p. 124.

13 A revealing journal entry reads:

> Art for Art's sake Why not?
> Art for Life's sake Why not?
> Art for Pleasure's sake Why not?
> What does it matter, as long as it is art?

Gauguin, *Intimate Journals*, p. 246.

14 In Gauguin's famous painting, *The Delightful Land*, better known as 'The Tahitian Eve', a young Tahitian woman strikes a pose inspired by some European paintings of nude figures. However, the apple of this Tahitian Eve has turned into an imaginary flower in the shape of a peacock feather, and instead of a snake, there is a fabulous lizard with scarlet wings. Strindberg referred to this Tahitian Eve when he wrote to Gauguin: 'You have created a new heaven and a new earth, but I do not enjoy myself in the midst of your creation. It is too sun-drenched for me, who enjoys the play of light and shade. And in your paradise there dwells an Eve who is not my ideal – for I, myself, really have an ideal woman or two!' Gauguin, *Intimate Journals*, p. 46.

14

The Parting of the Ways

These few remarks are not necessarily confined to the pictures exhibited at the Könyves Kálmán Salon [Budapest]. The exhibition sparked a heated and bitter controversy, full of recrimination and pettiness, because these pictures express, in my view for the first time, clearly and unequivocally, the parting of the ways. Let me then comment briefly on the causes and importance of this parting.

For anyone who looks at these pictures, and who knows how to look at works of art, will not really understand what this controversy and uproar is all about. The exhibited works do not represent any trend (not even an artistic one); they show no particular aspiration, and do not go anywhere; they represent no new 'attitude' that might come into conflict with old 'attitudes'. These pictures convey stillness, peace and harmony – it is therefore quite inconceivable they would disturb anyone.

And yet these pictures amount to a declaration of war. But this war is unlike the ones that were fought by the innumerable 'artistic movements' and 'secessions' in the nineteenth century. There a new 'attitude' always attacked the old 'attitude'. When the latter proved inadequate, the people had to find a new 'attitude', or, in most cases, simply grew tired of viewing things in the same light. This led to a new way of looking at things, a new 'direction', and the two directions invariably struggled with each other until a third came on the scene, the newest one and, declaring war on the combined forces of the first and the second directions, the comedy continued *ad infinitum*.

However, the issue here is different. We are not talking about differences, but about opposition. Here the adversaries oppose each other not because they represent different trends, but simply because of the nature of their existence. What is at stake is not the ascendancy of new art, but the rebirth of old art, of art itself, and the life-and-death struggle provoked by its rebirth against the new, modern art.

Károly Kernstok has delineated clearly what is involved here.[1] Namely the pictures he and his friends paint (together with the poetry

of a few poets, and the philosophical ideas of a few thinkers) are trying
to express the essential nature of things.

The essential nature of things! These simple words indicate, without any polemics, the substance of the great controversy, and mark
the point where the ways part. For let's face it, the whole conception
of the world with which we grew up, the art from which we received
our first great impressions, was unfamiliar with reality and denied that
anything could have an essential nature. It treated with a condescending smile those who dared to think or talk about the essence of
things, and dismissed them as being old fashioned, medieval and
scholastic. The age in which we grew up – and the whole nineteenth
century – did not believe in the permanence of anything. A century
earlier it was already stated that the landscape was but a mood, but in
our world everything was a mood. There was nothing solid in it and
nothing permanent; there was nothing in it that could possibly have
been imagined or allowed to bring emancipation from the slavery of
the moment. Everything turned into mood; everything lasted but a
moment, as long as I was exposed to certain experiences and feelings
and saw things in a certain light. Only to alter completely the next
moment. And there was nothing that could have created order in the
chaotic swirl of moments. There was nothing that might have served
as a common denominator among things and thereby transcended the
moment: there was nothing that might have been permanent in a
thing and thus raise it above the moment. For things did not exist,
other than the endless sequence of moods, and between moods there
is not, nor can there ever be, any difference in value.

Even the sovereign ego, which shapes everything in conformity with
its own moods, dissolved itself into fluid moments. The ego flooded
into the world and – aided by its moods – absorbed it. But precisely
for this reason the world also invaded the ego, and there was nothing
that could have drawn the boundary line between them. Nor was
there anything that could have created an order within the submerged
and indistinct ego. With the end of the solidity of things the solidity
of the ego also ceased to exist; and the loss of facts meant the loss of
values. There remained nothing else but mood. Only a mood of equal
rank and importance within and between individuals. Everything
became a matter of concept; everything was a question of perception,
and of individual opinion. The only thing to lend significance to each
individual opinion was its individual nature, and there was no significant distinction between individual views. Everything being subjective,
all unanimity of meaning ceased to exist; statements had lost their
meaning for they no longer excluded the possibility of an opposing
statement. In this world everything coincided and coexisted with

everything else, and there was nothing that could have excluded anything at all.

The only possible art of this mood of life was the art of sensations. The art of communication of experience, the art of the merely subjective, the merely transient. But the more subjective something is and the more it clings to the moment, the more problematical is its ability to be communicated. For it is only what is genuinely common that can be communicated, whereas this art [Impressionism] wanted at any price to communicate one moment in the life of the artist, something incommunicable. And thereby every influence became fortuitous. It was the play of fortuitously pleasant twisting lines and harmoniously shaded colours, the pleasantly but fortuitously tuned voices, devoid of any meaning. Not surprisingly, the creative artist's sombre mood could precipitate a fortuitous mood of gaiety in the recipient. Or, conversely, the artist's infinite variety of nuances simply produced unpredictable responses.

Consequently, art became the art of surfaces; surfaces behind which there is nothing, surfaces which signify nothing,[2] nor do they express anything, but simply exist somehow fortuitously, and somehow, fortuitously, exert some effect. No matter how, provided they have an effect. The art of surfaces could only be the art of sensations, the art of the denial of profound depth, or evaluation, or the making of distinctions. New categories, paradoxical categories, came into being, values were created which simply by being realized had necessarily to destroy themselves: the new and interesting as values, as the only values. For if there only exist moods and sensations, then only their newness and their power distinguishes them from each other. And with every moment, every analogy and recurrence, each sensation becomes less new and less interesting, until finally it loses all its character as sensation; it ceases to have an effect, it expires, it is dead.

This art [Impressionism] lacks substance, for substance is something tangible, homogeneous which requires space; it is solid and permanent. In this art there are no forms because form is unequivocal and excludes other forms and what is unformed; because form is the principle of evaluation, differentiation and the creation of order.

But in our world, where everything coexisted and was compatible with everything else, this art even failed to notice the birth of its deadly adversary and executioner. Or rather, it took note of it but proved unable to act and feel like an adversary towards anything: it felt this too was merely a new sensation reconcilable with all the old ones. I have in mind here, first and foremost, the few advances in the natural sciences and breakthroughs in the humanistic disciplines (Marxism, for instance) that formed the first challenge to Impressionism. The first to deny the legitimacy of the subjective, impressionist conception of life: they insisted on unequivocal, verifiable statements and on order in things. And statements had consequences, either because they were true or untrue; either they were valid or invalid. Furthermore, every single admission of the truth, acknowledged and verified, meant the inevitable and necessary rejection of a thousand other unverifiable truths. The natural sciences and Marxism produced statements that were about something: about things. Things that could be discussed because there is something permanent in them, something which is independent of my own moods and sensations; things that were completely unaffected by how I see them at any particular moment or under such and such an influence. Things exist, and in them the important and unimportant, the invariable and the variable, surface and essence.

The Impressionists also acquiesced in these truths too. Their all-comprehending minds accepted these too as truths – and in their feelings and experience everything remained as it had been.

Today, however, these recognitions have finally become emotional values. Once again we long for order among things. We long to recognize order and recognize in ourselves that which is really ours. We long for permanence, we want our deeds to be measurable, our statements to be unequivocal and verifiable. We also want to assign meaning to all our experiences, so they would have consequences and exclude something. We long for evaluations. We long for differentiations. We long for profound thought.

The very belief that there is something palpably permanent in the vortex of moments, the conviction that things exist and have an essential nature, excludes Impressionism and all its manifestations. For permanence means we can have goals worthy of attainment and, indeed, that we must strive for them, and the road we choose to reach these goals is no longer irrelevant. We no longer can say what one of the finest critics of Hungarian Impressionism said, 'The artist may do anything he likes provided he knows how to do what he likes.'[3] For now our goal itself is subject to criticism, and an art which has chosen the wrong road is to be rejected all the more emphatically the more cleverness and virtuosity it employs in striving for an unworthy goal. Indeed, the road actually taken can be criticized because we can now measure achievements and unsuccessful attempts, both the correct and incorrect ones.

This new feeling has already made its presence known from numerous directions, and in many places it has already found expression in poetry and architecture, in paintings and tragedy, in sculpture and philosophy. But this multi-faceted new art, and the new *Weltan-*

schauung, have yet to gain conscious expression. As yet few people are cognizant of it in their own selves, let alone in others, in their own or in cognate arts. Perhaps herein lies the greatest significance of Károly Kernstok and his friends. Up to now, they provided the clearest and most artistic expression of this mode of feeling and seeing things.

This art [the art of The Eight] is an old art, the art of order and values; it is a constructive art. Impressionism has converted everything into a decorative surface, even architecture itself; and its colours, lines and words were given value only by their attractiveness and their sensation-producing effect, because they do not carry anything deeper, and do not express anything concrete. The new art is architectonic in the old, true sense. Its colours, words and lines are merely expressions of the essence, order and harmony of things, their emphasis and their equilibrium. Everything expresses the harmony of force and substance, and can only attain expression in the equilibrium of materials and forms. Every line and every patch of colour – as in architecture – is beautiful and of value only in so far as it expresses this: the equilibrium of force and substance that comprise things, in their simplest, clearest, most concentrated and essential way. Here too everything is confined to the surface. Our senses can only respond to surfaces, and colours and words, tones and lines can be the only means of expression at all times. But the means of expression are now indeed the means of expression, and not ends and terminations. Impressionism always came to a stop at the discovery of possibilities of expression; the appearance of a new trend in means of expression and its disappearance always turned into a rigid style. Impressionism invariably provided merely attitudes, with which it would have been possible to reach any goal.

But Kernstok had no desire to go anywhere. He felt attitudes themselves were the goals, since they too could be the carriers of sensations and moods. Kernstok considered his ideas as ends, provided they were sufficiently new and sufficiently interesting. To Kernstok, ideas denote ends, not means; sensations and stimuli, not tasks and duties. The new art is the art of the creation of the whole, that of going all the way, of profundity.

The ways have parted. It is no use invoking the geniuses of Impressionism. The really great Impressionists are truly great only to the extent that they are not Impressionists. They are great to the extent that profundity is artistic and their ideas are but roads for them to approach the real comprehension of things, their attitudes only means towards the creation of the whole. And just as he who conceives his ideas and visions not as a task and weapon, but as a goal and pleasure is unworthy of them, so the Impressionists are not worthy of the prominent artists who rose from their ranks. They have not deserved them and they have not understood them. The road the geniuses travelled, from the idea to the whole, the Impressionists travelled in reverse on seeing their works. The very things which the geniuses presented to the Impressionists as a gift, they have debased to a mere attitude. They have reduced to a mannerism the art which expressed it, and extracted merely sensations from the thoughts of geniuses.

The ways have parted. It avails nothing that the clever Impressionists without any conviction profess to 'comprehend' many of the artistic moments of this art. This comprehension too is no more than an idea, only the extraction of sensations from anything whatever, and there follows from it no transformation. The Impressionists see the cudgel about to fall on their heads and take refined pleasure in the powerful gesture of the menacing hand. But their discerning intelligence is of little use because this gesture is now more than a gesture. Because this cudgel will indeed crash down on their heads. For the art of Kernstok, which brings quiet, means a declaration of war on the Impressionists and a life-and-death struggle. This art of order must destroy all the anarchy of sensation and mood. The mere appearance and existence of this art amounts to a declaration of war. It is a declaration of war on all Impressionism, all sensation and mood, all disorder and denial of values, every *Weltanschauung* and the art which writes 'I' as its first and last word.

NOTES

[1] In his artistic manifesto, 'The Exploring Art', Kernstok focused on nature and how the artist finds his own terms for dealing with nature. As Kernstok put it, 'People who viewed our paintings, or stood before or next to us, flung nature in our face. Yes, there is nature. But the arguments that were thrown at us, these arguments do not exist. Nature is not like that they said, nature is different; there are no such figures in nature; nature is natural – this was the main argument. Nature – oh so patient – not only puts up with being gazed at, but will not even protest when it is expropriated by various schools.'

Disavowing Impressionism's virtuosity of brushstroke and colour, Kernstok's paintings try to revive the Renaissance theory that art expresses the idea, the idea of beauty, which resides in the mind. As Kernstok put it, 'Art cannot mirror nature; but to the degree that it extracts new values from nature, art is the mirror of the artist's intellect.' This notion is the basic premise of Renaissance art theory. See Erwin Panofsky, *Idea* (Columbia: University of South Carolina Press, 1968), especially chapter 4: 'The Renaissance'.

2 Lukács's claim that the Impressionist vision of the world signified nothing is untenable and unfair. That the Impressionist painters did not address psychological or philosophical questions when they painted portraits or human figures is true enough. But Lukács completely ignores the fact that Impressionist painters, from Degas and Manet to Renoir and Monet, gave expression to society's longings for signs of those values that were 'threatened by the organization of the urban-industrial world: spontaneity, individualism, and the freedom to find consolation among natural things'. Robert L. Herbert, *Impressionism* (Yale University Press, 1988), p. 193.

3 Lukács's friend Lajos Fülep, a neo-Platonist in love with Florentine art, disavowed Impressionism. Fülep fully subscribed to Michelangelo's statement, 'One paints, not with the hands, but with the brain.' In 1911, Lukács and Fülep launched the journal *Szellem* [The Spirit]. Edited in Florence, the journal waged a crusade against Impressionism, positivism, determinism and evolutionism. In a seminal article, entitled 'The Role of Meaning in Artistic Creation', Fülep took issue with Benedetto Croce's claim that the total effect of a work of art, no matter how saturated it might be with philosophical concepts, is 'an intuition'. As Croce put it, 'To intuit is to express; and nothing else (nothing more, but nothing less) than to express.' This convinced Fülep that Croce was the 'aesthetician of Impressionism'. In place of intuition, Fülep placed memory. Like a good neo-Platonist, Fülep countered Croce by declaring, 'We remember not what we had seen, but we see what we remember, or can remember.' See Fülep, 'The Role of Meaning in Artistic Creation', *Szellem* (March 1911), p. 69; Croce, *Aesthetic*, tr. Douglas Ainslie (Boston: Nonpareil Books, 1983), p. 3.

15

Stavrogin's Confession

The much-maligned 'barbarism' of the Soviet government has made Dostoevsky's posthumous work accessible at last. Several boxes full of manuscripts have been discovered, and it is likely that we shall soon be able to read in full the literary work of Russia's greatest writer, whose influence on European intellectual life continues to grow. The first sample to appear has been 'Stavrogin's Confession',[1] a hitherto unpublished chapter from the novel *The Possessed* which Dostoevsky wrote, more or less as a pamphlet, in opposition to Russia's first revolutionary movements.[2]

The novel itself, considered as a whole, is not counted among Dostoevsky's outstanding works: its tendentious nature flaws it. And it is not because Dostoevsky opposes the revolution, but because the novel itself – partly because of its anti-revolutionary stand but mostly because of the way it is structured – appears ambiguous and contradictory. Evidently the politician and pamphleteer in Dostoevsky were by no means in such perfect agreement with the imaginative writer as Dostoevsky tended to assume. On the contrary, the honesty and audacity of his vision, and his identifying with the lived experience of his characters forced the writer – so characteristic of Dostoevsky – to take a standpoint antithetical to the aims of the pamphleteer.[3] The great writer created characters evoking the human background to the Russian revolution, its social and intellectual milieu (and hence its 'justification') more vividly than the pamphleteer would have liked. Consequently, Dostoevsky had no alternative but to bridge this inherent contradiction by the means of the pamphlet [Stavrogin's Confession] whereby the contradiction – from an artistic standpoint – became even deeper and more visible. Dostoevsky, as Gorky once rightly observed, libels his own characters.

Nevertheless, or for that very reason, *The Possessed* is one of Dostoevsky's most interesting works. Whereas in his other works the perfectly portrayed individual destinies partly conceal the inherent duality of Dostoevsky's essence, in *The Possessed* the contradiction between political bias and poetic vision receives a clear and full expression. Dostoevsky's greatness as a writer resides in his unique ability to strip without effort, as it were, every character, human relationship and conflict of the reified shell in which they are presented today, and to pare them down, to reduce them to their purely spiritual core. Thus Dostoevsky discloses for us a world completely devoid of capitalist society's inhuman mechanism and soulless objectification of things, but which still contains the deeper inner conflicts of our age. This is also the source of his utopian outlook, the notion that the remedy for all hardship may be found in pure human relationships, in recognizing and loving the human heart in every human being, in love and kindness. But this purely individual and individualistic solution undergoes a subtle metamorphosis – in a way that is imperceptible to the writer – and appears as a Christian message of love, indeed as the mission of the Russian Orthodox Church.[4] Inevitably, this gives rise to manifold complications and contradictions.

In the first place, it forces Dostoevsky to reconcile his own old sectarian faith, partly influenced by Feuerbach's anti-Christian theology, with Christianity – thereby forcing him to falsify both positions. In the second place, aware as Dostoevsky is of the social roots of his characters' sufferings and problems, he nevertheless portrays them as purely personal, pathological manifestations of individuals. And yet Dostoevsky cannot remain content with the purely individual solution as long as he professes to see Christianity as the remedy.

The result is that the characters in his novels, in a pure and profound sense, are riven and caught in an atmosphere of internal contradictions. The contours of these contradictions remain clear as long as the individual's fate is completely reduced to purely personal human relationships. But as soon as this reduction is not entirely attainable or, as in *The Possessed*, not even sought, it inevitably obscures the work as a whole. The recently published fragment of *The Possessed* is a powerful testament to Dostoevsky's creative genius. His inner contradictions are less conspicuous here than they are elsewhere in the novel itself. The two poles of Dostoevsky's world, the floundering man in contemporary society consumed by inner doubts and sufferings [Stavrogin], and the Christian message of love [Father Tikhon], confront each other in this fragment, in a lonely nocturnal dialogue, and recognize each other as brothers. And not only in the sense that for the man of goodwill every man must be a brother, but also in a more authentic and intimate sense: that their inner kinship appears and becomes conscious for both of them.

In so many words, the dialogue expresses clearly (without dogmatism)

Dostoevsky's often repeated religious thesis that 'the complete atheist still stands on the next-to-the-top rung of the ladder of perfect faith',[5] that nobody comes closer to real faith than the real atheist. But at the same time, it also confirms that Christianity plays no recognizable role in Dostoevsky's 'Christian' practice of love and sacrifice. Love and goodness take the form of an intuitive understanding of the human essence of a fellow being. And the beneficial effect of love and goodness is that they chart the path for the lost souls to follow (Sonya in *Crime and Punishment*, Prince Myshkin in *The Idiot*).[6]

Here, however, it is precisely the decisive actions of Dostoevsky's saintly human type, the triumph of Dostoevsky's world, that reveals the profound inner contradiction in his world picture. Though a visionary goodness lifts the curtain on the dark despair of human existence, and conscience casts its luminous light on the inner darkness of the self, its sufferings, sin and madness, it is incapable of transforming this knowledge into an act of redemption. True, Sonya may lead Raskolnikov out of the labyrinth of his abstract sins, which had removed him from society and deprived him of human intercourse. But the positive element, the new life that was to unfold for Raskolnikov, remains but a dream. And in the late works where Dostoevsky sought to portray this very conversion, his artistic integrity compelled him time and again to depict the failure of his supreme human type at the very moment he is faced with a real decision (the end of *The Idiot*).

Dostoevsky the writer has no faith in his own professed theories and their consequences. This confirms the abyss – which he never admitted – dividing him from Christianity, even the schismatic revivals of early Christianity. In effect, this Christianity is founded upon the invincible power of love: the soul turns towards love, and this love, born of recognition, uncovers suffering and points to the right path. Although the errant path may have social causes, salvation from it takes place independently of all non-spiritual constraints. But here Dostoevsky is unconsciously a non-believer. His visionary goodness illuminates suffering, and takes the form of a sort of cynicism that mercilessly identifies weakness, filth and debasement – that acknowledges and presupposes the worst of human beings. Although love perceives suffering and sin, it is unable to help because both are rooted much too deeply in the fallen nature of man, and neither the power of human understanding nor the power of loving human relationships can eradicate suffering and sin. This is because aberration and sinful ways are rooted in the human situation which men cannot overcome.

Thus Dostoevsky's desperate struggle to convert the social basis of human existence into that of pure spirit was, of necessity, doomed to failure. However, this failure has yielded a fascinating artistic triumph. For no writer before him has ever analysed so rigorously and consistently the social roots of tragedy of certain human types, and illuminated them in such depth.

Herein lies the incomparable literary value of Stavrogin's Confession. Stavrogin, the hero of *The Possessed*, who occasionally seems somewhat Lermontov-like, gives an exaggeratedly romantic impression in the novel whereas, in the Christian and oral confession of his most depraved deeds, he for the first time shows himself fully as the person he is: as the most authentic embodiment of that transitional Russian type also portrayed as the 'superfluous man' in various forms by Turgenev, Goncharov and Tolstoy. Here is the Russian intelligentsia who, as a human type, possesses strength and talent (Stavrogin commands demonic power and talent), but who is unable to make any use of these in the Russian context. Consequently, those qualities which in Turgenev's and Goncharov's heroes dissolve into nothing, in Dostoevsky's heroes may lead to meaningless, absurd, debased, even ridiculous crimes.

There now yawns the bottomless abyss of despair and hopelessness which turned the most honest members of the Russian intelligentsia into revolutionaries so early. We shudder when we witness the intelligentsia's genuine search for the meaning and the purpose of life, only to be left at the end with no other alternative but suicide, depravity or revolution (Stavrogin chose suicide).[7] And however passionately Dostoevsky resisted revolution as a pamphleteer, and with whatever conviction he preached a religious solution to these sufferings, it is precisely this Dostoevsky who convinces one most clearly of revolution's necessity. The political anathema he pronounced on revolution unexpectedly turns into an artistic glorification of its absolute, spiritual necessity.

NOTES

[1] In Dostoevsky's original version of *The Possessed*, chapter 9 in Part Two, 'At Tikhon', generally referred to as 'Stavrogin's Confession', was left out by his publisher, who felt that it was too shocking and would compromise both the author and the novel. Dostoevsky agreed and so this chapter was never included in the novel during the author's lifetime. Lukács's trenchant essay, 'Stavrogin's Confession', is based on the German publication of Dostoevsky's work, *Die Beichte Stawrogins* (Munich: Musarion Verlag, 1923).

[2] No other novel of Dostoevsky provoked as much controversy as *The Possessed*. Under the Soviets the novel became the emblem of reactionary

ideology and was categorized as 'socially obnoxious and detrimental to the cause of socialism'. The communist press never missed an opportunity to attack it for political reasons while dwelling on its literary defects. Lukács's claim that 'Stavrogin's Confession' discredits revolutionary ideals and dogmas is valid. For Stavrogin, this Mephistophelian apostle of destruction, full of demons and negations, everything is permissible because he does not obey any moral code. He personifies Dostoevsky's 'transgressors', those who challenge God and society with the force of their own nihilistic egos, by wilful actions beyond 'good and evil'.

3 Dostoevsky once wrote, 'I mean to utter certain thoughts whether all the artistic side of it goes to the dogs or not . . . Even if it turns into a mere pamphlet, I shall say all that I have in my heart.' For a more extensive treatment of this, see Irving Howe, 'Dostoevsky: The Politics of Salvation', in *Dostoevsky. A Collection of Critical Essays*, ed. Rene Wellek (Englewood Cliffs: Prentice Hall, 1962), pp. 63–70.

4 When Shatov, who in many ways is Dostoevsky's alter ego in *The Possessed*, argues that 'God's personality is the synthesis of the entire nation from the beginning of its existence to its end,' Stavrogin chastises him for boiling 'God down to a mere national attribute'. Shatov retorts, 'It's just the other way around; I'm raising the nation to God. And indeed, has it ever been otherwise.' Dostoevsky, *The Possessed*, tr. Andrew R. MacAndrew (Penguin, 1962), pp. 237–8.

5 *The Possessed*, p. 412.

6 It has been often observed that Dostoevsky, like Milton before him, did better by his Satan than by his God. Thus Dostoevsky's good and saintly characters, Prince Myshkin in *The Idiot*, Father Tikhon in *The Possessed*, and Father Zosima in *The Brothers Karamazov* are less convincing and dramatic than the human devils that abound in his novels. To this, of course, one could answer that saintly and undramatic figures are unassertive and hence undramatic, dull.

7 Stavrogin, the rich landowner married to a crippled and demented beggar, the demon-driven sadist who pushes to suicide the girl-child he had raped, the soulless intellectual who plays with revolutionary ideas, the citizen of the Canton of Uri, was found dangling just by the door. On the table he had left a note with the words: 'Accuse no one, I did it myself.' *The Possessed*, p. 692.

16

Integrated Civilizations

Happy are those ages when the starry sky is the map of all possible paths – ages whose paths are illuminated by the light of the stars. Everything in such ages is new and yet familiar, full of adventure and yet their own. The world is wide and yet it is like a home, for the fire that burns in the soul is of the same essential nature as the stars; the world and the self, the light and the fire, are sharply distinct, yet they never become permanent strangers to one another, for fire is the soul of all light and all fire clothes itself in light. Thus each action of the soul becomes meaningful and rounded in this duality: complete in meaning – in *sense* – and complete for the senses; rounded because the soul rests within itself even while it acts; rounded because its action separates itself from it and, having become itself, finds a centre of its own and draws a closed circumference round itself. 'Philosophy is really homesickness', says Novalis: 'it is the urge to be at home everywhere.'

This is why philosophy, as a form of life or as that which determines the form and supplies the content of literary creation, is always a symptom of the rift between 'inside' and 'outside', a sign of the essential difference between the self and the world, the incongruence of the soul and deed. That is why the happy ages have no philosophy, or why (it comes to the same thing) all men in such ages are philosophers, sharing the utopian aim of every philosophy. For what is the task of true philosophy if not to draw the archetypal map? What is the problem of the transcendental *locus* if not to determine how every impulse which springs from the innermost depths is co-ordinated with a form that it is ignorant of, but that has been assigned to it from eternity and thus must develop it in liberating symbols? When this is so, passion is the way, predetermined by reason, towards complete self-realization, and from madness come enigmatic yet decipherable messages of a transcendental power, otherwise condemned to silence. There is not yet any interiority, for there is not yet any exterior, any 'otherness' for the soul. The soul goes out to seek adventure; it lives through adventures, but it does not know the real torment of seeking and the real danger of finding; such a soul never stakes itself; it does not yet know that it can lose itself, it never thinks of having to look for itself. Such an age is the age of the epic.

It is not absence of suffering, not security of being, which in such an age encloses men and deeds in contours that are both joyful and severe (for what is meaningless and tragic in the world has not increased since the beginning of time; it is only that the songs of comfort ring out more loudly or are more muffled): it is the adequacy of the deeds to the soul's inner demand for greatness, for unfolding, for wholeness. When the soul does not yet know any abyss within itself which may tempt it to fall or encourage it to discover pathless heights, when the divinity that rules the world and distributes the unknown and unjust gifts of destiny is not yet understood by man, but is familiar and close to him as a father is to his small child, then every action is only a well-fitting garment for the world. Being and destiny, adventure and accomplishment, life and essence are identical concepts. For the question which engenders the formal answers of the epic is: how can life become essence? And if no one has ever equalled Homer, nor even approached him – for, strictly speaking, his works alone are epics – it is because he found the answer before the progress of the human mind through history had allowed the question to be asked.

This line of thought can, if we wish, take us some way towards understanding the secret of the Greek world: its perfection, which is unthinkable for us, and the unbridgeable gulf that separates us from it. The Greeks knew only answers but no questions, only solutions (even if enigmatic ones) but no riddles, only forms but no chaos. They drew the creative circle of forms this side of paradox, and everything which, in our time of paradox, is bound to lead to triviality, led them to perfection.

When we speak of the Greeks we always confuse the philosophy of history with aesthetics, psychology with metaphysics, and we invent a relationship between Greek forms and our own epoch. Behind those taciturn, now forever silent masks, sensitive souls look for the fugitive, elusive moments when they themselves have dreamed of peace, forgetting that the value of those moments is in their very transience and that what they seek to escape from when they turn to the Greeks constitutes their own depth and greatness.

More profound minds, who try to forge an armour of purple steel out of their own streaming blood so that their wounds may be concealed forever and their heroic gesture may become a paradigm of the real heroism that is to come – so that it may call the new heroism into being – compare the fragmentariness of the forms they create with the Greeks' harmony, and their own sufferings, from which their forms have sprung, with the torments which they imagine the Greeks' purity had to overcome. Interpreting formal perfection, in their obstinately solipsistic way, as a function of inner devastation, they hope to hear in the Greek words the voice of a torment whose intensity exceeds theirs by as much as Greek art is greater than their own. Yet this is a complete reversal of the transcendental topography of the mind, that topography whose nature and consequences can certainly be described, whose metaphysical significance can be interpreted and grasped, but for which it will always be impossible to find a psychology, whether of empathy or of mere understanding. For all psychological comprehension presupposes a certain position of the transcendental *loci*, and functions only within their range. Instead of trying to understand the Greek world in this way, which in the end comes to asking unconsciously: what could we do to produce these forms? or: how would we behave if we had produced these forms? it would be more fruitful to inquire into the transcendental topography of the Greek mind, which was essentially different from ours and which made those forms possible and indeed necessary.

We have said that the Greeks' answers came before their questions. This, too, should not be understood psychologically, but, at most, in terms of transcendental psychology. It means that in the ultimate structural relationship which determines all lived experience and all formal creation, there exist no qualitative differences which are insurmountable, which cannot be bridged by a leap between the transcendental *loci* and the subject *a priori* assigned to them; that the ascent to the highest point, as also the descent to the point of utter meaninglessness, is made along the paths of differentiation, that is to say, at worst, by means of a long, graduated succession of steps with many transitions from one to the next. Hence the mind's attitude within such a home is a passively visionary acceptance of readymade, ever-present meaning. The world of meaning can be grasped, it can be taken in at a glance; all that is necessary is to find the *locus* that has been predestined for each individual. Error, here, can only be a matter of too much or too little, a failure only of measurement or insight. For knowledge is only the lifting of a veil, creation only the copying of visible and eternal essences, virtue a perfect knowledge of the paths; and what is alien to meaning is so only because its distance from meaning is too great.

It is a homogeneous world, and even the separation between man and world, between 'I' and 'you', cannot disturb its homogeneity. Like every other component of this rhythm, the soul stands in the midst of the world; the frontier that makes up its contours is not different in essence from the contours of things: it draws sharp, sure lines, but it separates only relatively, only in relation to and for the purpose of a homogeneous system of adequate balances. For man does not stand alone, as the sole bearer of substantiality, in the midst of reflexive forms: his relations to others and the structures which arise therefrom are as full of substance as he is himself, indeed they are more fully filled with substance because they are more general, more 'philosophic', closer and more akin to the archetypal home: love, the family, the state. What he should do or be is, for him, only a pedagogical question, an expression of the fact that he has not yet come home; it does not yet express his sole insurmountable relationship with the substance. Nor is there, within man himself, any compulsion to make the leap: he bears the stain of the distance that separates matter from substance, he will be cleansed by an immaterial soaring that will bring him closer to the substance; a long road lies before him, but within him there is no abyss.

Such frontiers necessarily enclose a rounded world. Even if menacing and incomprehensible forces make themselves felt outside the circle which the stars of ever-present meaning draw round the cosmos that has only to be experienced and formed, they cannot displace the presence of meaning; they can destroy life, but never tamper with being; they can cast dark shadows on the formed world, but even these are assimilated by the forms as contrasts that only bring them more clearly into relief.

The circle within which the Greeks led their metaphysical life was smaller than ours: that is why we cannot, as part of our life, place ourselves inside it. Or rather, the circle whose closed nature was the transcendental essence of their lives has, for us, been broken; we cannot breathe in a closed world. We have invented the productivity of the spirit: that is why the primeval images have irrevocably lost their objective self-evidence for us, and our thinking follows the endless path of an approximation that is never fully accomplished. We have invented the creation of forms: and that is why everything that falls from our weary and despairing hands must always be incomplete. We have found the only true substance within ourselves: that is why we have to place an unbridgeable chasm between cognition and action, between soul and created structure, between self and world; and why all substantiality has to be dispersed in reflexivity on the far side of that chasm; that is why our essence had to become a postulate for us, and had thus to create a still deeper, still more menacing abyss between us and our own selves.

Our world has become infinitely large and each of its corners is richer in gifts and dangers than the world of the Greeks, but such wealth cancels out the positive meaning – the totality – upon which their life was based. For totality as the formative prime reality of every individual phenomenon implies that something closed within itself can be completed; completed because everything occurs within it, nothing is excluded from it and nothing points at a higher reality outside it; completed because everything within it ripens to its own perfection and, by attaining itself, submits to limitation. Totality of being is possible only where everything is already homogeneous before it has been contained by forms; where forms are not a constraint but only the emerging of consciousness, the coming to the surface of everything that had been lying dormant as a vague longing in the innermost depths of that which cried out for form; where knowledge is virtue and virtue is happiness, where beauty is the meaning of the world made visible.

That is the world of Greek philosophy. But such thinking was born only when the substance had already begun to pale. If, properly speaking, there is no such thing as a Greek aesthetic, because metaphysics anticipated everything aesthetic, then there is no difference, properly speaking, between Greek history and the philosophy of history: the Greeks travelled in history itself through all the stages that correspond *a priori* to the great forms; their history of art is a metaphysico-genetic aesthetic, their cultural development a philosophy of history. Within this process, substance was reduced from Homer's absolute immanence of life to Plato's likewise absolute yet tangible and graspable transcendence; and the stages of the process, which are clearly and sharply distinct from one another (no gradual transitions here!) and in which the meaning of the process is laid down as though in eternal hieroglyphics – these stages are the great and timeless paradigmatic forms of world literature: epic, tragic, philosophical. The world of the epic answers the question: how can life become essential? But the answer ripened into a question only when the substance had retreated to a far horizon. Only when tragedy had supplied the creative answer to the question: how can essence come alive? Only then did men become aware that life as it was (the notion of life as it should be cancels out life) had lost the immanence of the essence. In form-giving destiny and in the hero who, creating himself, finds himself, pure essence awakens to life, mere life sinks into not-being in the face of the only true reality of the essence; a level of being beyond life, full of richly blossoming plenitude, has been reached, to which ordinary life cannot serve even as an antithesis. Nor was it a need or a problem which gave birth to the existence of the essence; the birth of Pallas Athene is the prototype for the emergence of Greek forms. Just as the reality of the essence, as it discharges into life and gives birth to life, betrays the loss of its pure immanence in life, so this problematic basis of tragedy becomes visible, becomes a problem, only in philosophy; only when the essence, having completely divorced itself from life, became the sole and absolute, the transcendent reality, and when the creative act of philosophy had revealed tragic destiny as the cruel and senseless arbitrariness of the empirical, the hero's passion as earthbound and his self-accomplishment merely as the limitation of the contingent subject, did tragedy's answer to the question of life and essence appear no longer as natural and self-evident but as a miracle, a slender yet firm rainbow bridging bottomless depths.

The tragic hero takes over from Homer's living man, explaining and transfiguring him precisely because he has taken the almost extinguished torch from his hands and kindled it anew. And Plato's new man, the wise man with his active cognition and his essence-creating vision, does not merely unmask the tragic hero but also illuminates the dark peril the hero has vanquished; Plato's new wise man, by surpassing the hero, transfigures him. This new wise man, however, was the last type of man and his world was the last paradigmatic life-structure the Greek spirit was to produce. The questions which determined and supported Plato's vision became clear, yet they bore no fruit; the world became Greek in the course of time, but the Greek spirit, in that sense, has become less and less Greek; it has created new eternal problems (and solutions, too), but the essential Greek quality of [τόπος νοητός] the realm of the intelligible, where things may be grasped by the intellect] is gone forever. The new spirit of destiny would indeed seem 'a folly to the Greeks'.

Truly a folly to the Greeks! Kant's starry firmament now shines only in the dark night of pure cognition, it no longer lights any solitary wanderer's path (for to be a man in the new world is to be solitary). And the inner light affords evidence of security, or its illusion, only to the wanderer's next step. No light radiates any longer from within into the world of events, into its vast complexity to which the soul is a stranger. And who can tell whether the fitness of the action to the essential nature of the subject – the only guide that still remains – really touches upon the essence, when the subject has become a phenomenon, an object unto itself; when his innermost and most particular essential nature appears to him only as a never-ceasing demand written upon the imaginary sky of that which 'should be'; when this innermost nature must emerge from an unfathomable chasm which lies within the subject himself, when it can only be what emerges from the furthermost depths of his essential nature, and when no one can ever plumb or even glimpse the bottom of those depths? Art, the visionary reality of the world made to our measure, has thus become independent: it is no longer a copy, for all the models have gone; it is a created totality, for the natural unity of the metaphysical spheres has been destroyed forever.

To propose a philosophy of history relating to this transformation of the structure of the transcendental *loci* is not our intention here, nor would it be possible. This is not the place to inquire whether the reason for the change is to be found in our progress (whether upward or downward, no matter) or whether the gods of Greece were driven away by other forces. Neither do we intend to chart, however approximately, the road that led to our own reality, nor to describe the seductive power of Greece even when dead and its dazzling brilliance which, like Lucifer's, made men forget again and again the irreparable cracks in the edifice of their world and tempted them to dream of new unities – unities which contradicted the world's new essence and were therefore always doomed to come to naught. Thus the Church became the new *polis*, and the paradoxical link between the soul, lost in irredeemable sin, and its impossible yet certain redemption, became an almost Platonic ray of heavenly light in the midst of earthly reality: the leap became a ladder of earthly and heavenly hierarchies.

In Giotto and Dante, Wolfram von Eschenbach and Pisano, St Thomas and St Francis, the world became round once more, a totality capable of being taken in at a glance; the chasm lost the threat inherent in its actual depth; its whole darkness, without forfeiting any of its sombrely gleaming power, became pure surface and could thus be fitted easily into a closed unity of colours; the cry for redemption became a dissonance in the perfect rhythmic system of the world and thereby rendered possible a new equilibrium no less perfect than that of the Greeks: an equilibrium of mutually inadequate, heterogeneous intensities. The redeemed world, although incomprehensible and forever unattainable, was in this way brought near and given visible form. The Last Judgement became a present reality, just another element in the harmony of the spheres, which was thought to be already established; its true nature, whereby it transforms the world into a wound of Philoctetus that only the Paraclete can heal, was forgotten. A new and paradoxical Greece came into being: aesthetics became metaphysics once more.

For the first time, but also for the last. Once this unity disintegrated, there could be no more spontaneous totality of being. The source whose flood-waters had swept away the old unity was certainly exhausted; but the river beds, now dry beyond all hope, have forever marked the face of the earth.

Henceforth, any resurrection of the Greek world is a more or less conscious hypostasy of aesthetics into metaphysics – a violence done to the essence of everything that lies outside the sphere of art, and a desire to destroy it; an attempt to forget that art is only one sphere among many, and that the very disintegration and inadequacy of the world is the precondition for the existence of art and its becoming conscious. This exaggeration of the substantiality of art is bound to weigh too heavily upon its forms: they have to produce out of themselves all that was once simply accepted as given; in other words, before their own *a priori* effectiveness can begin to manifest itself, they must create by their own power alone the preconditions for such effectiveness – an object and its environment. A totality that can be simply accepted is no longer available to the forms of art: therefore they must either narrow down and volatilize their potential to the point where they can encompass it, or else they must show polemically the impossibility of achieving their necessary object and the inner nullity of their own means. And in this case they carry the fragmentary nature of the world's structure into the world of forms.

17

The Ideology of Modernism

It is in no way surprising that the most influential contemporary school of writing should still be committed to the dogmas of 'modernist' anti-realism. It is here that we must begin our investigation if we are to chart the possibilities of a bourgeois realism. We must compare the two main trends in contemporary bourgeois literature, and look at the answers they give to the major ideological and artistic questions of our time.

We shall concentrate on the underlying ideological basis of these trends (ideological in the above-defined, not in the strictly philosophical, sense). What we must avoid at all costs is the approach generally adopted by bourgeois-modernist critics themselves: that exaggerated concern with formal criteria, with questions of style and literary technique. This approach may appear to distinguish sharply between 'modern' and 'traditional' writing (i.e. contemporary writers who adhere to the styles of the last century). In fact it fails to locate the decisive formal problems and turns a blind eye to their inherent dialectic. We are presented with a false polarization which, by exaggerating the importance of stylistic differences, conceals the opposing principles actually underlying and determining contrasting styles.

To take an example: the *monologue intérieur*. Compare, for instance, Bloom's monologue in the lavatory or Molly's monologue in bed, at the beginning and at the end of *Ulysses*, with Goethe's early-morning monologue as conceived by Thomas Mann in his *Lotte in Weimar*. Plainly, the same stylistic technique is being employed. And certain of Thomas Mann's remarks about Joyce and his methods would appear to confirm this.

It is not easy to think of any two novels more basically dissimilar than *Ulysses* and *Lotte in Weimar*. This is true even of the superficially rather similar scenes I have indicated. I am not referring to the – to my mind – striking difference in intellectual quality. I refer to the fact that with Joyce the stream-of-consciousness technique is no mere stylistic device; it is itself the formative principle governing the narrative pattern and the presentation of character. Technique here is something absolute; it is part and parcel of the aesthetic ambition informing *Ulysses*. With Thomas Mann, on the other hand, the *monologue intérieur* is simply a technical device, allowing the author to explore aspects of Goethe's world which would not have been otherwise available. Goethe's experience is not presented as confined to momentary sense-impressions. The artist reaches down to the core of Goethe's personality, to the complexity of his relations with his own past, present and even future experience. The stream of association is only apparently free. The monologue is composed with the utmost artistic rigour: it is a carefully plotted sequence gradually piercing Goethe's personality to the core. Every person or event, emerging momentarily from the stream and vanishing again, is given a specific weight, a definite position, in the pattern of the whole. However unconventional the presentation, the compositional principle is that of the traditional epic, in the way the pace is controlled, the transitions and climaxes are organized, and the ancient rules of epic narration are faithfully observed.

It would be absurd, in view of Joyce's artistic ambitions and his manifest abilities, to qualify the exaggerated attention he gives to the detailed recording of sense-data, and his comparative neglect of ideas and emotions, as artistic failure. All this was in conformity with Joyce's artistic intentions; and, by the use of such techniques, he may be said to have achieved them satisfactorily. But between Joyce's intentions and those of Thomas Mann there is a total opposition. The perpetually oscillating patterns of sense and memory-data, their powerfully charged – but aimless and directionless – fields of force, give rise to an epic structure which is *static*, reflecting a belief in the basically static character of events.

These opposed views of the world – dynamic and developmental on the one hand, static and sensational on the other – are of crucial importance in examining the two schools of literature I have mentioned. I shall return to the opposition later. Here, I want only to point out that an exclusive emphasis on formal matters can lead to serious misunderstanding of the character of an artist's work.

What determines the style of a given work of art? How does the intention determine the form? (We are concerned here, of course, with the intention realized in the work; it need not coincide with the writer's conscious intention). The distinctions that concern us are not those between stylistic 'techniques' in the formalistic sense. It is the view of the world, the ideology or *Weltanschauung* underlying a writer's work, that counts. And it is the writer's attempt to reproduce this view of the world which constitutes his 'intention' and is the formative principle underlying the style of a given piece of writing. Looked at in this way, style ceases to be a formalistic category. Rather, it is rooted in content; it is the specific form of a specific content.

Content determines form. But there is no content of which man himself is not the focal point. However various the *données* of literature (a particular experience, a didactic purpose), the basic question is, and will remain: what is man?

Here is a point of division: if we put the question in abstract, philosophical terms, leaving aside all formal considerations, we arrive – for the realistic school – at the traditional Aristotelian dictum (which was also reached by other than purely aesthetic considerations): Man is *zoion politikon*, a social animal. The Aristotelian dictum is applicable to all great realistic literature. Achilles and Werther, Oedipus and Tom Jones, Antigone and Anna Karenina: their individual existence – their *Sein an sich*, in the Hegelian terminology, their 'ontological being' as a more fashionable terminology has it – cannot be distinguished from their social and historical environment. Their human significance, their specific individuality cannot be separated from the context in which they were created.

The ontological view governing the image of man in the work of leading modernist writers is the exact opposite of this. Man, for these writers, is by nature solitary, asocial, unable to enter into relationships with other human beings. Thomas Wolfe once wrote: 'My view of the world is based on the firm conviction that solitariness is by no means a rare condition, something peculiar to myself or to a few specially solitary human beings, but the inescapable, central fact of human existence.' Man, thus imagined, may establish contact with other individuals, but only in a superficial, accidental manner; only, ontologically speaking, by retrospective reflection. For 'the others', too, are basically solitary, beyond significant human relationship.

This basic solitariness of man must not be confused with that individual solitariness to be found in literature of traditional realism. In the latter case, we are dealing with a particular situation in which a human being may be placed, due either to his character or to the circumstances of his life. Solitariness may be objectively conditioned, as with Sophocles' Philoctetes, put ashore on the bleak island of Lemnos. Or it may be subjective, the product of inner necessity, as with Tolstoy's Ivan Ilyich or Flaubert's Frédéric Moreau in *Sentimental Education*. But it is always merely a fragment, a phase, a climax or anti-climax, in the life of the community as a whole. The fate of such individuals is characteristic of certain types in specific social or historical circumstances. Besides and beyond their solitariness, the common life, the strife of togetherness of other human beings, goes on as before. In a word, their solitariness is a specific social fate, not a universal *condition humaine*.

The latter, of course, is characteristic of the theory and practice of modernism. I would like, in the present study, to spare the reader tedious excursions into philosophy. But I cannot refrain from drawing the reader's attention to Heidegger's description of human existence as the 'thrownness-into-being' (*Geworfenheit ins Dasein*). A more graphic evocation of the ontological solitariness of the individual would be hard to imagine. Man is 'flung-into-being'. This implies, not merely that man is constitutionally unable to establish relationships with things or persons outside himself; but also that it is impossible to determined theoretically the origin and the goal of human existence.

Man, thus conceived, is an historical being. (The fact that Heidegger does admit a form of 'authentic' historicity in his system is not really relevant. I have shown elsewhere [*Reader* chapter 21] that Heidegger tends to belittle history as 'vulgar'; while his 'authentic' historicity is not distinguishable from ahistoricity.) This negation of history takes two different forms in modernist literature. First, the hero is strictly confined within the limits of his own experience. There is for him – and apparently for his creator – no pre-existent reality beyond his own self, acting upon him or being acted upon by him. Secondly, the hero himself is without personal history. He is 'flung-into-the-world', meaninglessly, unfathomably. He does not develop through contact with the world; he neither forms nor is formed by it. The only 'development' in this literature is the gradual revelation of the human condition. Man is now what he has always been and always will be. The narrator, the examining subject, is in motion; the examined reality is static.

Of course, dogmas of this kind are only really viable in philosophical abstraction, and then only with a measure of sophistry. A gifted writer, however extreme his theoretical modernism, will in practice have to compromise with the demands of historicity and of the social environment. Joyce uses Dublin, Kafka and Musil the Hapsburg Empire, as the *loci* of their masterpieces. But the places they lovingly depict are little more than backcloths; they are not basic to their artistic intention.

This view of human existence has specific literary consequences. Particularly in one category, of primary theoretical and practical importance, to which we must now give our attention: that of *potentiality*. Philosophy distinguishes between *abstract* and *concrete* (in Hegel, 'real') *potentiality*. These two categories, their interrelation and opposition, are rooted in life itself. *Potentiality* – seen abstractly or subjectively – is richer than actual life. Innumerable possibilities for man's development are imaginable, only a small percentage of which will be realized. Modern subjectivism, taking these imagined possibilities for the actual complexities of life, oscillates between melancholy and fascination. When the world declines to realize these possibilities, this melancholy becomes tinged with contempt. Hofmannsthal's Sobeide expressed the reaction of the generation first exposed to this experience:

> The burden of those endlessly pored-over
> And now forever perished possibilities . . .

How far were those possibilities even concrete or 'real'? Plainly, they existed only in the imagination of the subject, as dreams or day-dreams. Faulkner, in whose work this subjective potentiality plays an important part, was evidently aware that reality must thereby be subjectivized and made to appear arbitrary. Consider this comment of his: 'They were all talking simultaneously, getting flushed and excited, quarrelling, making the unreal into a possibility, then into a probability, then into an irrefutable fact, as human beings do when they put their wishes into words.' The possibilities in a man's mind, the particular pattern, intensity and aggressiveness they assume, will of course be characteristic of that individual. In practice, their number will border on the infinite, even with the most unimaginative individual. It is thus a hopeless undertaking to define the contours of individuality, let alone to come to grips with a man's actual fate, by means of potentiality. The *abstract* character of potentiality is clear from the fact that it cannot determine development – subjective mental states, however permanent or profound, cannot here be decisive. Rather, the development of personality is determined by inherited gifts and qualities; by the factors, external or internal, which further or inhibit their growth.

But in life potentiality can, of course, become reality. Situations arise in which a man is confronted with a choice; and in the act of choice a man's character may reveal itself in a light that surprises even himself. In literature – and particularly in dramatic literature – the denouement often consists in the realization of just such a potentiality, which circumstances have kept from coming to the fore. These potentialities are, then, 'real' or concrete potentialities. The fate of the character depends upon the potentiality in question, even if it should condemn him to a tragic end. In advance, while still a subjective potentiality in the character's mind, there is no way of distinguishing it from the innumerable abstract potentialities in his mind.

It may even be buried away so completely that, before the moment of decision, it has never entered his awareness even as an abstract potentiality. The subject, after taking his decision, may be unconscious of his own motives. Thus Richard Dudgeon, Shaw's Devil's Disciple, having sacrificed himself as Pastor Andersen, confesses: 'I have often asked myself for the motive, but I find no good reason to explain why I acted as I did.'

Yet it is a decision which has altered the direction of his life. Of course, this is an extreme case. But the leap of the denouement, cancelling and at the same time renewing the continuity of individual consciousness, can never be predicted. The concrete potentiality cannot be isolated from the myriad abstract potentialities. Only actual decision reveals the distinction.

The literature of realism, aiming at a truthful reflection of reality, must demonstrate both the concrete and abstract potentialities of human beings in extreme situations of this kind. A character's concrete potentiality once revealed, his abstract potentialities will appear essentially inauthentic. Moravia, for instance, in his novel *The Indifferent Ones*, describes the young son of a decadent bourgeois family, Michel, who makes up his mind to kill his sister's seducer. While Michel, having made his decision, is planning the murder, a large number of abstract – but highly suggestive – possibilities are laid before us. Unfortunately for Michel the murder is actually carried out; and, from the sordid details of the action, Michel's character emerges as what it is – representative of that background from which, in subjective fantasy, he imagined he could escape.

Abstract potentiality belongs wholly to the realm of subjectivity; whereas concrete potentiality is concerned with the dialectic between an individual's subjectivity and objective reality. The literary presentation of the latter thus implies a description of actual persons inhabiting a palpable, identifiable world. Only in the interaction of character and environment can the concrete potentiality of a particular individual be singled out from the 'bad infinity' of purely abstract potentialities, and emerge as the determining potentiality of just this individual at just this point in his development. This principle alone enables the artist to distinguish concrete potentiality from a myriad abstractions.

But the ontology on which the image of man in modernist literature is based invalidates this principle. If the 'human condition' – man as a solitary being, incapable of meaningful relationships – is identified with reality itself, the distinction between abstract and concrete potentiality becomes null and void. The categories tend to merge. Thus Cesare Pavese notes with John Dos Passos, and his German contemporary, Alfred Döblin, a sharp oscillation between 'superficial verism' and 'abstract expressionist schematism'. Criticizing Dos Passos, Pavese writes that fictional characters 'ought to be created by deliberate selection and description of individual features' – implying that Dos Passos' characterizations are transferable from one individual to another. He describes the artistic consequences: by exalting man's subjectivity, at the expense of the objective reality of his environment, man's subjectivity itself is impoverished.

The problem, once again, is ideological. This is not to say that the ideology underlying modernist writings is identical in all cases. On the contrary, the ideology exists in extremely various, even contradictory forms. The rejection of narrative objectivity, the surrender to subjectivity, may take the form of Joyce's stream of consciousness, or of Musil's 'active passivity', his 'existence without quality', or of Gide's '*action gratuite*', where abstract potentiality achieves pseudo-realization. As individual character manifests itself in life's moments of decision, so too in literature. If the distinction between abstract and concrete potentiality vanishes, if man's inwardness is identified with an abstract subjectivity, human personality must necessarily disintegrate.

T. S. Eliot described this phenomenon, this mode of portraying human personality as:

Shape without form, shade without colour,
Paralysed force, gesture without motion.

The disintegration of personality is matched by a disintegration of the outer world. In one sense, this is simply a further consequence of our argument. For the identification of abstract and concrete human potentiality rests on the assumption that the objective world is inherently inexplicable. Certain leading modernist writers, attempting a theoretical apology, have admitted this quite frankly. Often this theoretical impossibility of understanding reality is the point of departure, rather than the exaltation of subjectivity. But in any case the connection between the two is plain. The German poet Gottfried Benn, for instance, informs us that 'there is no outer reality, there is only human consciousness, constantly building, modifying, rebuilding a new world out of its own creativity.' Musil, as always, gives a moral twist to this line of thought. Ulrich, the hero of his *The Man Without Qualities*, when asked what he would do if he were in God's place, replies: 'I should be compelled to abolish reality'. Subjective existence 'without qualities' is the complement to the negation of outward reality.

The negation of outward reality is not always demanded with such theoretical rigour. But it is present in almost all modernist literature. In conversation, Musil once gave as the period of his great novel, 'between 1912 and 1914'. But he was quick to modify this statement by adding: 'I have not, I must insist, written a historical novel. I am not concerned with actual events . . . Events, anyhow, are interchangeable. I am interested in what is typical, in what one might call the ghostly aspect of reality'. The word 'ghostly' is interesting. It points to a major tendency in modernist literature: the attenuation of actuality. In Kafka, the descriptive detail is of an extraordinary immediacy and authenticity. But Kafka's artistic ingenuity is really directed towards substituting his angst-ridden vision of the world for objective reality; the realistic detail is the expression of a ghostly unreality, of a nightmare world, whose function is to evoke angst. The same phenomenon can be seen in writers who attempt to combine Kafka's techniques with a critique of society – like the German writer, Wolfgang Koeppen, in his satirical novel about Bonn, *Das Treibhaus*. A similar attenuation of reality underlies Joyce's stream of consciousness. It is, of course, intensified where the stream of consciousness is itself the medium through which reality is presented. And it is carried *ad absurdum* where the stream of consciousness is that of an abnormal subject or of an idiot – consider the first part of Faulkner's *Sound and Fury* or, a still more extreme case, Beckett's *Molloy*.

Attenuation of reality and dissolution of personality are thus interdependent: the stronger the one, the stronger the other. Underlying both is the lack of a consistent view of human nature. Man is reduced to a sequence of unrelated experiential fragments; he is as inexplicable to others as to himself. In Eliot's *Cocktail Party* the psychiatrist, who voices the opinions of the author, describes the phenomenon:

> Ah, but we die to each other daily.
> What we know of other people
> Is only our memory of the moments
> During which we knew them. And they have changed since then.
> To pretend that they and we are the same
> Is a useful and convenient social convention
> Which must sometimes be broken. We must also remember
> That at every meeting we are meeting a stranger. (I, iii)

The dissolution of personality, originally the unconscious product of the identification of concrete and abstract potentiality, is elevated to a deliberate principle in the light of consciousness. It is no accident that Gottfried Benn called one of his theoretical tracts '*Doppelleben*'. For Benn, this dissolution of personality took the form of a schizophrenic dichotomy. According to him, there was in man's personality no coherent pattern of motivation or behaviour. Man's animal nature is opposed to his denaturalized, sublimated thought processes. The unity of thought and action is 'backwoods philosophy'; thought and being are 'quite separate entities'. Man must be either a moral or a thinking being – he cannot be both at once.

These are not, I think, purely private, eccentric speculations. Of course, they are derived from Benn's specific experience. But there is an inner connection between these ideas and a certain tradition of bourgeois thought. It is more than a hundred years since Kierkegaard first attacked the Hegelian view that the inner and outer world form an objective dialectical unity, that they are indissolubly married in spite of their apparent opposition. Kierkegaard denied any such unity. According to Kierkegaard, the individual exists within an opaque, impenetrable 'incognito'.

This philosophy attained remarkable popularity after the Second World War – proof that even the most abstruse theories may reflect social reality. Men like Martin Heidegger, Ernst Jünger, the lawyer Carl Schmitt, Gottfried Benn and others, passionately embraced this doctrine of the eternal incognito which implies that a man's external deeds are no guide to his motives. In this case, the deeds obscured behind the mysterious incognito were, needless to say, these intellectuals' participation in Nazism: Heidegger, as Rector of Freiburg University, had glorified Hitler's seizure of power at his inauguration; Carl Schmitt had put his great legal gifts at Hitler's disposal. The facts were too well known to be simply denied. But, if this impenetrable incognito were the true '*condition humaine*', might not Heidegger or Schmitt, concealed within their incognito, have been secret opponents of Hitler all the time, only supporting him in the world of appearances? Ernst von Salomon's cynical frankness about his opportunism in *The Questionnaire* (keeping his reservations to himself or declaring them only in the presence of intimate friends) may be read as an ironic commentary on this ideology of incognito as we find it, say, in the writings of Ernst Jünger.

This digression may serve to show, by means of an extreme example, what the social implications of such an ontology may be. In the literary field, this particular ideology was of cardinal importance; by destroying the complex tissue of man's relations with his environment, it furthered the dissolution of personality. For it is precisely the opposition between a man and his environment that determines the development of his personality. There is no great hero of fiction –

from Homer's Achilles to Mann's Adrian Leverkuhn or Solohov's Grigory Melyekov – whose personality is not the product of such an opposition. I have shown how disastrous the denial of the distinction between abstract and concrete potentiality is for the presentation of character. The destruction of the complex tissue of man's interaction with his environment likewise saps the vitality of this opposition. Certainly, some writers who adhere to this ideology have attempted, unsuccessfully, to portray this opposition in concrete terms. But the underlying ideology deprives these contradictions of their dynamic, developmental significance. The contradictions coexist, unresolved, contributing to the further dissolution of the personality in question.

It is to the credit of Robert Musil that he was quite conscious of the implications of this method. Of his hero Ulrich he remarked: 'One is faced with a simple choice: either one must run with the pack (when in Rome, do as the Romans do); or one becomes a neurotic.' Musil here introduces the problem, central to all modernist literature, of the significance of psychopathology.

This problem was first widely discussed in the naturalist period. More than fifty years ago, that doyen of Berlin dramatic critics, Alfred Kerr, was writing: 'Morbidity is the legitimate poetry of naturalism. For what is poetic in everyday life? Neurotic aberration, escape from life's dreary routine. Only in this way can a character be translated to a rarer clime and yet retain an air of reality.' Interesting, here, is the notion that the poetic necessity of the pathological derives from the prosaic quality of life under capitalism. I would maintain – we shall return to this point – that in modern writing there is a continuity from naturalism to the modernism of our day – a continuity restricted, admittedly, to underlying ideological principles. What at first was no more than dim anticipation of approaching catastrophe developed, after 1914, into an all-pervading obsession. And I would suggest that the ever-increasing part played by psychopathology was one of the main features of the continuity. At each period – depending on the prevailing social and historical conditions – psychopathology was given a new emphasis, a different significance and artistic function. Kerr's description suggests that in naturalism the interest in psycho-pathology sprang from an aesthetic need; it was an attempt to escape from the dreariness of life under capitalism. The quotation from Musil shows that some years later the opposition acquired a moral slant. The obsession with morbidity had ceased to have a merely decorative function, bringing colour into the greyness of reality, and become a moral protest against capitalism.

With Musil – and with many other modernist writers – psychopa-thology became the goal, the *terminus ad quem*, of their artistic intention, which follows from its underlying ideology. There is, first, a lack of definition. The protest expressed by this flight into psychopathology is an abstract gesture; its rejection of reality is wholesale and summary, containing no concrete criticism. It is a gesture, moreover, that is destined to lead nowhere; it is an escape into nothingness. Thus the propagators of this ideology are mistaken in thinking that such a protest could ever be fruitful in literature. In any protest against particular social conditions, these conditions themselves must have the central place. The bourgeois protest against feudal society, the proletarian against bourgeois society, made their point of departure a criticism of the old order. In both cases the protest – reaching out beyond the point of departure – was based on a concrete *terminus ad quem*: the establishment of a new order. However indefinite the structure and content of this new order, the will towards its more exact definition was not lacking.

How different the protest of writers like Musil! The *terminus a quo* (the corrupt society of our time) is inevitably the main source of energy, since the *terminus ad quem* (the escape into psychopathology) is a mere abstraction. The rejection of modern reality is purely subjective. Considered in terms of man's relation with his environment, it lacks both content and direction. And this lack is exaggerated still further by the character of the *terminus ad quem*. For the protest is an empty gesture, expressing nausea, or discomfort, or longing. Its content – or rather lack of content – derives from the fact that such a view of life cannot impart a sense of direction. These writers are not wholly wrong in believing that psychopathology is their surest refuge; it is the ideological complement of their historical position.

This obsession with the pathological is not only to be found in literature. Freudian psychoanalysis is its most obvious expression. The treatment of the subject is only superficially different from that in modern literature. As everybody knows, Freud's starting point was 'everyday life'. In order to explain 'slips' and day-dreams, however, he had to have recourse to psychopathology. In his lectures, speaking of resistance and repression, he says: 'Our interest in the general psychology of symptom formation increases as we understand to what extent the study of pathological conditions can shed light on the workings of the normal mind'. Freud believed he had found the key to the understanding of the normal personality in the psychology of the abnormal. This belief is still more evident in the typology of Kretschner, which also assumes that psychological abnormalities can explain normal psychology. It is only when we compare Freud's psychology with that of Pavlov, who takes the Hippocratic view that mental abnormality is a deviation from the norm, that we see it in its true light.

Clearly, this not strictly a scientific or literary-critical problem. It is an ideological problem, deriving from the ontological dogma of the solitariness of man. The literature of realism, based on the Aristotelian concept of man as *zoion politikon*, is entitled to develop a new typology for each new phase in the evolution of society. It displays the contradictions within society and within the individual in the context of a dialectical unity. Here, individuals embodying violent and extraordinary passions are still within the range of a socially normal typology (Shakespeare, Balzac, Stendhal). For, in this literature, the average man is simply a dimmer reflection of the contradictions always existing in man and society; eccentricity is a socially conditioned distortion. Obviously, the passions of the great heroes must not be confused with 'eccentricity' in the colloquial sense: Christian Buddenbrook is an 'eccentric'; Adrian Leverkuhn is not.

The ontology of *Geworfenheit* makes a true typology impossible; it is replaced by an abstract polarity of the eccentric and the socially average. We have seen why this polarity – which in traditional realism serves to increase our understanding of social normality – leads in modernism to a fascination with morbid eccentricity. Eccentricity becomes the necessary complement of the average; and this polarity is held to exhaust human potentiality. The implications of this ideology are shown in another remark of Musil's: 'If humanity dreamt collectively, it would dream Moosbrugger.' Moosbrugger, you will remember, was a mentally retarded sexual pervert with homicidal tendencies.

What served, with Musil, as the ideological basis of a new typology – escape into neurosis as a protest against the evils of society – becomes with other modernist writers an immutable *condition humaine*. Musil's statement loses its conditional 'if' and becomes a simple description of reality. Lack of objectivity in the description of the outer world finds its complement in the reduction of reality to a nightmare. Beckett's *Molloy* is perhaps the *ne plus ultra* of this development, although Joyce's vision of reality as an incoherent stream of consciousness had already assumed, in Faulkner, a nightmare quality. In Beckett's novel we have the same vision twice over. He presents us with an image of the utmost human degradation – an idiot's vegetative existence. Then, as help is imminent from a mysterious unspecified source, the rescuer himself sinks into idiocy. The story is told through the parallel streams of consciousness of the idiot and of his rescuer.

Along with the adoption of perversity and idiocy as types of the *condition humaine*, we find what amounts to its frank glorification. Take Montherlant's *Pasiphaé*, where sexual perversity – the heroine's infatuation with a bull – is presented as a triumphant return to nature, as the liberation of impulse from the slavery of convention. The chorus – i.e., the author – puts the following question (which, though rhetorical, clearly expects an affirmative reply): '*Si l'absence de pensée et l'absence de morale ne contribuent pas beaucoup à la dignité des bêtes, des plantes et des eaux . . .* ' Montherlant expresses as plainly as Musil, though with different moral and emotional emphasis, the hidden – one might say repressed – social character of the protest underlying this obsession with psychopathology, its perverted Rousseauism, its anarchism. There are many illustrations of this in modernist writing. A poem of Benn's will serve to make the point:

> O that we were – our primal ancestors,
> Small lumps of plasma in hot, sultry swamps;
> Life, death, conception, parturition
> Emerging from those juices soundlessly.
>
> A frond of seaweed or a dune of sand,
> Formed by the wind and heavy at the base;
> A dragon or gull's wing – already, these
> Would signify excessive suffering.

This is not overtly perverse in the manner of Beckett or Montherlant. Yet, in this primitivism, Benn is at one with them. The opposition of man as animal to man as social being (for instance, Heidegger's devaluation of the social as '*das Man*', or Klage's assertion of the incompatibility of *Geist* and *Seele*, or Rosenberg's racial mythology) leads straight to a glorification of the abnormal and to un undisguised anti-humanism.

A typology limited in this way to the *homme moyen sensuel* and the idiot also opens the door to 'experimental' stylistic distortion. Distortion becomes as inseparable a part of the portrayal of reality as the recourse to the pathological. But literature must have a concept of the normal if it is to 'place' distortion correctly; that is to say, to see it *as* distortion. With such a typology this placing is impossible, since the normal is no longer a proper object of literary interest. Life under capitalism is, often rightly, presented as a distortion (a petrification or paralysis) of the human substance. But to present psychopathology as a way of escape from this distortion is itself a distortion. We are invited to measure one type of distortion against another and arrive, necessarily, at universal distortion. There is no principle to set against the general pattern, no standard by which the petit-bourgeois and the pathological can be seen in their social context. And these tendencies, far from being relativized with time, become ever more absolute.

Distortion becomes the normal condition of human existence; the proper study, the formative principle of art and literature.

I have demonstrated some of the literary implications of this ideology. Let us now pursue the argument further. It is clear, I think, that modernism must deprive literature of a sense of *perspective*. This would not be surprising; rigorous modernists such as Kafka, Benn and Musil have always indignantly refused to provide their readers with any such thing. I will return to the ideological implications of the idea of perspective later. Let me say here that, in any work of art, perspective is of overriding importance. It determines the course and content; it draws together the threads of the narration; it enables the artist to choose between the important and the superficial, the crucial and the episodic. The direction in which characters develop is determined by perspective, only those features being described which are material to their development. The more lucid the perspective – as in Molière or the Greeks – the more economical and striking the selection.

Modernism drops the selective principle. It asserts that it can dispense with it, or can replace it with its dogma of the *condition humaine*. A naturalistic style is bound to be the result. This state of affairs – which to my mind characterizes all modernist art of the past fifty years – is disguised by critics who systematically glorify the modernist movement. By concentrating on formal criteria, by isolating technique from content and exaggerating its importance, these critics refrain from judgement on the social or artistic significance of subject matter. They are unable, in consequence, to make the aesthetic distinction between *realism* and *naturalism*. This distinction depends on the presence or absence in a work of art of a 'hierarchy of significance' in the situations and characters presented. Compared with this, formal categories are of secondary importance. That is why it is possible to speak of the basically *naturalistic* character of modernist literature – and to see here the literary expression of an ideological continuity. This is not to deny that variations in style reflect changes in society. But the particular form this principle of naturalistic arbitrariness, this lack of hierarchic structure, may take is not decisive. We encounter it in the all-determining 'social conditions' of naturalism, in symbolism's impressionist methods and its cultivation of the exotic, in the fragmentation of objective reality in futurism and constructivism and the German *Neue Sachlichkeit*, or, again, in surrealism's stream of consciousness.

These schools have in common a basically static approach to reality. This is closely related to their lack of perspective. Characteristically, Gottfried Benn actually incorporated this in his artistic programme. One of his volumes bears the title, *Static Poems*. The denial of history, of development, and thus of perspective, becomes the mark of true insight into the nature of reality.

The wise man is ignorant
of change and development
his children and his children's children
are no part of his world.

The rejection of any concept of the future is for Benn the criterion of wisdom. But even those modernist writers who are less extreme in their rejection of history tend to present social and historical phenomena as static. It is, then, of small importance whether this condition is 'eternal', or only a transitional stage punctuated by sudden catastrophes (even in early naturalism the static presentation was often broken up by these catastrophes, without altering its basic character). Musil, for instance, writes in his essay, *The Writer in our Age*: 'One knows just as little about the present. Partly, this is because we are, as always, too close to the present. But it is also because the present into which we were plunged some two decades ago is of particularly all-embracing and inescapable character.' Whether or not Musil knew of Heidegger's philosophy, the idea of *Geworfenheit* is clearly at work here. And the following reveals plainly how, for Musil, this static state was upset by the catastrophe of 1914: 'All of a sudden, the world was a sudden rift . . .' In short: this static apprehension of reality in modernist literature is no passing fashion; it is rooted in the ideology of modernism.

To establish the basic distinction between modernism and that realism which, from Homer to Thomas Mann and Gorky, has assumed change and development to be the proper subject of literature, we must go deeper into the underlying ideological problem. In *The House of the Dead* Dostoevsky gave an interesting account of the convict's attitude to work. He described how the prisoners, in spite of brutal discipline, loafed about, working badly or merely going through the motions of work until a new overseer arrived and allotted them a new project, after which they were allowed to go home. 'The work was hard', Dostoevsky continues, 'but, Christ, with what energy they threw themselves into it! Gone was all their former indolence and pretended incompetence.' Later in the book Dostoevsky sums up his experiences: 'If a man loses hope and has no aim in view, sheer boredom can turn him into a beast . . .' I have said that the problem of perspective in literature is directly related to the principle of selection. Let me go further: underlying the problem is a profound ethical complex, reflected in the composition of the work itself. Every human action is based on a presupposition of its inherent meaningfulness, at least to the subject. Absence of meaning makes a mockery of action and reduces art to naturalist description.

Clearly, there can be no literature without at least the appearance of change or development. This conclusion should not be interpreted in a narrowly metaphysical sense. We have already diagnosed the obsession with psychopathology in modernist literature as a desire to escape from the reality of capitalism. But this implies the absolute primacy of the *terminus a quo*, the condition from which it is desired to escape. Any movement towards a *terminus ad quem* is condemned to impotence. As the ideology of most modernist writers asserts the unalterability of outward reality (even if this is reduced to a mere state of consciousness) human activity is, *a priori*, rendered impotent and robbed of meaning.

The apprehension of reality to which this leads is most consistently and convincingly realized in the work of Kafka. Kafka remarks of Josef K., as he is being led to execution: 'He thought of flies, their tiny limbs breaking as they struggle away from the fly-paper.' This mood of total impotence, of paralysis in the face of the unintelligible power of circumstances, informs all his work. Though the action of *The Castle* takes a different, even an opposite, direction to that of *The Trial*, this view of the world, from the perspective of a trapped and struggling fly, is all-pervasive. This experience, this vision of a world dominated by angst and of man at the mercy of incomprehensible terrors, makes Kafka's work the very type of modernist art. Techniques, elsewhere of merely formal significance, are used here to evoke a primitive awe in the presence of an utterly strange and hostile reality. Kafka's angst is the experience *par excellence* of modernism.

Two instances from musical criticism – which can afford to be both franker and more theoretical than literary criticism – shows that it is indeed a universal experience with which we are dealing. The composer, Hanns Eisler, says of Schoenberg: 'Long before the invention of the bomber, he expressed what people were to feel in the air raid shelters.' Even more characteristic – though seen from a modernist point of view – is Theodor W. Adorno's analysis (in *The Ageing of Modern Music*) of the symptoms of decadence in modernistic music: 'The sounds are still the same. But the experience of angst, which made their originals great, has vanished.' Modernist music, he continues, has lost touch with the truth that was its *raison d'être*. Composers are no longer equal to the emotional presuppositions of their modernism. And that is why modernist music has failed. The diminution of the original angst-obsessed vision of life (whether due, as Adorno thinks, to inability to respond to the magnitude of the horror or, as I believe, to the fact that this obsession with angst among bourgeois intellectuals has already begun to recede) has brought about a loss of substance in modern music, and destroyed its authenticity as a modernist artform.

This is a shrewd analysis of the paradoxical position of the modernist artist, particularly where he is trying to express deep and genuine experience. The deeper the experience, the greater the damage to the artistic whole. But this tendency towards disintegration, this loss of artistic unity, cannot be written off as a mere fashion, the product of experimental gimmicks. Modern philosophy, after all, encountered these problems long before modern literature, painting or music. A case in point is the problem of *time*. Subjective idealism had already separated time, abstractly conceived, from historical change and particularly of place. As if this separation were insufficient for the new age of imperialism, Bergson widened it further. Experienced time, subjective time, now became identical with real time; the rift between this time and that of the objective world was complete. Bergson and other philosophers who took up and varied this theme claimed that their concept of time alone afforded insight into authentic, i.e. subjective, reality. The same tendency soon made its appearance in literature.

The German left-wing critic and essayist of the twenties, Walter Benjamin, has well described Proust's vision and the techniques he used to present it in his great novel: 'We all know that Proust does not describe a man's life as it actually happens, but as it is remembered by a man who has lived through it. Yet this puts it far too crudely. For it is not actual experience that is important, but the texture of reminiscence, the Penelope's tapestry of a man's memory.' The connection with Bergson's theories of time is obvious. But whereas with Bergson, in the abstraction of philosophy, the unity of perception is preserved, Benjamin shows that with Proust, as a result of the radical disintegration of the time sequence, objectivity is eliminated: 'A lived event is finite, concluded at least on the level of experience. But a remembered event is infinite, a possible key to everything that preceded it and to everything that will follow it.'

This is the distinction between a philosophical and an artistic vision of the world. However hard philosophy, under the influence of idealism, tries to liberate the concepts of space and time from temporal and spatial particularity, literature continues to assume their unity. The fact that, nevertheless, the concept of subjective time has cropped up in literature only shows how deeply subjectivism is rooted in the experience of the modern bourgeois intellectual. The individual, retreating into himself in despair at the cruelty of the age, may experience an intoxicated fascination with its forlorn condition. But then a new horror breaks through. If reality cannot be understood (or no effort is made to understand it), then the individual's subjectivity – alone in the universe, and reflecting only itself – takes on an equally incomprehensible and horrific character. Hugo von Hofmannsthal was to experience this condition very early in his poetic career:

> It is a thing that no man cares to think on,
> And far too terrible for mere complaint,
> That all things slip from us and pass away.
>
> And that my ego, bound by no outward force –
> Once a small child's before it became mine –
> Should now be strange to me, like a strange dog.

By separating time from the outer world of objective reality, the inner world of the subject is transformed into a sinister, inexplicable flux and acquires – paradoxically, it may seem – a static character.

In literature this tendency towards disintegration will, of course, have an even greater impact than on philosophy. When time is isolated in this way, the artist's world disintegrates into a multiplicity of partial worlds. The static view of the world, now combined with diminished objectivity, here rules unchanged. The world of man – the only subject matter of literature – is shattered if a single component is removed. I have shown the consequences of isolating time and reducing it to a subjective category. But time is by no means the only component whose removal can lead to such disintegration. Here, again, Hofmannsthal anticipated later developments. His imaginary 'Lord Chandos' reflects: 'I have lost the ability to concentrate my thoughts or set them out coherently.' The result is that a condition tending towards a definitely pathological outcry is anticipated here – admittedly in glamorous, romantic guise. But it is the same disintegration that is at work.

Previous realistic literature, however violent its criticism of reality, had always assumed the unity of the world it described and seen it as a living whole inseparable from man himself. But the major realists of our time deliberately introduce elements of disintegration into their work – for instance, the subjectivizing of time – and use them to portray the contemporary world more exactly. In this way, the once natural unity becomes a conscious, constructed unity. But in modernist literature the disintegration of the world of man – and consequently the disintegration of personality – coincides with the ideological intention. Thus angst, this basic modern experience, this by-product of *Geworfenheit,* has its emotional origin in the experience of a disintegrating society. But it attains its effects by evoking the disintegration of the world of man.

To complete our examination of modernist literature, we must consider for a moment the question of allegory. Allegory is that aesthetic genre which lends itself *par excellence* to a description of man's alienation from objective reality. Allegory is a problematic genre because it rejects that assumption of an immanent meaning to human existence which – however unconscious, however combined with religious concepts of transcendence – is the basis of traditional art. Thus in medieval art we observe a new secularity (in spite of the continued use of religious subjects) triumphing more and more, from the time of Giotto, over the allegorizing of an earlier period.

Certain reservations should be made at this point. First, we must distinguish between literature and the visual arts. In the latter, the limitations of allegory can be the more easily overcome in that the transcendental, allegorical subject can be clothed in an aesthetic immanence (even if of a merely decorative kind) and the rift with reality can in some sense be eliminated – we have only to think of Byzantine mosaic art. This decorative element has no real equivalent in literature; it exists only in a figurative sense, and then only as a secondary component. Allegorical art of the quality of Byzantine mosaic is only rarely possible in literature. Secondly, we must bear in mind in examining allegory – and this is of great importance for our argument – a historical distinction: does the concept of transcendence in question contain within itself tendencies toward immanence (as in Byzantine art or Giotto), or is it the product precisely of a rejection of these tendencies?

Allegory, in modernist literature, is clearly of the latter kind. Transcendence implies here, more or less consciously, the negation of any meaning immanent in the world or the life of man. We have already examined the underlying ideological basis of this view and its stylistic consequences. To conclude our analysis, and to establish the allegorical character of modernist literature, I must refer again to the work of one of the finest theoreticians of modernism – Walter Benjamin. Benjamin's examination of allegory was a product of his researches into German baroque drama. Benjamin made his analysis of these relatively minor plays the occasion for a general discussion of the aesthetics of allegory. He was asking, in effect, why it is that transcendence, which is the essence of allegory, cannot but destroy aesthetics itself.

Benjamin gives a very contemporary definition of allegory. He does not labour the analogies between modern art and the baroque (such analogies are tenuous at best, and were much overdone by the fashionable criticism of the time). Rather, he uses the baroque drama to criticize modernism, imputing the characteristics of the latter to the former. In so doing, Benjamin became the first critic to attempt a philosophical analysis of the aesthetic paradox underlying modernist art. He writes:

> In allegory, the *facies hippocratica* of history looks to the observer like a petrified primeval landscape. History, all the suffering and failure it contains, finds expression in the human face – or, rather, in the human skull. No sense of freedom, no classical proportion, no human emotion lives in its features. Not only human existence in general, but the fate of every individual human being is symbolized in this most palpable token of mortality. This is the core of the allegorical vision, of the baroque idea of history as the passion of the world. History is significant only in the stations of its corruption. Significance is a function of morality – because it is death that marks the passage from corruptibility to meaningfulness.

Benjamin returns again and again to this link between allegory and the annihilation of history.

> In the light of this vision history appears, not as the gradual realization of the eternal, but as a process of inevitable decay. Allegory thus goes beyond beauty. What ruins are in the physical world, allegories are in the world of the mind.

Benjamin points to the aesthetic consequences of modernism – though projected into the baroque drama – more shrewdly and consistently than any of his contemporaries. He sees that the notion of objective time is essential to any understanding of history, and that the notion of subjective time is a product of a period of decline. 'A thorough knowledge of the problematic nature of art' thus becomes for him – correctly, from his point of view – one of the hallmarks of allegory in baroque drama. It is problematic, on the one hand, because it is an art intent on expressing absolute transcendence, that fails to do so because of the means at its disposal. It is also problematic because it is an art reflecting the corruption of the world and bringing about its own dissolution in the process. Benjamin discovers 'an immense, anti-aesthetic subjectivity' in baroque literature, associated with a 'theologically-determined subjectivity'. Romantic – and, on a higher plane, baroque – writers were well aware of this problem, and gave their understanding, not only theoretical, but artistic – that is to say allegorical – expression. 'The image', Benjamin remarks, 'becomes a flaw in the sphere of allegorical intuition. When touched by the light of technology, its symbolic beauty is gone. The false appearance of totality vanishes. The image dies; the parable no longer holds true: the world it once contained disappears.'

The consequences for art are far reaching, and Benjamin does not hesitate to point them out: 'Every person, every object, every relation-ship can stand for something else. This transferability constitutes a devastating, though just, judgement on the profane world – which is thereby branded as a world where such things are of small importance.' Benjamin knows, of course, that although details are 'transferable', and thus insignificant, they are not banished from art altogether. On the contrary. It is precisely in modern art, with which he is ultimately concerned, that descriptive detail is often of an extraordinarily sensuous, suggestive power – we think again of Kafka. But this, as we showed in the case of Musil (a writer who does not consciously aim at allegory) does not prevent the substance of the world from undergoing permanent alteration, from becoming transferable and arbitrary. It is just this, modernist writers maintain, that is typical of their own apprehension of reality. Yet presented in this way, the world becomes, as Benjamin puts it, 'exalted and depreciated at the same time'. Even the conviction that phenomena are *not* ultimately transferable is rooted in a belief in the world's rationality and in man's ability to penetrate its secrets. In realistic literature each descriptive detail is both *individual* and *typical*. By de-stroying the coherence of the world, they reduce detail to the level of mere particularity (once again, the connection between modernism and naturalism is plain). Detail, in its allegorical transferability, though brought into a direct, if paradoxical connection with transcendence, becomes an abstract function of the transcendence to which it points. Modernist literature thus replaces concrete typicality with abstract par-ticularity.

We are here applying Benjamin's paradox directly to aesthetics and criticism, and particularly to the aesthetics of modernism. And, though we have reversed his scale of values, we have not deviated from the course of his argument. Elsewhere, he speaks out even more plainly – as though the baroque mask had fallen, revealing the modernist skull underneath:

> Allegory is left empty-handed. The forces of evil, lurking in its depths, owe their very existence to allegory. Evil is, precisely, the non-existence of that which allegory purports to present.

The paradox Benjamin arrives at – that his investigation of the aesthetics of baroque tragedy has culminated in a negation of aesthe-tics – sheds a good deal of light on modernist literature, and particu-larly on Kafka. In interpreting his writings allegorically I am not, of course, following Max Brod, who finds a specifically religious allegory in Kafka's works. Kafka refuted any such interpretation in a remark he is said to have made to Brod himself. 'We are nihilistic figments, all of us; suicidal notions forming in God's mind.' Kafka rejected, too, the gnostic concept of God as an evil demiurge: 'The world is a cruel whim of God, an evil day's work.' When Brod attempted to give this an optimistic slant, Kafka shrugged off the attempt ironically: 'Oh, hope enough, hope without end – but not, alas, for us.' These remarks, quoted by Benjamin in his brilliant essay on Kafka, point to the general spiritual climate of his work: 'His profoundest experience is of the hopelessness, the utter meaninglessness of man's world, and particularly that of present-day bourgeois man.' Kafka, whether he says so openly or not, is an atheist. An atheist, though, of that modern species who regard God's removal from the scene not as a liberation – as did Epicurus and the Encyclopedists – but as a token of the 'God-forsakenness' of the world, its utter desolation and futility. Jacobsen's *Niels Lyhne* was the first novel to describe this state of mind of the atheistic bourgeois intelligentsia. Modern religious atheism is characterized, on the one hand, by the fact that unbelief has lost its revolutionary élan – the empty heavens are the projection of a world beyond hope or redemption. On the other hand, religious atheism shows that the desire for salvation lives on with undiminished force in a world without God, worshipping the void created by God's absence.

The supreme judges in *The Trial*, the castle administration in *The Castle*, represent transcendence in Kafka's allegories: the transcendence of nothingness. Everything points to them, and they could give meaning to everything. Everybody believes in their existence and omnipotence; but nobody knows them, nobody knows how they can be reached. If there is a God here, it can only be the God of religious atheism: *atheos absconditus*. We become acquainted with a repellent host of subordinate authorities; brutal, corrupt, pedantic and, at the same time, unreliable and irresponsible. It is a portrait of the bourgeois society Kafka knew, with a dash of Prague local colouring. But it is also allegorical in that the doings of this bureaucracy and of those dependent on it, its impotent victims, are not concrete and realistic, but a reflection of that nothingness which governs existence. The hidden, non-existent God of Kafka's world derives his spectral character from the fact that his own non-existence is the ground of all existence; and the portrayed reality, uncannily accurate as it is, is spectral in the shadow of that dependence. The only purpose of transcendence – the intangible *nichtendes Nichts* – is to reveal the *facies hippocratica* of the world.

The abstract particularity which we saw to be the aesthetic consequence of allegory reaches its high point in Kafka. He is a marvellous observer; the spectral character of reality affects him so deeply that the simplest episodes have an oppressive, nightmarish immediacy. As an artist, he is not content to evoke the surface of life. He is aware that individual detail must point to general significance. But how does he go about the business of abstraction? He has emptied everyday life of meaning by using the allegorical method; he has allowed detail to be annihilated by his transcendental nothingness. This allegorical transcendence bars Kafka's way to realism, prevents him from investing observed detail with the significance of the typical. Kafka is not able, in spite of his extraordinarily evocative power, in spite of his unique sensibility, to achieve that fusion of the particular and the general which is the essence of realistic art. His aim is to raise the individual detail in its immediate particularity (without generalizing its content) to the level of abstraction. Kafka's method is typical, here, of modernism's allegorical approach. Specific subject matter and stylistic variation do not matter; what matters is the basic ideological determination of form and content. The particularity we find in Beckett and Joyce, in Musil and Benn, various as the treatment of it may be, is essentially of the same kind.

If we combine what we have up to now discussed separately we arrive at a consistent pattern. We see that modernism leads not only to the destruction of traditional literary forms; it leads to the destruction of literature as such. And this is true not only of Joyce, or of the literature of expressionism and surrealism. It was not André Gide's ambition, for instance, to bring about a revolution in literary style; it was his philosophy that compelled him to abandon conventional forms. He planned his *Faux-Monnayeurs* as a novel. But its structure suffered from a characteristically modernist schizophrenia: it was supposed to be written by the man who was also the hero of the novel. And, in practice, Gide was forced to admit that no novel, no work of literature could be constructed in that way. We have here a practical demonstration that – as Benjamin showed in another context – modernism means not the enrichment, but the negation of art.

Part IV

Philosophy and Politics

Introduction

Philosophy and Politics

Lukács's path to Marxism and ultimately communism is fascinating, engrossing and instructive because it led from his Socratic quest for an examined life to a leap of faith. On the eve of the First World War, Lukács categorically rejected socialism, saying that 'redemption has no plural'.[1]

In November 1918, one month before Lukács joined the newly formed communist party in Hungary, Max Weber warned against the 'Russian danger'. But while Weber, an ardent nationalist, cautioned German intellectuals not to be tempted by the Bolshevik Revolution of 1917, the disenchanted world entered a revolutionary phase in Budapest. And Lukács, Weber's close friend, made the leap of faith.

By the time Lukács's 'Bolshevism as an Ethical Problem', his *summa contra* communism appeared in the *Szabadgondolat* [Free Thought] in December 1918, Lukács was already a party member. Lukács's conversion stunned his friends, above all Max Weber. Our translation of 'Bolshevism as an Ethical Problem' is based on its original publication in *Szabadgondolat*. Max Weber, in his famous lectures known as the 'Science of a Vocation' and 'Politics as a Vocation', delivered in Munich in January 1919, named and took issue with Lukács who, he claimed, in turning communist had failed to distinguish between the 'ethic of responsibility' and the 'ethic of ultimate ends' (*Gesinnungsethik*).

As death was closing on Weber (June 1920), he edited and reorganized his most systematic work, *Economy and Society*, which Guenther Roth called 'the sum of Max Weber's scholarly vision of society'.[2] But as Weber worked on the galley proofs of *Economy and Society*, he again took issue with Lukács.[3] Weber was familiar with at least three of Lukács's Marxist essays, notably 'What is Orthodox Marxism?' (March 1919), 'The Changing Function of Historical Materialism' (June 1920), and 'Class Consciousness' (March 1920), which reappeared in somewhat revised form in *History and Class Consciousness*. Lukács's essay, 'Class Consciousness' (*Reader* chapter 19) is reprinted, with some deletions, from *History and Class Consciousness*. Though Lukács's original notes are retained, the editor has updated the quoted texts by using contemporary and easily available English editions of the cited works.

In sharp disagreement with Lukács, Weber equated revolution with usurpation and non-legitimate domination. In contrast to Lukács, who dwelled on the 'movement of the whole', Weber's sociological focus remained the 'charismatic leader'. It is safe to assume that Weber had also Lukács in mind when he inserted this passage into the galley proofs of *Economy and Society*:

> Before this, every revolution which has been attempted under modern conditions has failed completely because of the indispensability of trained officials and the lack of its own organized staff . . . See below, the ch[apter] on the revolution [unwritten].[4]

Had Weber lived a few months longer, he would most likely have written his 'theory of revolution' in response to Lukács's revolutionary politics.

Lukács's *History and Class Consciousness* is a recognized classic. Jürgen Habermas quotes with approval Herbert Schnädelbach who, in his *Philosophy in Germany 1831–1933* (Cambridge, 1984) wrote: 'Our contemporary philosophy has been decisively shaped by Ludwig Wittgenstein's *Tractatus Logico-philosophicus* (1921), Georg Lukács's *History and Class Consciousness* (1923), and Martin Heidegger's *Being and Time* (1926).' That there is an implicit connection between the thought of Lukács and Heidegger has been convincingly demonstrated by Lucien Goldmann.[5]

As Goldmann has shown, the philosophical and existential line which starts from Lukács's *Soul and Form* and runs through *History and Class Consciousness* ends in Heidegger's *Being and Time*. It should also be kept in mind that both Lukács and Heidegger were fascinated and influenced by Kierkegaard. Hence the question of being, its authenticity, and the analysis of totality, that featured so prominently in Lukács's *Soul and Form*, also engaged Heidegger in *Being and Time*. There is also a basic disagreement between Lukács and Heidegger. Lukács's concept of the philosophy of consciousness, as it appears in *History and Class Consciousness*, received a critical analysis in Heidegger's *Being and Time*. As Jürgen Habermas rightly pointed out, 'The path-breaking achievement of *Being and Time* consists in Heidegger's decisive argumentative step towards dismantling the philosophy of consciousness.'[6]

Not surprisingly, in his *Being and Time*, Heidegger denies 'authentic' existence to the Marxist Lukács – without actually naming him – the leading figure of Western Marxism whom Heidegger held responsible for Bolshevism. Whereas Lukács names Heidegger as the philosopher in league with Nazism.

Lukács's essays on Heidegger and Nietzsche are excerpted from his polemical work, *The Destruction of Reason*, completed at the height of the Cold War in 1952. Whatever one may say about the polemical zeal and wilful distortion of the book, which George Lichtheim judged to be an 'intellectual crime',[7] *The Destruction of Reason* is, none the less, a historical document on the political atmosphere and intellectual miscarriages at the height of the Cold War.

In his early years it was with Nietzsche that Lukács pierced life's dumb abyss to make it alive with speech. Like Ibsen, Nietzsche exerted a powerful influence on Lukács. And like the great transvaluator himself, Lukács called for 'new tables' with 'new values' in Hungary. But as a Marxist, at the height of the Cold War, Lukács launched a furious attack on Heidegger and Nietzsche.

In the case of Nietzsche, it was part of Lukács's effort as a Marxist to dethrone his youthful idols and abandon the temples where he once worshipped.

NOTES

[1] Lukács, *Early Works*, p. 717.

[2] Max Weber, *Economy and Society* (3 vols., New York, 1968), ed. Guenther Roth and Claus Wittich, vol. 1, p. xxvii.

[3] Arpad Kadarkay, 'The Demonic Self: Max Weber and Georg Lukács' in *Hungarian Studies*, vol. 9, Nos. 1–2 (1994), pp. 77–102.

[4] Max Weber, *Economy and Society*, vol. 1, p. 266.

[5] Lucien Goldmann, *Lukács and Heidegger* (London: Routledge Kegan Paul, 1977).

[6] Jürgen Habermas, 'Work and *Weltanschauung*: The Heidegger Controversy from a German Perspective' in *Heidegger: A Critical Reader*, ed. Hubert L. Dreyfus & Harrison Hall (Oxford: Blackwell, 1992), p. 190.

[7] See *Encounter* (August 1963), p. 95.

18

Bolshevism as an Ethical Problem

It is not my intention here to discuss either the practical feasibility of Bolshevism, or its good or bad consequences when in power. Apart from the fact that this writer feels the least qualified to resolve such questions, it seems advisable for the time being, in order to pose the question clearly, to overlook the practical aspects of the question. For the answer – like every answer to an important question – is ethical in nature, though its immanent clarification, from the specific perspective of pure action, is essentially a practical task.

Furthermore, there is at least partial support for putting the question this way in the frequently heard argument, in debates that swirl around Bolshevism,[1] over whether the socio-economic situation is 'ripe' enough for the immediate realization of Bolshevism. This in itself presents us with an insoluble problem. In my opinion, there never is a situation where one can actually know and foresee things with an absolute certainty. For the human will, intent on immediate self-realization at all costs, forms an integral part of the 'ripe' situation as part of its objective relations.

On the other hand, the realization that the triumph of Bolshevism may eventually destroy great values essential for culture and civilization, is never a decisive counter-argument for those who choose Bolshevism, either on philosophical or ethical grounds. With or without regret, they acknowledge this fact but, aware of Bolshevism's inevitability, will not modify their goals – and rightly so. They know full well that such a global historical exchange of values is inconceivable without the destruction of old values, and are confident that their will to create new values is strong enough to compensate future generations amply for any loss of values.

In the light of this, it appears there is no ethical problem for a real socialist, as if his choice of Bolshevism was a foregone conclusion. After all, if the advanced development of social relations and the loss of values present no major obstacles, then obviously the question is: what is our chance of realizing our convictions immediately and without any compromise. Can one be a true socialist under these circumstances while still preferring to deliberate and wait for things? In other words, while entertaining compromise. By contrast, to a non-Bolshevik who invokes democratic principles, which the dictatorship of the minority consciously and inevitably precludes, the disciples of Lenin, faithful to their leader's doctrine, respond by saying they will remove from their party and its programme the concept of democracy, and simply profess to be communists. The question of morality therefore hinges upon the following question. Is democracy nothing but a tactic of socialism (merely a tactical weapon when socialism as a minority movement opposes the ruling class's unlawful terror based on law), or is democracy so integral to socialism that it cannot be omitted until one clarifies its moral and ideological consequences? Without this clarification, the repudiation of the principles of democracy constitutes a grave ethical problem for every responsible and rational socialist.

Marx's philosophy of history has seldom been properly and deliberately separated from his sociology. As a result, it has escaped many people's attention that Marxism's two principal tenets, class struggle and class division, and with it the creation of a non-oppressive socialist state, no matter how closely related they are, do not constitute a single concept. The first tenet states the cardinal historical fact of Marxist sociology:[2] until now the social order always existed and its causes always existed by necessity; this is the most important fact in the real disposition of social relations. The other tenet is that utopian postulate of the Marxist philosophy of history: the ethical prescription for the coming world order. (Marx's Hegelianism, which projects the various aspects of reality on to a single plane, had something to do with blurring this distinction.) In short, the proletarian class struggle, whose appointed task is to create a new world order, *qua* class struggle, does not yet contain this world order.[3] Just because the emancipation of the proletariat puts an end to capitalist class rule, it does not follow that all class rule ceases, just as it did not cease with the triumph of the bourgeois wars of liberation. In terms of pure sociological necessity, the emancipation of the proletariat merely inverts the class structure, the ruled become the rulers. Though the indispensable precondition for preventing its occurrence, and thus inaugurating the realm of freedom without rulers and ruled, is the victory of the proletariat – whose victory liberates the last oppressed class – it is but a precondition, and a negative one at that. This realm of freedom transcends sociological postulates and laws, it presupposes the will to a world order; a democratic world order.[4] However, this will – precisely because it cannot be derived from any sociological fact – forms such an integral part of the socialist world view, that it cannot be removed without endangering the collapse of the whole edifice. The will to new order designates the proletariat as the socialist redeemers of humanity, the messianic class of world history.

Without this messianic pathos, the unprecedented triumphal march of social democracy would have been inconceivable. Engels had every right to see in the proletariat the successor of German classical philosophy. That ethical idealism which broke all its earthly bonds, and which Kantian–Fichtean thought utilized in its attempt to lift the old world off its hinges – metaphysically – that idealism became a deed in Marxism. But what became a deed in Marxism was but a thought in Kant and Fichte; Marx's ethical idealism took a straight line to its goal, while in Schelling's aesthetics and in Hegel's philosophy of state, it deviated from the path of progress and became reactionary.

Marx may have modelled his philosophy of history on the Hegelian image of *List der Idee*, namely that the proletariat, fighting for its own class interest, creates a world free of tyranny. When the moment of decision arrives – and that moment has arrived – it is impossible not to see the divorce between soulless empirical reality and the human, utopian ethical will. And then one must decide whether socialism indeed personifies the will and power to redeem this world – or whether socialism is really just an ideological cover for class interest, which differs from other class interests only in content, but not qualitatively or in terms of ethical legitimacy. (The eighteenth-century bourgeois liberal ideals of universal rights also proclaimed and believed in the transformation of the world, e.g., free trade; but that these rights were a class-based ideology was revealed in the French Revolution – the moment of decision.)

In other words, if a state recognized no class rule, if pure social democracy was no more than an ideology, then one could hardly talk here about ethical questions, and ethical dilemmas. The ethical question arises precisely because social democracy's real and final goal, the one that determines and crowns everything is that the proletarian class struggle has an ultimate value: the end of all class struggle and the creation of a social order where the very idea of class struggle is inconceivable. At this moment [December 1918] it is seductively within our reach to realize this goal, but it is precisely the immediacy of the goal that gives rise to the ethical dilemma confronting us. We either seize the opportunity and realize communism, and then we must embrace dictatorship, terror and class oppression, and raise the proletariat to the position of ruling class in place of class-rule as we have known it, convinced that – just as Beelzebub chased out Satan –

this last form of class rule, by its very nature the cruelest and most naked, will destroy itself, and with it all class rule. Or we insist on creating a new world order with new means, the means of democracy (for real democracy was but a demand and never a reality even in the so-called democratic states), and thereby run the risk that most of humanity is disinterested in the new world. And if we are subsequently unwilling to impose our will on humanity, we must wait and while waiting continue to instruct others and spread the faith until humanity's own conscience and will gives birth to what its conscious members have already known for a long time as the only possible solution.

The source of the ethical dilemma is that each of these positions conceals and succours potentially terrifying sins and countless errors which must be shouldered by those who want to decide in one way or other. The danger inherent in the second position is quite clear: it means the necessity – temporary – of collaborating with classes and parties that, though they agree with some of the direct goals of social democracy, none the less remain hostile to its ultimate goal. The task: find a form of collaboration which would make this possible, without social democracy endangering the purity of its goals in any way, and the true pathos of its will to self-realization. Here the danger and the possibility of getting lost is this. It is extremely difficult, if not impossible, to prevent our deviation from the straight path of conviction becoming a self-serving act, and our conscious delay in realizing our conviction having no adverse effect on the pathos of will. The dilemma which confronts socialism, with its demand for democracy, is the need for an external compromise which, as such, must not be internalized.

The key to Bolshevism's fascinating power is that it frees us from this compromise. But those who are mesmerized by Bolshevism may not be always fully conscious of what they have accepted in order to avoid the dilemma. Their dilemma can be stated as follows: can the good be achieved by evil means, and freedom by tyranny; can there be a new world if the means to its realization are only technically different from the rightly abhorred and abjured means of the old order? One could perhaps invoke here the axiomatic statement of Marxist sociology, namely, that history and the historical process of all hitherto existing society is always the history of class struggles, the struggle of rulers and ruled, and not even the proletariat is exempt from this 'law'. But if this is true, then – as we have already stated – the whole intellectual content of socialism, apart from fulfilling the material needs of the proletariat, remains only an ideology. And this is impossible. And because it is impossible, the historical axiom cannot be turned into an ethical tenet, the pillar of the new world. Because then we have to accept evil *as* evil, tyranny *as* tyranny, and class rule *as* class rule. And we must possess faith – the true *credo qua absurdum est* – that oppression will not precipitate as always the oppressed's struggle for power (an opportunity for new tyranny) – and so on, in an endless, senseless chain of struggle – but rather lead to the self-negation of oppression.

The question of faith therefore, like every ethical question, involves a choice between two alternatives. According to some sharp-eyed observers, though in this case rather superficial ones, the loss of faith in socialism explains why so many old, battle-tested socialists refuse to identify with the Bolshevik position. I confess I do not share this belief. For I do not believe one needs more faith for the 'sudden heroism' of choosing Bolshevism, than one needs for siding with the rather sluggish, seemingly non-heroic democracy, with its profound demand for responsibility, and long struggles that instruct and educate. In Bolshevism the individual can, if he so desires, preserve – no matter at what cost – the apparent purity of his conviction. In democracy, the individual consciously surrenders his conviction so that, though he sacrifices himself, social democracy as a whole can be realized; not only its parts, not merely a fragment of its lost centre.

Let me repeat: Bolshevism rests on the metaphysical assumption that good can issue from evil, that it is possible, as Razumikhin says in *Crime and Punishment*, to lie our way through to the truth. This writer cannot share this faith and therefore sees at the root of Bolshevism an insoluble ethical dilemma. Democracy in his view requires only superhuman self-abnegation and self-sacrifice from those who, consciously and honestly, persevere to the very end. But this, though it requires a superhuman effort, is not in essence such an insoluble question as is Bolshevism's moral problem.

NOTES

[1] The Bolshevik seizure of power in Russia in November 1917 had a galvanizing effect on intellectual circles in Hungary. The radical journal *Szabadgondolat* [Free Thought], edited by Karl Polányi, devoted a special December 1918 issue to the 'great Russian transformation'. Polányi invited leading sociologists like Oscár Jászi and intellectuals, including Lukács, close friend of Polányi, to evaluate Lenin's communist experiment. The ever pragmatic Jászi proposed sending 'experts' to Russia to make an on-the-spot study of a society in the 'most advanced' state of

crisis. Jászi wanted to use the hard 'facts' gathered in Lenin's Russia to counteract the hotheads in Budapest. For his contribution to the debate on Bolshevism, Lukács chose the title 'Bolshevism as a Moral Problem'.

2 Lukács here takes issue with Marx who, in a letter to his friend Joseph Weydemeyer, wrote: 'What I did that was new was to prove: 1) that the existence of classes is only bound up with the particular historical phases in the development of production, 2) that the class struggle necessarily leads to the dictatorship of the proletariat, 3) that this dictatorship itself only constitutes the transition to the abolition of all classes and to a classless society.' Robert C. Tucker, ed., *The Marx-Engels Reader* (New York: W. W. Norton, 1978), p. 220.

3 Lukács clearly dissents from Marx who, in *The Holy Family: A Critique of Critical Criticism*, argued that the socialist future is prefigured in the very existence of the proletariat and its situation. As Marx put it, the proletariat 'cannot liberate itself without destroying its own living conditions. It cannot do so without destroying all the inhuman living conditions of contemporary society which are concentrated in its own situation.' *The Marx-Engels Reader*, p. 134.

4 Whereas to Marx the raising of the proletariat to the position of ruling class presages the victory of democracy, to Lukács democracy or, more precisely, the ethical will to democracy, is antithetical to making the proletariat the ruling class. See Marx-Engels, *The Communist Manifesto* (Penguin, 1967), especially chapter 2: 'Proletarians and Communists'.

19

Class Consciousness

> The question is not what goal is *envisaged* for the time being by this or that member of the proletariat, or even by the proletariat as a whole. The question is *what is the proletariat* and what course of action will it be forced historically to take in conformity with its own *nature*.
>
> Marx *The Holy Family*

Marx's chief work breaks off just as he is about to embark on the definition of class. This omission was to have serious consequences both for the theory and the practice of the proletariat. For in this vital point the later movement was forced to base itself on interpretations, on the collation of occasional utterances by Marx and Engels and on the independent extrapolation and application of their method. In Marxism the division of society into classes is determined by their position within the process of production. But what, then, is the meaning of class consciousness? The question at once branches out into a series of closely interrelated problems. First of all, how are we to understand class consciousness (in theory)? Second, what is the (practical) function of class consciousness, so understood, in the context of the class struggle? This leads to the further question: is the problem of class consciousness a 'general' sociological problem or does it mean one thing for the proletariat and another for every other class that has hitherto emerged? And lastly, is class consciousness homogeneous in nature and function or can we discern different gradations and levels in it? And if so, what are their practical implications for the class struggle of the proletariat?

I

In his celebrated account of historical materialism[1] Engels proceeds from the assumption that although the essence of history consists in the fact that 'nothing happens without a conscious purpose or an intended aim', to understand history it is necessary to go further than this. For on the one hand, 'the many individual wills active in history for the most part produce results quite other than those intended – often quite the opposite; *their motives, therefore, in relation to the total result are likewise of only secondary importance.* On the other hand, the further question arises: *what driving forces in turn stand behind these motives?* What are the historical causes which transform themselves into these motives in the brain of the actors?' He goes on to argue that these driving forces ought themselves to be determined, in particular those which 'set in motion great masses, whole people and again whole classes of the people; and which create *a lasting action resulting in a great transformation.*' The essence of scientific Marxism consists, then, in the realization that the real driving forces of history are independent of man's (psychological) consciousness.

At a more primitive stage of knowledge this independence takes the form of the belief that these forces belong, as it were, to nature and that in them and in their causal interactions it is possible to discern the 'eternal' laws of nature. As Marx says of bourgeois thought:

> Reflections on the forms of human life, hence also scientific analysis of those forms, takes a course directly opposite to their real development. Reflection begins *post festum* [after the feast], and therefore with the results of the process of development ready to hand. The forms which stamp products as commodities and which are therefore the preliminary requirements for the circulation of commodities, already possess the fixed quantity of natural forms of social life before man seeks to give an account, not of their historical character, for in his eyes they are immutable, but of their content and meaning.[2]

This is dogma whose most important spokesman can be found in the political theory of classical German philosophy and in the economic theory of Adam Smith and Ricardo. Marx opposes to them a critical philosophy, a theory of theory and a consciousness of consciousness. This critical philosophy implies above all historical criticism. It dissolves the rigid, unhistorical, natural appearance of social institutions; it reveals their historical origins and shows therefore that they are subject to history in every respect including historical decline. Consequently history does not merely unfold *within* the terrain mapped out by these institutions. It does not resolve itself into the evolution of *contents*, of men and situations, etc., while the *principles* of society remain eternally valid. Nor are these institutions the *goal* to which all history aspires, such that when they are realized history will have fulfilled her mission and will then be at an end. On the contrary, history is precisely *the history of these institutions*, of the changes they undergo as institutions which bring men together in societies. Such institutions start by controlling economic relations between men and go on to permeate all human relations (and hence also man's relations with himself and with nature, etc.).

At this point bourgeois thought comes up against an insuperable obstacle, for its starting point and its goal are always, if not always consciously, an apologia for the existing order of things or at least the proof of their immutability.[3] 'Thus there has been history, but there is no longer any,'[4] Marx observes with reference to bourgeois economics, a dictum which applies with equal force to all attempts by bourgeois thinkers to understand the process of history. (It has often been pointed out that this is also one of the defects of Hegel's philosophy of history.) As a result, while bourgeois thought is indeed able to conceive history as a problem, it remains an *intractable* problem. Either it is forced to abolish the process of history and regard the institutions of the present as eternal laws of nature which for 'mysterious' reasons and in a manner wholly at odds with the principles of a rational science were held to have failed to establish themselves firmly, or indeed at all, in the past. (This is characteristic of bourgeois sociology.) Or else, everything meaningful or purposive is banished from history. It then becomes impossible to advance beyond the mere 'individuality' of the various epochs and their social and human representatives. History must then insist with Ranke that every age is 'equally close to God', i.e., has attained an equal degree of perfection and that – for quite different reasons – there is no such thing as historical development.

In the first case it ceases to be possible to understand the *origin* of social institutions.[5] The objects of history appear as the objects of immutable, eternal laws of nature. History becomes fossilized in a *formalism* incapable of comprehending that the real nature of socio-historical institutions is that they consist of *relations between men*. On the contrary, men become estranged from this, the true source of historical understanding and cut off from it by an unbridgeable gulf. As Marx points out,[6] people fail to realize 'that these determined social relations are as much produced by men as are the cloth, the linen, etc.'

In the second case, history is transformed into the irrational rule of blind forces which is embodied at best in the 'spirit of the people' or in 'great men'. It can therefore only be described pragmatically but it cannot be rationally understood. Its only possible organization would be aesthetic, as if it were a work of art. Or else, as in the philosophy of history of the Kantians, it must be seen as the instrument, senseless in itself, by means of which timeless, suprahistorical, ethical principles are realized.

Marx resolves this dilemma by exposing it as an illusion. The dilemma means only that the contradictions of the capitalist system of production are reflected in these mutually incompatible accounts of the same object. For in this historiography with its search for 'sociological' laws or its formalistic rationale, we find the reflection of man's plight in bourgeois society and of his helpless enslavement by the forces of production. 'Their own movement within society', Marx remarks[7] 'has for them the form of a movement made by things, and these things, far from being under their control, in fact control them.' This law was expressed most clearly and coherently in the purely natural and rational laws of classical economics. Marx retorted with the demand for a historical critique of economics which resolves the totality of the reified objectivities of social and economic life into *relations between men*. Capital and with it every form in which the national economy objectifies itself is, according to Marx, 'not a thing but a social relation between persons mediated through things.'

However, by reducing the objectivity of the social institutions so hostile to man to relations between men, Marx also does away with the false implications of the irrationalist and individualist principle, i.e. the other side of the dilemma. For to eliminate the objectivity attributed both to social institutions inimical to man and to their historical evolution means the restoration of this objectivity to their underlying basis, to the relations between men; it does not involve the elimination of laws and objectivity independent of the will of man and in particular the wills and thoughts of individual men. It simply means that this objectivity is the self-objectification of human society at a particular stage in its development; its laws hold good only within the framework of the historical context which produced them and which is in turn determined by them.

It might look as though by dissolving the dilemma in this manner we were denying consciousness any decisive role in the process of history. It is true that the conscious reflexes of the different stages of economic growth remain historical facts of great importance; it is true that while dialectical materialism is itself the product of this process, it does not deny that men perform their historical deeds themselves and that they do so consciously. But as Engels emphasizes in a letter to Mehring,[8] this consciousness is false. However, the dialectical method does not permit us simply to proclaim the 'falseness' of this consciousness and to persist in an inflexible confrontation of true and false. On the contrary, it requires us to investigate this 'false consciousness' concretely as an aspect of the historical totality and as a stage in the historical process.

Of course bourgeois historians also attempt such concrete analyses; indeed they reproach historical materialists with violating the concrete uniqueness of historical events. Where they go wrong is in their belief that the concrete can be located in the empirical individual of history ('individual' here can refer to an individual man, class or people) and in his empirical given (and hence psychological or mass-psychological) consciousness. And just when they imagine that they have discovered the most concrete thing of all: *society as a concrete totality*, the system of production at a given point in history and the resulting division of society into classes – they are in fact at the furthest remove from it. In missing the mark they mistake something wholly abstract for the concrete. 'These relations', Marx states, 'are not the relations of individual to individual, but of workman to capitalist, of farmer and landlord. Efface these relations and you have extinguished the whole of society, and your Prometheus is nothing more than a phantom without arms or legs . . .'[9]

Concrete analysis means then: the relation of society *as a whole*. For only when this relation is established does the consciousness of their existence that men have at any given time emerge in all its essential characteristics. It appears, on the one hand, as something which is *subjectively* justified in the social and historical situation, as something which can and should be understood, i.e., as 'right'. At the same time, *objectively*, it by-passes the essence of the evolution of society and fails to pinpoint it and express it adequately. That is to say, objectively, it appears as a 'false consciousness'. On the other hand, we may see the same consciousness as something which fails *subjectively* to reach its self-appointed goals, while furthering and realizing the *objective* aims of a society of which it is ignorant and which it did not choose.

This twofold dialectical determination of 'false consciousness' constitutes an analysis far removed from the naive description of what men *in fact* thought, felt and wanted at any moment in history and from any given point in the class struggle. I do not wish to deny the great importance of this, but it remains after all merely the *material* of genuine historical analysis. The relation with concrete totality and the dialectical determinants arising from it transcend pure description and yield the category of objective possibility. By relating consciousness to the whole of society it becomes possible to infer the thoughts and feelings which men would have in a particular situation if they were *able* to assess both it and the interests arising from it in their impact on immediate action and on the whole structure of society. That is to say, it would be possible to infer the thoughts and feelings appropriate to their objective situation. The number of such situations is not unlimited in any society. There will always be a number of clearly distinguished basic types whose characteristics are determined by the types of position available in the process of production, however much detailed research is able to refine social typologies. Now class consciousness consists in fact of the appropriate and rational reactions 'imputed' [*zugerechnet*] to a particular position typical in the process of production.[10] This consciousness is, therefore, neither the sum nor the average of what is thought or felt by the single individuals who make up the class. And yet the historically significant actions of the class as a whole are determined in the last resort by this consciousness and not by the thought of the individual – and these actions can be understood only by reference to this consciousness.

This analysis establishes right from the start the distance that separates class consciousness from the empirically given, and from the psychologically describable and explicable ideas which men form about their situation in life. But it is not enough just to state that this distance exists or even to define its implications in a formal and general way. We must discover, firstly, whether it is a phenomenon that differs according to the manner in which the various classes are related to society as a whole and whether the differences are so great as to produce *qualitative distinctions*. And we must discover, secondly, the *practical* significance of these different possible relations between the objective economic totality, the imputed class consciousness and the real, psychological thoughts of men about their lives. We must discover, in short, the *practical, historical function* of class consciousness.

Only after such preparatory formulations can we begin to exploit the category of objective possibility systematically. The first question we must ask is how far is it *in fact* possible to discern the whole economy of a society from inside it? It is essential to transcend the limitations of particular individuals caught up in their narrow prejudices. But it is no less vital not to overstep the frontier fixed for them by the economic structure of society and their position in it.[11] Regarded abstractly and formally, then, class consciousness implies a class-conditioned *unconsciousness* of one's own socio-historical and economic condition.[12] This condition is given as a definite structural relation, a definite formal nexus which appears to govern the whole of life. The 'falseness', the illusion implicit in this situation is in no sense arbitrary; it is simply the intellectual reflection of the objective economic structure. Thus, for example, 'the value or price of labour-power takes on the appearance of the price or value of labour itself . . .' and 'the illusion is created that the totality is paid labour . . . In contrast to that, under slavery even that portion of labour which is paid for appears unpaid for.'[13] Now it requires the most painstaking historical analysis to use the category of objective possibility so as to isolate the conditions in which this illusion can be exposed and a real connection with the totality established. For if from the vantage point of a particular class the totality of existing society is not visible; if a class thinks the thoughts imputable to it and which bear upon its interests right through to their logical conclusion and yet fails to strike at the heart of that totality, then such a class is doomed to play only a subordinate role. It can never influence the course of history in either a conservative or progressive direction. Such classes are normally condemned to passivity, to an unstable oscillation between the ruling and the revolutionary classes, and if perchance they do erupt then such explosions are purely elemental and aimless. They may win a few battles but they are doomed to ultimate defeat.

For a class to be ripe for hegemony means that its interests and consciousness enable it to organize the whole of society in accordance with those interests. The crucial question in every class struggle is this: which class possesses this capacity and this consciousness at the decisive moment? This does not preclude the use of force. It does not mean that the class interests destined to prevail and thus to uphold the interests of society as a whole can be guaranteed an automatic victory. On the contrary, such a transfer of power can often be brought about only by the most ruthless use of force (as, e.g., the primitive accumulation of capital). But it often turns out that questions of class consciousness prove to be decisive in just those situations where force is unavoidable and where classes are locked in a life-and-death struggle. Thus the noted Hungarian Marxist Ervin Szabó is mistaken in criticizing Engels for maintaining that the Great Peasant War (of 1525) was essentially a reactionary movement. Szabó argues that the peasants' revolt was suppressed *only* by the ruthless use of force and that its defeat was not grounded in socio-economic factors and in the class consciousness of the peasants. He overlooks the fact that the deepest reason for the weakness of the peasantry and the superior strength of the princes is to be sought in class consciousness. Even the most cursory student of the military aspects of the Peasant War can easily convince himself of this.

It must not be thought, however, that all classes ripe for hegemony have a class consciousness with the same inner structure. Everything hinges on the extent to which they can become conscious of the actions they need to perform in order to obtain and organize power. The question then becomes: how far does the class concerned perform the actions history has imposed on it 'consciously' or 'unconsciously'? And is that consciousness 'true' or 'false'? These distinctions are by no means academic. Quite apart from problems of culture where such fissures and dissonances are crucial, in all practical matters too the fate of a class depends on its ability to elucidate and solve the problems with which history confronts it. And here it becomes transparently obvious that class consciousness is concerned neither with the thoughts of individuals, however advanced, nor with the state of scientific knowledge. For example, it is quite clear that ancient society was broken economically by the limitations of a system built on slavery. But it is equally clear that neither the ruling classes nor the classes that rebelled against them in the name of revolution or reform could perceive this. In consequence the practical emergence of these problems meant that the society was necessarily and irremediably doomed.

The situation is even clearer in the case of the modern bourgeoisie, which, armed with the knowledge of the workings of economics, clashes with feudal and absolutist society. For the bourgeoisie is quite unable to perfect its fundamental science, its own science of classes: the reef on which it founders is its failure to discover even a theoretical solution to the problem of crises. The fact that a scientifically acceptable solution does exist is of no avail. For to accept that solution, even in theory, would be tantamount to observing society *from a class standpoint other than that of the bourgeoisie*. And no class can do that – unless it is willing to abdicate its power freely. Thus the barrier which converts the class consciousness of the bourgeoisie into 'false' consciousness is objective; it is the class situation itself. It is the objective result of the economic set-up, and is neither arbitrary, subjective nor psychological. The class consciousness of the bourgeoisie may well be able to reflect all the problems of organization entailed by its hegemony and by the capitalist transformation and penetration of total production. But it becomes obscured as soon as it is called upon to face problems that remain within its jurisdiction but which point beyond the limits of capitalism. The discovery of the 'natural laws' of economics is pure light in comparison with medieval feudalism or even the mercantilism of the transitional period, but by an internal dialectical twist they become 'natural laws based on the unconsciousness of those who are involved in them'.[14] [. . .]

II

It follows from the above that for pre-capitalist epochs and for the behaviour of many strata within capitalism whose economic roots lie in pre-capitalism, class consciousness is unable to achieve complete clarity and to influence the course of history consciously.

This is true above all because class interests in pre-capitalist society never achieve full (economic) articulation. Hence the structuring of society into classes and estates means that economic elements are *inextricably* joined to political and religious factors. In contrast to this, the rule of the bourgeoisie means the abolition of the estates system and this leads to the organization of society along class lines . . .

This situation has its roots in the profound difference between capitalist and pre-capitalist economics. The most striking distinction, and the one that directly concerns us, is that pre-capitalist societies are much less *cohesive* than capitalist societies. The various parts are much more self-sufficient and less closely interrelated than in capitalism. Commerce plays a smaller role in society, the various sectors are more autonomous (as in the case of village communes) or else play no part at all in the economic life of the community and the process of production (as was true of large numbers of citizens in Greece and Rome). In such circumstances, the state, i.e., the organized unity, remains insecurely anchored in the real life of society. One sector of society simply lives out its 'natural' existence in what amounts to total independence of the fate of the state.

> The simplicity of the productive organism of these self-sufficing communities which constantly reproduce themselves in the same form and, when accidentally destroyed, spring up again on the same spot and with the same name – this simplicity supplies the key to the riddle of the unchangeability of Asiatic societies, which is in such striking contrast to the constant dissolution and refounding of Asiatic states, and never-ceasing changes of dynasty. The structure of the fundamental economic elements of society remains untouched by the storms which blow up in the cloudy regions of politics.[15]

Even commerce is not able, in the forms it assumes in pre-capitalist societies, to make decisive inroads into the basic structure of society. Its impact remains superficial and the process of production above all in relation to labour, remains beyond its control. 'The merchant could buy every commodity, but labour as a commodity he could not buy. He existed only on sufferance, as a dealer in the products of handicrafts.'[16]

Despite all this, every such society constitutes an economic unity. The only question that arises is whether this unity enables the individual sectors of society to relate to society as a whole in such a way that their imputed consciousness can assume an economic form. Marx emphasizes[17] that in Greece and Rome the class struggle 'chiefly took the form of a conflict between debtors and creditors'. But he also makes the further, very valid point: 'Nevertheless, the money-relationship – and the relationship of creditor to debtor is one of money – reflects only the deeper antagonism between the economic conditions of existence.' Historical materialism showed that this reflection was no more than a reflection, but we must go on to ask: was it at all possible – objectively – for the classes in such a society to become conscious of the economic basis of these conflicts and of the economic problems with which the society was afflicted? Was it not inevitable that these conflicts and problems should assume either natural, religious forms,[18] or else political and legal ones, depending on circumstances?

[. . .] Thus class consciousness has quite a different relation to history in pre-capitalist and capitalist periods. In the former case the classes could only be deduced from the immediately given historical reality *by the method of historical materialism*. In capitalism they themselves constitute this immediately given historical *reality*. It is therefore no accident that (as Engels too has pointed out) this knowledge of history only became possible with the advent of capitalism. Not only – as Engels believed – because of the greater simplicity of capitalism in contrast to the 'complex and concealed relations' of earlier ages. But primarily because only with capitalism does capitalist class interest emerge in all its starkness as the motor of history. In pre-capitalist periods man could never become conscious (not even by virtue of an 'imputed' consciousness) of the 'true driving forces which stand behind the motives of human actions in history'. They remained hidden behind motives and were in truth the blind forces of history. Ideological factors do not merely 'mask' economic interests, they are not merely the banners and slogans: they are the parts, the components of which the real struggle is made. Of course, if historical materialism is deployed to discover the *sociological meaning* of these struggles, economic interests will doubtless be revealed as the decisive factors in any explanations.

But there is still an unbridgeable gulf between this and capitalism where economic factors are not concealed 'behind' consciousness but are present *in* consciousness itself (albeit unconsciously or repressed). With capitalism, with the abolition of the feudal estates and with the creation of a society with a *purely economic* articulation, class consciousness arrived at the point where *it could become conscious*. From then on social conflict was reflected in an ideological struggle for consciousness and for the veiling or the exposure of the class character of society. But the fact that this conflict became possible points forward to the dialectical contradictions and the internal dissolution of pure class society. In Hegel's words, 'When philosophy paints its gloomy picture a form of life has grown old. It cannot be rejuvenated by the gloomy picture, but only understood. Only when the dusk starts to fall does the owl of Minerva spreads its wings and fly.'

III

Bourgeoisie and proletariat are the only pure classes in bourgeois society. They are the only classes whose existence and development are entirely dependent on the course taken by the modern evolution of production and only from the vantage point of these classes can a plan for total organization of society *even be imagined*. The outlook of the other classes (petit-bourgeoisie or peasants) is ambiguous or sterile because their existence is not based exclusively on their role in the capitalist system of production but is indissolubly linked with the vestiges of feudal society. Their aim, therefore, is not to advance capitalism or to transcend it, but to reverse its action or at least to prevent it from developing fully. Their class interest concentrates on the *symptoms of development* and not on development itself, and on elements of society rather than on the construction of society as a whole.

The question of consciousness may make its appearance in terms of the objectives chosen or in terms of action, as for instance in the case of the petit-bourgeoisie. This class lives at least in part in the capitalist big city and every aspect of its existence is directly exposed to the influence of capitalism. Hence it cannot possibly remain wholly unaffected by the *fact* of class conflict between bourgeoisie and proletariat. But the 'democrat, because he represents the petit-bourgeoisie, that is, a *transition class*, in which the interests of the two classes are simultaneously, mutually blunted, imagines himself elevated above class antagonism generally.'[19] Accordingly he will search for ways whereby he will 'not indeed eliminate the two extremes of capital and wage labour, but will weaken their antagonism and transform it into harmony.'[20] In all decisions crucial to society its actions will be irrelevant and it will be forced to fight on both sides in turn but always without consciousness. In so doing its own objectives – which exist exclusively in its own consciousness – must become progressively weakened and increasingly divorced from social action. Ultimately they will assume purely 'ideological' forms. The petit bourgeoisie will only be able to play an active role in history as long as these objectives happen to coincide with the real economic interests of capitalism. This was the case with the abolition of the feudal estates during the French Revolution. With the fulfilment of this mission its utterances, which for the most part remain unchanged in form, become more and more remote from the real events and finally turned into mere caricatures (this was true, e.g., of the Jacobinism of the Montagne 1818–51).

[. . .] The tragedy of the bourgeoisie is reflected historically in the fact that even before it had defeated its predecessor, feudalism, its new enemy, the proletariat, had appeared on the scene. Politically it became evident when, at the moment of victory, the 'freedom' in whose name the bourgeoisie had joined battle with feudalism was transformed into a new repressiveness. Sociologically, the bourgeoisie did everything in its power to eradicate the fact of class conflict from the consciousness of society, even though class conflict had only emerged in its purity and become established as an historical fact with the advent of capitalism. Ideologically, we see the same contradiction in the fact that the bourgeoisie endowed the individual with an unprecedented importance, but at the same time that same individuality was annihilated by the economic conditions to which it was subjected, by the reification created by commodity production.

All these contradictions, and the list might be extended indefinitely, are only the reflection of the deepest contradictions in capitalism itself as they appear in the consciousness of the bourgeoisie in accordance with their position in the total system of production. For this reason they appear as dialectical contradictions in the class consciousness of the bourgeoisie. They do not merely reflect the inability of the bourgeoisie to grasp the contradictions inherent in its own social order. For, on the other hand, capitalism is the first system of production able to achieve a total economic penetration of society[21] and this implies that in theory the bourgeoisie should be able to progress from this central point to the possession of an (imputed) class consciousness of the whole system of production. On the other hand, the position held by the capitalist class and the interests which determine its actions ensure that it will be unable to control its own system of production even in theory.

There are many reasons for this. In the first place, it seems to be true that only for capitalism does production occupy the centre of class consciousness and hence provide the theoretical starting point for analysis. With reference to Ricardo, 'who had been reproached with an exclusive concern with production', Marx emphasized[22] that he 'defined distribution as the sole subject of economics'. And the detailed analysis of the process by which capital is concretely realized shows in every single instance that the interest of the capitalist (who produces not goods but commodities) is necessarily confined to matters that must be peripheral in terms of production. Moreover, the capitalist, enmeshed in what is for him the decisive process of the expansion of capital, must have a standpoint from which the most important problems become quite invisible.[23]

The discrepancies that result are further exacerbated by the fact that there is an insoluble contradiction running through the internal structure of capitalism between the social and the individual principle, i.e., between the function of capital as private property and its objective economic function. As the *Communist Manifesto* states: 'Capital is a social force and not a personal one.' But it is a social force whose movements are determined by the individual interests of the owners of capital – who cannot see and who are necessarily indifferent to all the social implications of their activities. Hence the social principle and the social function implicit in capital can only prevail unbeknown to them and, as it were, against their will and behind their backs. Because of this conflict between the individual and the social, Marx rightly characterized the stock companies as the 'negation of the capitalist mode of production itself'.[24] Of course, it is true that stock companies differ only in inessentials from individual capitalists and even the so-called abolition of the anarchy of production through cartels and trusts only shifts the contradiction elsewhere without, however, eliminating it. This situation forms one of the decisive factors governing the class consciousness of the bourgeoisie. It is true that the bourgeoisie acts as a class in the objective evolution of society. But it understands the process (which it is itself instigating) as something external which is subject to objective laws which it can only experience passively.

Bourgeois thought observes economic life consistently and necessarily from the standpoint of the individual capitalist and this naturally produces a sharp confrontation between the individual and the overpowering supra-personal 'law of nature' which propels all social phenomena.[25] This leads both to the antagonism between individual and class interests in the event of conflict (which, it is true, rarely becomes as acute among the ruling classes as in the bourgeoisie), and also to the logical impossibility of discovering theoretical and practical solutions to the problems created by the capitalist system of production.

> The *summum bonum*, the sole form of wealth for which people clamour at such times, is money, hard cash, and compared with it all other commodities – just because they are use-values – appear to be useless, mere baubles and toys, as our Doctor Martin Luther says, mere ornament and gluttony. This sudden transformation of the credit system into a monetary system adds theoretical dismay to the actually existing panic, and the agents of the circulation process are overawed by the impenetrable mystery surrounding their own relations.[26]

This terror is not unfounded, that is to say, it is much more than the bafflement felt by the individual capitalist when confronted by his own individual fate. The facts and the situations which induce this panic force something into the consciousness of the bourgeoisie which is too much of a brute fact for its existence to be wholly denied or repressed. But equally it is something that the bourgeoisie can never fully understand. For the recognizable background to this situation is the fact that 'the *real barrier* of capitalist production is *capital itself*'.[27] And if this insight were to become conscious it would indeed entail the self-negation of the capitalist class.

In this way the objective limits of capitalist production become the limits of the class consciousness of the bourgeoisie. The older 'natural' and 'conservative' forms of domination had left unmolested the forms of production of whole sections of the people they ruled and therefore exerted by and large a traditional and unrevolutionary influence. Capitalism, by contrast, is a revolutionary form *par excellence. The fact that it must necessarily remain in ignorance of the objective economic limitations of its own system expresses itself as an internal, dialectical contradiction in its class consciousness.*

This means that *formally* the class consciousness of the bourgeoisie is geared to economic consciousness. And indeed the highest degree of unconsciousness, the crassest form of 'false consciousness' always manifests itself when the conscious mastery of economic phenomena appears to be at its greatest. From the point of view of the relation of consciousness to society this contradiction is expressed as the *irreconcilable antagonism between ideology and economic base.* Its dialectics are grounded in the irreconcilable antagonism between the (capitalist) individual, i.e., the stereotyped individual of capitalism, and the 'natural' and inevitable process of development, i.e., the process not subject to consciousness. In consequence theory and practice are brought into irreconcilable opposition to each other. But the resulting dualism is anything but stable; in fact it constantly strives to harmonize principles that have been wrenched apart and thenceforth oscillate between a new 'false' synthesis and its subsequent cataclysmic disruption.

This internal dialectical contradiction in the class consciousness of the bourgeoisie is further aggravated by the fact that the objective limits of capitalism do not remain purely negative. That is to say that capitalism does not merely set 'natural' laws in motion that provoke crises which it cannot comprehend. On the contrary, those limits acquire a historical embodiment with its own consciousness and its own actions: the proletariat.

Most 'normal' shifts of perspective produced by the capitalist point of view in the image of the economic structure of society tend to 'obscure and mystify the true origin of surplus value'.[28] In the 'normal', purely theoretical view this mystification only attaches to the organic composition of capital, namely to the place of the employer in the productive system and the economic function of interest, etc. In other words, it does no more than highlight the failure of observers to perceive the true driving forces that lie beneath the surface. But when it comes to practice this mystification touches upon the central fact of capitalist society: the class struggle.

In the class struggle we witness the emergence of all the hidden forces that usually lie concealed behind the façade of economic life, at which the capitalists and their apologists gaze as though transfixed. These forces appear in such a way that they cannot possibly be ignored. So much so that even when capitalism was in the ascendant and the proletariat could only give vent to its protests in the form of vehement spontaneous explosions, even the ideological exponents of the rising bourgeoisie acknowledged the class struggle as a basic fact of history. (For example, Marat and later historians such as Mignet.) But in proportion as the theory and practice of the proletariat made society conscious of this unconscious, revolutionary principle inherent in capitalism, the bourgeoisie was thrown back increasingly on to a conscious defensive. The dialectical contradiction in the 'false' consciousness of the bourgeoisie became more and more acute: the 'false' consciousness was converted into a mendacious consciousness. What had been at first an objective contradiction now became subjective also: the theoretical problem turned a moral posture which decisively influenced every practical class attitude in every situation and on every issue.

Thus the situation in which the bourgeoisie finds itself determines the function of its class consciousness in its struggle to achieve control of society. The hegemony of the bourgeoisie really does embrace the whole of society; it really does attempt to organize the whole of society in its own interests (and in this it has had success). To achieve this it was forced both to develop a coherent theory of economics, politics and society (which in itself presupposes and amounts to a '*Weltanschauung*'), and also to make conscious and sustain its faith in its own *mission* to control and organize society. The tragic dialectics of the bourgeoisie can be seen in the fact that it is not only desirable but essential for it to clarify its own class interests on *every particular issue*, while at the same time such a clear awareness becomes fatal when it is extended to *the question of the totality*. The chief reason for this is that the rule of the bourgeoisie can only be the rule of a minority. Its hegemony is exercised not merely *by* a minority but *in the interest* of that minority, so the need to deceive the other classes and to ensure that their class consciousness remains amorphous is inescapable for a bourgeois regime. (Consider here the theory of the state that stands 'above' class antagonisms, or the notion of an 'impartial' system of justice.)

But the veil drawn over the nature of bourgeois society is indispensable to the bourgeoisie itself. For the insoluble internal contradictions of the system become revealed with increasing starkness and so confront its supporters with a choice. Either they must consciously ignore insights which become increasingly urgent or else they must suppress their own moral instincts in order to be able to support with a good conscience an economic system that serves their own interests.

Without overestimating the efficacy of such ideological factors it must be agreed that the fighting power of a class grows with its ability to carry out its own mission with a good conscience and to adapt all phenomena to its own interests with unbroken confidence in itself. If we consider Sismondi's criticism of classical economics, German criticism of natural law and the youthful critiques of Carlyle it becomes evident that from a very early stage the ideological history of the bourgeoisie was *nothing but a desperate resistance to every insight into the true nature of the society it had created and thus to a real understanding of its class situation.* When the *Communist Manifesto* makes the point that the bourgeoisie produces its own gravediggers this is valid ideologically as well as economically. The whole of bourgeois thought in the nineteenth century made the most strenuous efforts to mask the real foundations of bourgeois society; everything was tried: from the greatest falsification of fact to the 'sublime' theories about the 'essence' of history and the state. But in vain: with the end of the century the issue was resolved by the advances of science and their corresponding effects on the consciousness of the capitalist elite.

This can be seen very clearly in the bourgeoisie's greater readiness to accept the idea of conscious organization. A greater measure of concentration was achieved first in the stock companies and in the cartels and trusts. This process revealed the social character of capital more and more clearly without affecting the general anarchy of production. What it did was to confer near-monopoly on a number of giant individual capitalists. Objectively, then, the social character of capital was brought into play with great energy but in such a manner as to keep its nature concealed from the capitalist class. Indeed this illusory elimination of economic anarchy successfully diverted their attention from the true situation. With the crises of the War [1914] and the post-war period this tendency has advanced still further: the idea of a 'planned' economy has gained ground at least among the more progressive elements of the bourgeoisie. Admittedly this applies only within quite narrow strata of the bourgeoisie and even there it is thought of more as a theoretical experiment than as a practical way out of the impasse brought about by the crises.

When capitalism was still expanding it rejected every sort of social organization on the grounds that it was 'an inroad upon such sacred things as the rights of property, freedom and unrestricted play of the initiative of the individual capitalist.'[29] If we compare that with the current attempts to harmonize a 'planned' economy with the class interests of the bourgeoisie, we are forced to admit that what we are witnessing is *the capitulation of the class consciousness of the bourgeoisie before that of the proletariat*. Of course, the section of the bourgeoisie that accepts the notion of a 'planned' economy does not mean the same by it as does the proletariat: which regards it as a last attempt to save capitalism by driving its internal contradictions to breaking point. Nevertheless this means jettisoning the last theoretical line of defence. (As a strange counterpart to this we may note that *at just this point in time* certain sectors of the proletariat *capitulate before the bourgeoisie* and adopt this, the most problematic form of bourgeois organization.)

With this the whole existence of the bourgeoisie and its culture is plunged into the most terrible crisis. On the one hand, we find the utter sterility of an ideology divorced from life, of a more or less conscious attempt at forgery. On the other hand, a jejune cynicism, no less terrible, lives on in the utter irrelevances and nullities of its own existence and its own naked self-interest. This ideological crisis is an unfailing sign of decay. The bourgeoisie has already been thrown on to the defensive; however aggressive its *weapons* may be, it is fighting for self-preservation. *Its power to dominate has vanished beyond recall.* [. . .]

IV

The relationship between class consciousness and class situation is really very simple in the case of the proletariat, but the obstacles which prevent its consciousness being realized in practice are correspondingly greater. In the first place this consciousness is divided within itself. It is true that society as such is highly unified and that it evolves in a unified manner. But in a world where the reified relations of capitalism have the appearance of a natural environment there does not appear to be unity but a diversity of mutually independent objects and forces.

The most striking division in proletarian class consciousness and the one most fraught with problems is the separation of the economic struggle from the political one. Marx repeatedly exposed the fallacy of this split and demonstrated that it is in the nature of every economic struggle to develop into a political one (and vice versa).[30] Nevertheless it has not proved possible to eradicate this heresy from the theory of the proletariat. The cause of this aberration is to be found in the dialectical separation of immediate objectives and ultimate goal and, hence, in the dialectical division within the proletarian revolution itself.

Classes that successfully carried out the revolution in earlier societies had their task made easier *subjectively* by this very fact of the discrepancy between their own class consciousness and the objective economic set-up; i.e., by their very unawareness of their own function in the process of change. They had only to use the power at their disposal to enforce their *immediate* interests while the social import of their actions was hidden from them and left to the 'ruse of reason' of the course of events.

But as the proletariat has been entrusted by history with the task of *transforming society consciously*, its class consciousness must develop a dialectical contradiction between its immediate interests and its long-term objectives, and between discrete factors and the whole. For the discrete factor, the concrete situation with its concrete demands is by its very nature an integral part of the existing capitalist society; it is governed by the laws of that society and is subject to its economic structure. Only when the immediate interests are integrated into a total view and related to the final goal of the process do they become revolutionary, pointing concretely and consciously beyond the confines of capitalist society.

This means that subjectively, i.e., for the class consciousness of the proletariat, the dialectical relationship between immediate interests and objective impact on the whole of society is located *in the consciousness of the proletariat itself*. It does not work itself out as a purely objective process quite apart from all (imputed) consciousness – as was the case with all classes hitherto. Thus the revolutionary victory of the proletariat does not imply, as with former classes, *the immediate realization of the socially given existence of the class*, but, as the young Marx already saw and defined, *its self-annihilation*. The *Communist Manifesto* formulates the distinction in this way: 'All the preceding classes that got the upper hand, sought to fortify their already acquired status by subjecting society at large to their conditions of appropriation. The proletarians cannot become masters of the productive forces of society, except *by abolishing their own previous mode of appropriation*, and thereby every other previous mode of appropriation.' (My italics.)

This inner dialectic makes it hard for the proletariat to develop its class consciousness in opposition to that of the bourgeoisie which, by cultivating the crudest and most abstract kind of empiricism, was able to make do with a superficial view of the world. Whereas even when the development of the proletariat was still at a very primitive stage it discovered that one of the elementary rules of class warfare was to advance beyond what was immediately given. [. . .]

The dialectical cleavage in the consciousness of the proletariat is a product of the same structure that makes the historical mission of the proletariat possible by pointing forward and beyond the existing social order. In the case of the other classes we found an antagonism between the class's self-interest and that of society, between individual deed and social consequences. This antagonism set an external limit on consciousness. Here, in the centre of proletarian class consciousness we discover an antagonism between momentary interest and ultimate goal. The outward victory of the proletariat can only be achieved if this antagonism is inwardly overcome.

As we stressed in the epigraph to this essay the existence of this conflict enables us to perceive that class consciousness is identical with neither the psychological consciousness of individual members of the proletariat, nor with the (mass-psychological) consciousness of the proletariat as a whole; but it is, on the contrary, *the sense, become conscious, of the historical role of the class*. This sense will crystallize into particular interests of the moment which may only be omitted at the price of allowing the proletarian class struggle to slip back into the most primitive utopianism. Every momentary interest may have one of two functions: either it will be a step towards the ultimate goal or else it will conceal it. Which of the two it will be depends *entirely upon the class consciousness of the proletariat and not on victory or defeat in isolated skirmishes*. Marx drew attention very early on to this danger, which is particularly acute on the economic 'trade union' front:

> At the same time the working class ought not to exaggerate to themselves the ultimate consequences of these struggles. They ought not to forget that they are fighting with effects, but not with the causes of those effects . . . that they are applying palliatives, not curing the malady. They ought, therefore, not to be exclusively absorbed in these unavoidable guerilla fights . . . instead of simultaneously trying to cure it, instead of using their organized forces as a lever for the final emancipation of the working class, that is to say, the ultimate abolition of the wages system.[31]

[. . .] To say that class consciousness has no psychological reality does not imply that it is a mere fiction. Its reality is vouched for by its ability to explain the infinitely painful path of the proletarian revolution, with its many reverses, its constant return to its starting point and the incessant self-criticism of which Marx speaks in the celebrated passage in *The Eighteenth Brumaire*.

Only the consciousness of the proletariat can point to the way that leads out of the impasse of capitalism. As long as this consciousness is lacking, the crisis remains permanent, it goes back to its starting point, repeats the cycle until after infinite sufferings and terrible detours the school of history completes the education of the proletariat and confers upon it the leadership of mankind. But the proletariat is not given any choice. As Marx says, it must become a class not only 'against capital' but also 'for itself'; that is to say, the class struggle must be raised from the level of economic necessity to the level of conscious aim and effective class consciousness. The pacifist and humanitarians of the class struggle whose efforts tend, whether they intend it or not, to retard this lengthy, painful and crisis-ridden process would be horrified if they could see what sufferings they inflict on the proletariat by extending this course of education. But the proletariat cannot abdicate its mission. The only question at issue is how much it has to suffer before it achieves ideological maturity, before it acquires a true understanding of its class situation and a true class consciousness.

Of course this uncertainty and lack of clarity are themselves the symptoms of the crisis in bourgeois society. As the product of capitalism the proletariat must necessarily be subject to the modes of existence of its creator. This mode of existence is inhumanity and reification. No doubt the very existence of the proletariat implies criticism and the negation of this form of life. But until the objective crisis of capitalism has matured and until the proletariat has achieved true class consciousness, and the ability to understand the crisis fully, it cannot go beyond the criticism of reification and so it is only negatively superior to its antagonists. Indeed, if it can do no more than negate some aspects of capitalism, if it cannot at least aspire to a critique of the whole, then it will not even achieve a negative superiority.
[. . .]

It would be foolish to believe that this criticism and the recognition that a post-utopian attitude to history has become *objectively possible* means that utopianism can be dismissed as a factor in the proletarian struggle for freedom. That is true only for those stages of class consciousness that have really achieved the unity of theory and practice described by Marx, the real and practical intervention of class consciousness in the course of history and hence the practical understanding of reification. And this did not all happen at a single stroke and in a coherent manner. For there are not merely national and 'social' stages involved but there are also gradations within the class consciousness of workers in the same strata. The separation of economics from politics is the most revealing and also the most important instance of this. It appears that some sections of the proletariat have absolutely the right instincts as far as the economic struggle goes and can even raise them to the level of class consciousness. At the same time, however, when it comes to political questions they manage to persist in a completely utopian point of view. It does not need to be emphasized that there is no question here of a mechanical duality. The utopian view of the function of politics must impinge dialectically on their views about economics and, in particular, on their notions about the economy as a totality (as, for example, in the Syndicalist theory of revolution). In the real absence of a real understanding of the interaction between politics and economics, a war against the whole economic system, to say nothing of its reorganization, is quite out of the question. [. . .]

These gradations are, then, on the one hand, objective historical necessities, nuances in the objective possibilities of consciousness (such as the relative cohesiveness of politics and economics in comparison to cultural questions). On the other hand, where consciousness already exists as an objective possibility, they indicate degrees of distance between the psychological class consciousness and the adequate understanding of the total situation. *These* gradations, however, can no longer be referred back to the socio-economic causes. *The objective theory of class consciousness is the theory of its objective possibility.* The stratification of the problems and economic interests *within* the proletariat is, unfortunately, almost wholly unexplored, but research would undoubtedly lead to discoveries of the very first importance. But however useful it would be to produce a typology of the various strata, we would still be confronted at every turn with the problem of whether it is actually possible to make the objective possibility of class consciousness into a reality. Hitherto the question could only occur to extraordinary individuals (consider Marx's completely non-utopian prescience with regard to the problems of dictatorship). Today [1920] it has become a real and relevant question for a whole class: the question of the inner transformation of the proletariat, of its development to the stage of achieving its own objective historical mission. It is an ideological crisis which must be solved before a practical solution to the world's economic crisis can be found.

In view of the great distance that the proletariat has to travel ideologically it would be disastrous to foster any illusions. But it would be no less disastrous to overlook the forces at work within the proletariat which are tending towards the ideological defeat of capitalism. Every proletarian revolution has created workers' councils in an increasingly radical and conscious manner. When this weapon increases in power to the point where it becomes the organ of the state, this is a sign that the class consciousness of the proletariat is on the verge of overcoming the bourgeois outlook of its leaders.

The revolutionary workers' council (not to be confused with its opportunist caricatures) is one of the forms which the consciousness of the proletariat has striven to create ever since its inception. The fact that it exists and is constantly developing shows that the proletariat already stands on the threshold of its own consciousness and hence on the threshold of victory. The workers' council spells the political and economic defeat of reification. In the period following the dictatorship it will eliminate the bourgeois separation of the legislature, administration and judiciary. During the struggle for control its mission is twofold. On the one hand, it must overcome the fragmentation of the proletariat in time and space, and on the other, it has to bring economics and politics together into the true synthesis of proletarian praxis. In this way it will help to reconcile the dialectical conflict between immediate interest and ultimate goal.

Thus we must never overlook the distance that separates the consciousness of even the most revolutionary worker from the authentic class consciousness of the proletariat. But even this situation can be explained on the basis of the Marxist theory of class struggle and class consciousness. *The proletariat only perfects itself by annihilating and transcending itself, by creating the classless society through the successful conclusion of its own class struggle.* The struggle for this society, in which the dictatorship of the proletariat is merely a phase, is not just a battle waged against an external enemy, the bourgeoisie. It is equally the struggle of the proletariat *against itself*: against the devastating and degrading effects of the capitalist system upon its class consciousness. The proletariat will only have won the real victory when it has overcome these effects within itself. The separation of the areas that should be united, the diverse stages of consciousness which the proletariat has reached in the various spheres of activity are a precise index of what has been achieved and what remains to be done. The proletariat must not shy away from self-criticism, for victory can only be gained by the truth and self-criticism must, therefore, be an essential part of its nature.

NOTES

All notes are by Lukács, unless otherwise indicated, but publication details are for recent editions of cited works where appropriate.

[1] Engels, *Ludwig Feuerbach and the End of Classical German Philosophy* (New York: International Publishers, 1935).

[2] Marx, *Capital*, tr. Ben Fowkes (Penguin, 1990), vol. 1, p. 168.

[3] And also of the 'pessimism' which *perpetuates* the present state of affairs

and represents it as the uttermost limit of human development just as much as does 'optimism'. In this respect (and in this respect alone) Hegel and Schopenhauer are on a par with each other.

[4] Marx, *The Poverty of Philosophy*, tr. H. Quelch (Chicago, 1910), p. 131.

[5] *Ibid.*, p. 114.

[6] *Ibid.*, p. 119.

[7] Marx, *Capital*, vol. 1, pp. 167–8. Cf. also Engels, *The Origin of the Family, Private Property and the State*, ed. Michele Barrett (Penguin, 1985), p. 110.

[8] *Dokumente des Sozialismus* II, p. 76.

[9] Marx, *The Poverty of Philosophy*, p. 109.

[10] In this context it is unfortunately not possible to discuss in greater detail some of the ramifications of these ideas in Marxism, e.g. the very important category of the 'economic persona'. Even less can we pause to glance at the relation of historical materialism to compare trends in bourgeois thought (such as Max Weber's ideal types).

[11] This is the point from which to gain an historical understanding of the great utopias such as those of Plato or Sir Thomas More. Cf. also Marx on Aristotle, *Capital*, vol. 1, pp. 151, 253–4, 532.

[12] Marx says about Benjamin Franklin: 'Yet he states this without knowing it. He speaks first of the "one labour", then of "the other labour", and finally of "labour", without further qualification, as the substance of the value of everything.' *Capital*, vol. 1, p. 142. And similarly: 'They do this without being aware of it.' *Ibid*, pp. 166–7.

[13] Marx, 'Wages, Prices and Profit' in Marx-Engels, *Selected Works*, 2 vols. (London: Lawrence and Wishart, 1950), vol. 1, pp. 388–9.

[14] Marx-Engels, *Collected Works*, vol. 3 (London, 1975), p. 433.

[15] Marx, *Capital*, vol. 1, p. 479.

[16] *Ibid.*, p. 479.

[17] Marx, *Capital*, vol. 1, pp. 135–6.

[18] Marx and Engels repeatedly emphasize the naturalness of these social formations, *Capital*, vol. 1, pp. 339, 351, etc. The whole structure of evolution in Engels' *The Origin of the Family, Private Property and the State* is based on this idea. I cannot enter here into the controversies on this issue – controversies involving Marxists too; I should just like to stress that here I also consider the views of Marx and Engels to be more profound and historically more correct than those of their 'improvers'.

[19] Marx, *The Eighteenth Brumaire of Louis Bonaparte* (New York: International Publishers, 1963), p. 54.

[20] *Ibid.*, p. 50.

[21] But this is no more than a tendency. It is Rosa Luxemburg's great achievement to have shown that this is not just a passing phase but that capitalism can only survive – economically – while it moves society in the direction of capitalism but has not yet fully penetrated it. This economic self-contradiction of any purely capitalist society is undoubtedly one of the reasons for the contradictions in the class consciousness of the bourgeoisie.

22 Marx, *A Contribution to the Critique of Political Economy* (New York: International Publishers, 1970), pp. 201–2.

23 Marx, *Capital*, vol. 3, pp. 136, 307–8, 318, etc. It is self-evident that the different groups of capitalists, such as industrialists and merchants, etc., are differently placed; but the distinctions are not relevant in this context.

24 *Ibid.*, p. 428.

25 [Ed.] On this see Lukács's essay, 'The Marxism of Rosa Luxemburg' in *History and Class Consciousness*, tr. Rodney Livingstone (Cambridge: The MIT Press, 1971).

26 Marx, *Critique of Political Economy*, p. 146.

27 Marx, *Capital*, vol. 3, pp. 245, 252.

28 *Ibid.*, vol. 3, pp. 165, 151, 373–5, 383.

29 *Ibid.*, vol. 1, p. 356.

30 Marx, *The Poverty of Philosophy*, chapter 2; Letters and extracts from letters to F. A. Sorge and others.

31 Marx, 'Wages, Price and Profit' in *Selected Works*, vol. 1, pp. 404–5.

20

Friedrich Nietzsche

What determined Nietzsche's particular position in the development of modern irrationalism was partly the historical situation at the time of his appearance, and partly his unusual personal gifts. With regard to the former, we have already touched on the most important social happenings of this period. Another circumstantial factor – one favourable to his development – was that Nietzsche concluded his activity on the eve of the imperialist age. This is to say that, on the one hand, he envisaged the impending conflicts of Bismarck's age from every perspective. He witnessed the founding of the German Reich, the hopes that were pinned to it and their disappointment, the fall of Bismarck, and the inauguration by Wilhelm II of an overly aggressive imperialism. And at the same time he witnessed the Paris Commune, the origins of the great party of the proletarian masses, the outlawing of socialists, and the workers' heroic struggle against it. On the other hand, however, Nietzsche did not personally live to see the imperialist period. He was thus offered a favourable opportunity to conjecture and to solve in mythical form – and from the perspective of the reactionary bourgeoisie – the main problems of the subsequent period. This mythical form furthered his influence not only because it was to become the increasingly dominant mode of philosophical expression in the imperialist age. But also because it enabled him to pose imperialism's cultural, ethical and other problems in such a general way that he could always remain the reactionary bourgeoisie's leading philosopher, whatever the variations in the situation and the reactionary tactics adopted to match them. Nietzsche had already acquired this status before the first imperialist world war, and he retained it even after the second.

But the lasting influence whose objective theory we have just outlined could never have become a reality, were it not for the peculiar features of Nietzsche's not inconsiderable talent. He had a special sixth sense, an anticipatory sensitivity to what the parasitical intelligentsia would need in the imperialist age, what would invariably move and disturb it, and what kind of answer would most appease it. Thus he was able to encompass very wide areas of culture, to illuminate pressing questions with clever aphorisms, and to satisfy the frustrated, indeed sometimes rebellious instincts of this parasitical class of intellectuals with gestures that appeared fascinating and hyper-revolutionary. And at the same time he could answer all these questions, or at least indicate the answers, in such a way that out of all his subtleties and fine nuances, it was possible for a robust and reactionary class insignia of the imperialist bourgeoisie to emerge.

This Jekyll and Hyde character corresponds to the social existence, and hence to the emotional and intellectual world, of this class in a triple sense. Firstly, an oscillation between the most acute feeling for nuance, the keenest over-sensitivity, and a suddenly erupting, often hysterical brutality is always an intrinsic sign of decadence. Secondly, it is very closely linked with a deep dissatisfaction concerning contemporary culture: an 'unease about the future' in Freud's phrase, and a revolt against it. Under no circumstances, however, would the 'rebel' stomach any interference with his own parasitical privileges and their basis in society. He therefore waxes enthusiastic when the revolutionary character of this discontent receives a philosophical sanction, but is at the same time deflected – by its social substance – into a rebuttal of democracy and socialism. And thirdly, it was just at the time of Nietzsche's activity that the decline of the bourgeois class, and its decadent tendencies reached such a pitch that their subjective evaluation within the bourgeois class also underwent a significant change. . .

Now as a diviner of the cultural psyche, as aesthetician and moralist, Nietzsche was perhaps the cleverest and most versatile exponent of this decadent self-knowledge. But his significance went further: in acknowledging decadence as the basic phenomenon of bourgeois development in his time, he undertook to chart the course of its self-conquest. For in the most spirited and vigilant intellectuals who succumbed to the influence of the decadent outlook, there ineluctably arose a desire to conquer it. Such a desire rendered the struggles of the burgeoning new class, the proletariat, extremely attractive for most of these intellectuals. Here, and particularly with regard to personal conduct and morality, they perceived auguries of a possible social recovery and, in connection with it – naturally this thought was uppermost – of their own recovery. At the same time, the majority of the intellectuals had no inkling of the economic and social implications of a real socialist transformation. Since they contemplated it in purely ideological terms, they had no clear notion how far and how profoundly such a realignment would mean a radical break with their own class; or how such a break, once accomplished, would affect the lives of the persons concerned. Confused though this movement may

have been, it did embrace wide sections of the more advanced bourgeois intelligentsia. Naturally enough, it revealed itself with particular
vehemence in times of crisis (for instance the ban on socialists, the
fate of naturalism, the First World War and the expressionist movement in Germany, *boulangisme* and the Dreyfus Affair in France, etc.).

Nietzsche's philosophy performed the 'social task' of 'rescuing' and
'redeeming' this type of bourgeois mind. It offered a road which
avoided the need for any break, or any serious conflict with the
bourgeoisie. It was a road whereby the pleasant moral feeling of being
a rebel could be sustained and even intensified, whilst a 'more thorough', 'cosmic biological' revolution was enticingly projected in contrast to the 'superficial', 'external' social revolution. A 'revolution',
that is, which would fully preserve the bourgeoisie's privileges, and
would first and foremost passionately defend the privileged existence
of the parasitical and imperialist intelligentsia. A 'revolution' directed
against the masses and lending an expression compounded of pathos
and aggressiveness to the veiled egoistic fears of the economically and
culturally privileged. The road indicated by Nietzsche never departed
from the decadence proliferating in the intellectual and emotional life
of this class. But the new-found self-knowledge placed it in a new
light: it was precisely in decadence that the true progressive seeds of
a genuine, thoroughgoing renewal of mankind were deemed to lie.
This 'social task' found itself in pre-established harmony, at it were,
with Nietzsche's talents, his deepest intellectual inclinations and his
learning. Like those sections of society at whom his work was aimed,
Nietzsche himself was principally concerned with cultural problems,
notably art and individual morality. Politics always appeared as
though an abstract, mythicized horizon, and Nietzsche's ignorance of
economics was as great as that of the average contemporary intellectual [. . .]

Academic schools of thought have often reproached Nietzsche with
having no system, something they held to be necessary to a real
philosopher. Nietzsche himself roundly condemned all systems: 'I
mistrust all systematizers and avoid them. The will to a system is a
lack of integrity.'[1] We have already observed this tendency in Kierkegaard, and it is not fortuitous. The bourgeoisie's philosophical crisis,
as demonstrated by the demise of Hegelianism, amounted to far more
than the recognition of a given system's inadequacy; it signified the
breakdown of a concept that had swayed men for thousands of years
[. . .]

Nietzsche's rejection of systems arose out of the relativistic, agnos-
ticizing tendencies of this age. The suggestion that he was the first and
most influential thinker with whom this agnosticism turned into the

sphere of myth we shall investigate later. His aphoristic mood of expression is no doubt intimately related to this outlook. But there was also another motive. It is a general phenomenon in ideological history that thinkers who can observe a social development only in embryo, but who can already perceive the key elements in it and who – especially in the moral area – are striving for an intellectual grasp of it prefer the essayistic, aphoristic forms. The reason is that these forms guarantee the expression most fitted to a mixture of a mere scenting of future developments on the one hand, and an acute observation and evaluation of their symptoms on the other. We see this in Montaigne and Mandeville, and in the French moralists from La Rochefoucauld to Vauvenargues and Chamfort. Stylistically, Nietzsche had a great liking for most of these authors. But a contrast in the basic tenor of his content accompanied this formal preference. The important moralists had already criticized – the majority in a progressive way – the morality of capitalism from within an absolutist, feudal society. Nietzsche's anticipation of the future was, on the contrary, approvingly oriented towards an impending reactionary movement, which in his particular context meant an imperialist reaction.

We must now ask whether, in Nietzsche's case, we are justified in speaking of a system. Are we entitled to interpret his individual aphorisms in a systematic context? We believe that the systematic coherence of a philosopher's thoughts is an older phenomenon than the idealist systems and can still survive when they have collapsed. No matter whether this systematic framework is an approximately correct reflection of the real world or one distorted by class considerations, idealist notions and so forth, such a systematic framework is to be found in every philosopher worth his salt. Admittedly, it does not tally with the structure which the individual philosopher himself intends to give his work. While indicating the need thus to reconstruct the real consistency in the fragments of Heraclitus and Epicurus, Marx added: 'Even with philosophers who give their works a systematic form, Spinoza for instance, the actual inner structure of the system is quite different from the form in which they consciously present it.'[2] We shall now venture to show that such a systematic coherence may be detected behind Nietzsche's aphorisms.

In our view, it was only little by little that the nodal points in the framework of Nietzsche's ideas took definite shape: the resistance to socialism, the effort to create an imperial Germany. There is ample evidence that in his youth, Nietzsche was an ardent Prussian patriot. This enthusiasm is one of the most significant factors in his early philosophy. It cannot possibly be regarded as a matter of chance or youthful whim that he wanted to be involved in the war of 1870–1; or that, since a Basel professor could not enlist as a soldier, he at least took part as a volunteer nurse. It is at any rate characteristic that his sister (although we must view her statements in a highly critical way) recorded the following memory of the war. At that time, she wrote, he first sensed 'that the strongest and highest will-to-live is expressed not in a wretched struggle for survival, but as the will to fight, the will to power and super-power'.[3] At all events this bellicose philosophical state of mind, which was an extremely Prussian one, in no way contradicts the young Nietzsche's other views. In his papers of autumn 1873, for example, we find the following; 'My starting-point is the Prussian soldier: here we have a true convention, we have coercion, earnestness and discipline, and that also goes for the form.'

Just as distinct as the source of the young Nietzsche's enthusiasm are the features of his principal enemy. Directly after the fall of the Paris Commune he wrote to his friend, Baron von Gersdorff:

> Hope is possible again! Our *German* mission isn't over yet! I'm in better spirit than ever, for not yet everything has capitulated to Franco-Jewish levelling and 'elegance', and to the greedy instincts of *Jetztzeit* ('now-time'). There is still bravery, and it's a German bravery that has something else to it than the *élan* of our lamentable neighbours. Over and above the war between nations, that international hydra which suddenly raised its fearsome heads has alarmed us by heralding quite different battles to come.[4]

And the content of this battle, which initially was waged directly against the movement obstructing the full fruition of his ideology, Nietzsche moreover defined in the draft, several months earlier, of his letter dedicating *The Birth of Tragedy* to Richard Wagner. Once more the Prussian victory was his point of departure. From it he drew such conclusions as these, '. . . because that power will destroy something which we loathe as the real enemy of all profound philosophy and aesthetics. This something is a disease from which German life has had to suffer since the great French Revolution in particular; ever-recurring in spasmodic fits, it has afflicted even the best type of German, to say nothing of the great mass of people among whom that affliction, in vile desecration of an honourable word, goes under the name of liberalism.' [. . .] As we see, Nietzsche's philosophical thinking was opposed to democracy and socialism from the beginning.

This attitude and these perspectives form the basis of Nietzsche's understanding of Ancient Greece. Here his opposition to the revolutionary traditions of bourgeois development is quite plainly perceptible. We are not thinking mainly of the Dionysian principle which made Nietzsche's first writings famous, for there the idea was still, in his own words, part of his 'artistic metaphysics'. It took on actual significance only after the conquest of decadence had become a central problem for the mature Nietzsche. But it is extremely revealing to note the principles upon which his new image of Ancient Greece was founded in the first place. Prominent among these is the idea that slavery is necessary to any real civilization.

If Nietzsche had stressed the role of slavery in Greek culture merely from the historical standpoint, this perfectly correct observation would be of no great importance; he himself referred to Friedrich August Wolf, who had made it before him.[5] It was bound to gain an even wider currency, and not only because of progress in historical studies. It followed also from a review of the 'heroic illusion' of the French Revolution, whose ideologists had ignored the slavery issue in order to create out of the democratic city-state a model of a modern revolutionary democracy. (These same views influenced the German image of Ancient Greece in the period from Winckelmann to Hegel.) What is new in Nietzsche is that he used slavery as a vehicle for his critique of *contemporary* civilization: 'And while it may be true that the Greeks perished because of their slave-holding, it is far more certain that we shall perish because of the *absence* of slavery.'[6] [. . .]

What Nietzsche contrasts with present times is the Greek dictatorship by an elite which clearly recognizes 'that work is an ignominy', and which creates immortal artworks at its leisure. 'In more recent times', he wrote, 'it is not the person who needs art but the slave who has determined the general outlook. Such phantoms as the dignity of man, the dignity of labour are the shabby products of a slave mentality hiding from its own nature. Unhappy the age in which the slave needs such ideas and is spurred to reflect upon himself and the world around him. Wretched the seducers who have deprived the slave of his innocence by means of the fruit of the Tree of Knowledge.'

Now what are the qualities of this 'elite' whose revival, assisted by a return to slavery, aroused in the young Nietzsche the hope of a cultural renaissance on a utopian and mythical plane? That it springs from a barbarian condition is something we might accept as confirming historical facts. Indeed Nietzsche depicted it in the most lurid colours in 'Homer's Contest' (1871–2). But if we are to understand Greek civilization, stated Nietzsche in a polemic against the Orphic thinkers – who held that 'a life rooted in such an urge [characterized by cruelty, a tigerish lust to annihilate] is not worth living' then, to understand it, 'we must start with the point that the Greek genius tolerated the terrible presence of this urge and considered it *justified*.'[7] Thus it is a matter not of conquering, civilizing and humanizing the barbarian instincts, but of constructing a great civilization on their bedrock and diverting them into suitable channels. Only in this context, not from the standpoint of some vague 'artist metaphysics', can the Dionysian principle be properly grasped and appreciated. Moreover, Nietzsche rightly said in a later draft of the preface to his debut work on the Dionysian principle: 'What a disadvantage my timidity is when I speak as a scholar of a subject of which I might have spoken from "experience".' [. . .]

If we now return to slavery as the alleged bedrock of any genuine civilization, we can see how much of the later Nietzsche this early work – albeit in an immature manner – anticipated. In this context the Schopenhauer and Wagner portraits which he produced with such fervent eloquence resemble mythicized pretexts for expressing something not fully developed, half in poetic and half in philosophical form. His own later criticism of his first writings – especially in *Ecce homo* – all tended in this direction:

> A psychologist might add that what I in my youthful years heard in Wagnerian music had nothing at all to do with Wagner; that when I described Dionysian music I described *that* which I had heard – that I had instinctively to translate and transfigure into the latest idiom all I had borne within me. The proof of this, *as strong a proof as can be*, is my essay 'Wagner in Bayreuth': in all the psychologically decisive passages I am the only person referred to – one may ruthlessly insert my name or the word 'Zarathustra' wherever the text gives the word Wagner . . . Wagner himself had an idea of this: he failed to recognize himself in the essay.[8]

Modified somewhat, this also applies to the Schopenhauer portrait in the work of Nietzsche's youth. The third, similarly mythologized, Socrates portrait is a totally different matter. In this debut work the great antithesis was already 'The Dionysian and the Socratic'.[9] And Nietzsche – at first in predominantly aesthetic terms – enlarged this antithesis to encompass that of instinct and reason. In *Ecce homo* he reached a conclusion: the discovery that Socrates was a 'decadent' and that one must rate 'morality itself as a symptom of decadence' the mature Nietzsche considered 'a novelty, a unique event of the first order in the history of knowledge.'[10]

When investigating in general the determining causes of Nietzsche's further development, one usually lays the chief stress on the Wagner disappointment. But the points just raised concerning Nietzsche's attitude to Wagner already show us that it was a symptom of his shift rather than its actual cause. In Wagner, and with increasing acuteness, Nietzsche challenged the art of his own German period in the name of the imperialist future. When, especially after the First World

War, it became the fashion to challenge the nineteenth century's ideology (the age of 'security') in the name of the twentieth, Nietzsche's split with Wagner and his late polemics against him furnished the methodological 'model' for this conflict. The fact that the ideological spokesmen of the Hitler period continued this tradition, though linking it with Wagner idolatry, does not prove anything. Their rejection of 'security' was combined also with the glorification of Bismarck, whom Nietzsche in his final period nearly always attacked in conjunction with Wagner. For the older Nietzsche, Wagner was the greatest artistic expression of that decadence whose most important political representative he saw in Bismarck. And in going beyond the philosophy of Schopenhauer he followed the same direction. We must not forget that even the young Nietzsche was never really an orthodox disciple of Schopenhauer with regard to radical a-historicism. From the start he toyed with the mythicizing of history, whereas his master had totally avoided history. This tendency, already present in *The Birth of Tragedy*, grew more pronounced in the second *Untimely Meditations*.[11] And thus, along with Wagner and Bismarck, Schopenhauer too came more and more within the area of that decadence he wanted to conquer. [. . .]

Only if we proceed from Nietzsche's ethics can we comprehend his attitude to what he called the 'ultimate questions' of philosophy, to religious belief or unbelief. As is widely known, Nietzsche declared a fervent allegiance to atheism; and with the same fervour he denounced all religions, but especially Christianity. That was of great importance for his influence on the intelligentsia, large sections of which were increasingly breaking away from the old religions. [. . .] Nietzsche carried religious atheism far beyond the Schopenhauerian stage. We see this from a negative angle above all in the fact that Nietzsche transformed the argument of his atheism into myth to an even greater extent than was the case with Schopenhauer's Buddhism. He dissociated himself more strongly still from the connection with the natural sciences, and his views ran increasingly and more deliberately counter to 'vulgar' atheism. A famous passage in *The Gay Science* states that God is dead, indeed that men have murdered him.[12] [. . .] Saying that Zarathustra had deprived men of God, Nietzsche linked atheism with the new ethics of 'All is permissible'. The killing of God was only the means of liberating men from the restraints acquired in the course of millennia and turning them into those immoralists which the tyrannical ruling class of the future was to become, in opposition to the herd. When Nietzsche happened to touch on the theme of 'back to nature' he at once stressed his differences with Rousseau. For Nietzsche, there is only one way that something purposeful can come of this: 'Nature, i.e., daring to be immoral like nature.'[13] And it would be equally false to draw a parallel between such passages and Hobbes's natural state, for the latter was concerned with the starting point of man's development, with a 'Whence?' whereas Nietzsche's concern was the goal to be realized, the 'Whither?' So here again we may clearly observe the contrast with the Enlightenment, with which individual commentators have tried to associate Nietzsche because of his atheism. In the Enlightenment, the idea was to prove that belief in God might not signify any kind of moral imperative for mankind, that the moral laws would operate in a society of atheists just as much as in one where religious patronage held sway (Bayle). Nietzsche, on the contrary, wanted to show that the demise of the idea of God (or the death of God) would entail a moral renaissance in the sense we have noted above. Apart, therefore, from the other ethical contradictions in the 'old' and 'new' Enlightenment, about which we again already know Nietzsche's opinion, we find another contrast here in respect of the socio-ethical role of religion. The 'old' Enlightenment regarded the religious concept as irrelevant to men's morality, actions, views etc., which in reality were adequately determined by a combination of society and men's reason. On the other hand, Nietzsche – and here he far exceeded Feuerbach's weaknesses in the realm of historico-philosophical idealism – regarded the switch to atheism as a turning-point for morality. At this point let us just briefly remark that here Nietzsche's world view is very close to certain tendencies in Dostoevsky. Since he had only read the *Notes from Underground*, *The House of the Dead* and *The Insulted and Injured*, and none of Dostoevsky's major novels, the parallels in the relationship of their religious atheism and morality appear all the more striking.

The extremely subjective and idealistic character of Nietzsche's atheism needs stressing immediately because on the most important philosophical questions, he continually and effectively stood against idealism . . . [But] Nietzsche's kind of 'radical' atheism blurs all religion's dividing lines and – within specific limits which we are coming to – offers an open house to the most diverse religious tendencies. Here again the uniqueness of Nietzsche's influence stands out: what he created was a blanket ideology for all that imperialist age's strongly reactionary tendencies. Socially and hence ethically, his *mythos* was quite unequivocal. In every other respect, however, it was wrapped in a mental haze which admitted of any interpretation one chose; and this lack of intellectual definition did not take away the immediate suggestive power of Nietzsche's symbols. That is why it was equally possible to find in Nietzsche a prop for the (fascist) myth of 'one's own kind' as opposed to the 'foreign' (Christian) myth, and to bring his 'radical' atheism into an amicable rapport with Christianity itself. This Nietzsche's sister tried from the start to achieve by heavy-handed pan-Germanic methods; later minds found a stylistically more refined expression for the same procedure. Thus Jaspers, for instance, writes of Nietzsche's relationship to Christianity: 'Although we may reproach Nietzsche with atheism and point to his "Anti-Christ", Nietzsche's atheism is not a flat straightforward denial of God, nor is it the indifference of a man so far from God, and so far from seeking him out, that God does not exist. The very manner in which Nietzsche decrees for his age that "God is dead" conveys his emotion . . . And even when he . . . is straightforward to the point of a radical "No" to all faith in God whatsoever, Nietzsche is still remarkably close to Christianity: "It is after all the best piece of idealism with which I have really become familiar: since childhood I have pursued it into many nooks and crannies, and I believe I have never dealt it an unfair blow at heart" '. (To Peter Gast, 21 July 1881).[14] And for a contemporary American such as Kaufmann, Nietzsche's conformity with Christianity outweighs his departures from it.

All these seemingly very marked contradictions are resolved if we consider more closely the socio-ethical content of Nietzsche's anti-Christian polemics. Here too we must refrain from taking tone and style as our criterion, or else we could easily say with Alfred Baeumler: 'He felt with acute clarity that his own position was infinitely bolder, infinitely more perilous than that of the eighteenth-century Church's most daring rationalist opponents.'[15] This paradox is not hard to account for. Even in the case of Voltaire – no atheist – the Enlightenment's attack on the Church was chiefly directed against it as the central pillar of feudal absolutism. And hence the attack embraced every area of human life and thought; it extended from the most general questions of philosophy and epistemology to the fields of ethics and aesthetics. Nietzsche's polemics, on the other hand, railed exclusively against the putative ideological forerunners of democracy and socialism, against the spokesmen for slave morality. The whole struggle against Christianity therefore took on a very narrow and firmly reactionary character, but beyond that, it lost its social reality. The Enlightenment was challenging the real ideological pillar of absolute monarchy; but was Nietzsche not berating ideologies and institutions that were actually his best allies in his central campaign against socialism and democracy? Of course there are elements in Christian teaching, and occasional proclivities in the development of Christian religion, where the idea of the equality of all human beings – which Nietzsche hated – finds powerful expression. But the

Church's development, and also that of the dominant religious mood, tends towards completely disarming that idea in the social sphere by interpreting it in such a way that it lends itself perfectly to the current system of exploitation and oppression, and to the resultant inequality. That is the social explanation of the fact that Elizabeth Forster-Nietzsche was just as assiduous as Jaspers or Kaufmann in detecting links between Nietzsche and Christianity or the Christian Church. And in this they are absolutely right from the social angle, for the political axis of the Pope, Cardinal Spellman, etc., has been in total agreement with the Nietzschean ethics we have outlined. The fact that the theoretical-ethical declarations accompanying this praxis hardly bear Nietzsche's frankly cynical tone is a secondary point compared with their essential unanimity. Hitlerian propaganda, on the other hand, could directly exploit just this side of Nietzsche's critique of Christianity.

We may now confine ourselves to the brief citing of several crucial passages from Nietzsche's works. They show quite clearly that the theme we have emphasized was not picked at random, but is at the very core of Nietzsche's anti-Christianity. We shall begin by quoting some concluding sentences from *Ecce homo*. Significantly, all that comes afterwards is the antithesis which was decisive for Nietzsche at the close of his career: '*Dionysus against the Crucified*'. It is equally characteristic that the passage about to be quoted ends with Voltaire's phrase '*Ecrasez l'infâme!*' Precisely this passages illustrates in the grossest way the extreme contrast between that which Voltaire wanted to abolish in Christianity, and that which Nietzsche thought should be abolished. Nietzsche wrote as follows:

> The *unmasking* of Christian morality is an event without equal, a real catastrophe . . . The concept 'God' invented as an antithetical concept of life – everything harmful, noxious, slanderous, the whole mortal enmity against life brought into one terrible unity! The concept 'the Beyond', 'real world' invented so as to deprive of value the *only* world which exists – so as to leave over no goal, no reason, no task for our earthly reality! The concept 'soul', 'sprit', finally even 'immortal soul', invented so as to despise the body, so as to make it sick – 'holy' . . . The concept 'sin' invented together with the instrument of torture which goes with it, the concept of 'free will', so as to confuse the instincts, so as to make mistrust of the instincts into second nature! In the concept of the 'selfless', of the 'self-denying' the actual badge of *decadence*, being *lured* by the harmful, no longer being *able* to discover where one's advantage lies, self-destruction, made the sign of value in general, made 'duty', 'holiness', the 'divine' in man! Finally – it is the most fearful – in the concept of the *good* man common cause made with everything

weak, sick, ill-constructed, suffering from itself, all that *which ought to
perish* – the law of *selection* crossed, an ideal made of opposition to the
proud and well-constituted, to the affirmative man, to the man certain of
the future and guaranteeing the future – the latter is henceforth called the
evil man . . . And all this was believed in *as morality*! – *Ecrasez l'infâme!*[16]

This hate-inspired lyrical effusion finds the requisite factual, ethi-
cal-social and historical culmination in Nietzsche's *Anti-Christ*, which
also appeared in his last period. We do not need direct quotation to show
that here Nietzsche, from first to last, was trying to make the idea of
human equality intellectually contemptible and to wipe it out: that was
his basic aim throughout his career. Let us just point out once more that
Nietzsche never, of course, rejected equality out of general ethical
considerations; his attitude was the direct result of his stance with regard
to democracy, revolution and socialism, which to his mind were necessary fruits of the dominion of Christianity. Nietzsche wrote:[17]

And let us not underestimate the fatality that has crept out of Christianity even into politics! No one any longer possesses today the courage to claim special privileges or the right to rule, the courage to feel a
sense of reverence towards himself and towards his equals – the courage for a *pathos of distance* . . . Our politics is *morbid* from this lack of
courage! – The aristocratic outlook has been undermined most deeply
by the life of equality of souls; and if the belief in the 'prerogative of the
majority' makes revolutions and *will continue to make them* – it is
Christianity, let there be no doubt about it, *Christian* value judgement
which translates every revolution into mere blood and crime! Christianity is a revolt of everything that crawls along the ground directed
against that which is *elevated*: the Gospel of the 'lowly' *makes* low.

And as a kind of historical-typological rider to this statement he added
somewhat later:[18]

The pathological conditionality of his perspective makes of the convinced man a fanatic – Savonarola, Luther, Rousseau, Robespierre,
Saint-Simon – the antithetical type of the strong, emancipated spirit.
But the larger-than-life attitudes of these *sick* spirits, these conceptual
epileptics, impresses the great masses – fanatics are picturesque, mankind would rather see gestures than listen to *reasons* . . .

The basic thinking here is clear: out of Christianity came the French
Revolution, out of this came democracy, and out of this came socialism. When, therefore, Nietzsche takes his stand as an atheist, the
truth is that he is out to destroy socialism.

In Nietzsche's polemics against Christianity, as indeed in all his social and ethical writings, the naive reader will gain the impression that all these phenomena are being examined as they are manifested in real, material existence, from the angle of biological needs and laws. But this is an illusion, which Nietzsche too was probably labouring under himself. Specific branches of classical philology apart, Nietzsche's knowledge was certainly very extensive, and his grasp of it lively and vivid, but this knowledge was always superficial and acquired at second and third hand. Jaspers concedes as much even for the philosophical classics with which Nietzsche was in vigorous dispute throughout his life. But much more than just superficiality is involved. For Nietzsche, biology was one of the means of arguing and making concrete on quasi-scientific lines an essential element in his methodology. The method itself, of course, came into being long before him. In all reactionary social–biological theories (it may not be an accident that the two make a regular habit of appearing together), the 'biological law' – the 'organic' in Restoration philosophy, the 'struggle for survival' in Social Darwinism – constantly appears as the basis from which the most diverse regressive conclusions are drawn in the fields of society, morals, etc. [. . .]

In Nietzsche's time, Social Darwinism emerged as one such ideology supporting the reactionary concept of social processes. The term 'reactionary' still holds good where the thinkers concerned, e.g., F. A. Lange in Germany, subjectively placed themselves on the side of progress. These thinkers chose a method which did not lead to a concrete examination of social phenomena; on the contrary it diverted them from concrete conception because, in every period, the 'universal law' of the 'struggle for survival' explains every event in the same way, i.e., it explains nothing at all. And with this methodology they supported the bias of declining liberalism: they substituted for class warfare various freely invented expressions of the 'laws of motion' of society.[19]

In books on Nietzsche there was at one time a sharp controversy as to whether and how far Nietzsche should be considered a Darwinist. We consider this discussion irrelevant for two reasons. In the first place, Nietzsche was never more than a *Social* Darwinist in the above sense of the term. And secondly, his relationship to Darwinism is the clearest illustration of the fact that it was not scientific discoveries and knowledge that guided his thinking into specific channels and forced specific roles upon him. On the contrary, his struggle against socialism shaped his pseudo-scientific attitudes. He only differed from his likeminded contemporaries in that the programmatic arbitrariness of his 'scientific' arguments was stated with cynical frankness, without bothering to wear a mask of objectivity.

If we recall our study of Nietzsche's interpretation of ancient society, we will realize that Social Darwinism strongly influenced his views of the *agon*, *Eris* [discord], and so on. Darwinism accordingly receives a positive emphasis in this phrase. For example, Nietzsche reproached David Strauss for praising Darwinism in general terms without having the courage to apply it rigorously to moral problems, but instead taking refuge in idealism.[20] Occasionally, moreover, and quite as a matter of course, he used images borrowed from Darwinism in order to elucidate individual phenomena: 'Darwinism is also right with regard to thinking in images: the stronger image devours the weaker ones.' Darwinism played a far slighter role for Nietzsche in the period of *Human, All Too Human*. Although he did not attack it, he drew on it in his explanations far less often. This consigning of it to the background is understandable if we consider at the same time the evolutionist tendencies of this transitional phase that we stressed earlier. Only when Nietzsche had overcome this illusion did he adopt a dismissive attitude of increasing sharpness towards Darwin and Darwinism. As early as *The Gay Science* [1882] he treated Darwinism with irony on account of its plebeian nature:

> The whole of English Darwinism breathes something like the musty air of English overpopulation, like the smell of the distress and overcrowding of small people. But a natural scientist should come out of his human nook; and in nature it is not conditions of distress that are *dominant* but overflow and squandering, even to the point of absurdity. The struggle for existence is only an *exception*, a temporary restriction of the will to life. The great and small struggle always revolves around superiority, around growth and expansion, around power – in accordance with the will to power which is the will of life.[21]

But we can study the actual content of this shift only in the more detailed statements of the last works and sketches, where its real motives are voiced with Nietzschean candour. In *The Twilight of the Idols* and *The Will to Power* the decisive motive of his new anti-Darwinism is now clearly expressed. Here again it becomes clear how Nietzsche resembled and how he differed from the general run of 'Social Darwinists'. Instead of considering the facts of natural evolution itself, both sides used the expression 'the struggle for survival' (Marx) from the standpoint of their view of the present and future that would result, from the class struggle between bourgeoisie and proletariat. Capitalism's ordinary 'Darwinist' apologists started with the experience of the period after 1860, which they superficially generalized. If, they thought, the 'struggle for survival' operated in society unchecked, it would end ineluctably in the victory of the 'strong' (the capitalists). This is where Nietzsche's sceptical, pessimistic critique begins. 'Normal' conditions for the social struggle for survival will inevitably lead the 'weak' (the workers, the masses, socialism) to a position of command. Here Nietzsche was not only, as in his ethics, a 'prophet' of imperialist barbarity, but was moreover looking for those *new* forms of dominion which could thwart the rise of the proletariat. The accent is on the word 'new' because Nietzsche, as we have seen, was highly sceptical about those methods of oppression practised in his own times (he had witnessed the failure of the anti-socialist laws). He did not believe that the contemporary capitalists, political conservatives as they were, were capable of carrying out such a policy.

That calling awaited none other than the 'lords of the earth' whose deliberate training was the principal idea behind Nietzsche's ethics . . . Now that we have presented the sharp contrast between Nietzsche and the ordinary direct apologists of capitalism, we must briefly remark on the methods they shared in connection with Darwinism. Each side started out not by examining the objective correctness and applicability of Darwinism to social phenomena, but from its own political aims and the perspectives they provided. Thus in the last resort, it boils down to the same method whether the ordinary apologists, out of a narrow optimism about capitalist evolution, are commending Darwin, or whether Nietzsche, as a result of the scepticism we have just indicated, is rejecting and attacking him. In both cases, Darwinism was only a mythologized pretext for the ideological war against the proletariat.

It was in the light of such considerations that Nietzsche taxed Darwin as follows in *Twilight of the Idols*:

> Darwin forgot the mind (-that is English!): *the weak possess more mind* . . . To acquire mind one must need mind – one loses it when one no longer needs it. He who possesses strength divests himself of mind (– 'let it depart!' they think today in Germany, '– the *Reich* will still be ours.' One will see that under mind I include foresight, patience, dissimulation, great self-control, and all that is mimicry (this last includes a great part of what is called virtue).[22]

In the above statements Nietzsche was, as we have already noted, contesting the struggle for survival as a universal phenomenon; the latter, for him, was the will to power, and the former only an exceptional instance. From this there now follows his programmatic rejection of the Social Darwinism of his contemporaries, which of course appears in his book as Darwinism itself:

Supposing, however, that this struggle exists – and it does indeed occur – its outcome is the reverse of that desired by the school of Darwin, of that which one *ought* perhaps to desire with them: namely, the defeat of the stronger, the more privileged, the fortunate exceptions. Species do *not* grow more perfect: the weaker dominate the stronger again and again – the reason being they are the great majority, and they are also *cleverer*.[23]

This problem receives more detailed treatment in *The Will to Power*. So as to avoid repetition, we shall pick out only the arguments which complement these statements, and which, indeed, became very significant for the development of the militantly reactionary world view of the imperialist age. Nietzsche summed up his opposition to Darwin in three statements: '*First proposition*: man as a species is not progressing. Higher types are indeed attained, but they do not last. The level of the species is *not* raised.'[24] It is clear how this proposition derives from the social reflections we have just cited: since the class struggle (the struggle for survival) does not automatically bring about the higher type of human being Nietzsche desired, survival cannot possibly be the basis of evolution in nature and society. But over and beyond this, Nietzsche's thesis points to the reactionary future: mankind's peak achievements are of equivalent merit, and the spontaneous dynamics of society can only corrupt them and condemn them to perish. Everything depends on creating devices whereby these peak achievements of nature can not only be preserved but also systematically produced. [. . .]

Nietzsche's second proposition states: 'man as a species does not represent any progress compared with any other animal. The whole animal and vegetable kingdom does not evolve from the lower to the higher – but all at the same time, in utter disorder, over and against each other.'[25] This thesis too, although objectively it hardly goes beyond the usual anti-Darwinist arguments, also gained ascendancy in imperialism's reactionary views. [. . .]

The third proposition includes nothing that is especially new for us. In it Nietzsche is chiefly opposed to the liberal interpreters of Social Darwinism, such as Spencer who, as Nietzsche put it, perceived that 'the domestication (the "culture") of man does not go deep – Where it does go deep it at once becomes degeneration (type: the Christian). The "savage" (or, in moral terms, the evil man) is a return to nature – and in a certain sense his recovery – his *cure* from "culture".' Nietzsche was scoring a valid point against the liberal apologists inasmuch as the humanizing of the instincts cannot possibly go really deep in capitalism. But it is perfectly evident from this very point how exclusively both Spencer and Nietzsche projected their own ideals on to Darwinism, from which they gained no fresh insights. [. . .]

For Nietzsche himself, eternal recurrence is the decisive counter to the concept of becoming. This counterbalance was needed because becoming cannot give rise to something new (in the context of capitalist society) without betraying its function in Nietzsche's system. We have already encountered the tendency to transform becoming into a simulated movement, to assign to it the mere role of providing variations within the 'eternally cosmic' laws of the will-to-power. Eternal recurrence narrows the scope even more: the emergence of something new is a 'cosmic' impossibility. 'The rotating cycle', wrote Nietzsche no later than the time of his *The Gay Science*, 'is not something that has become but a first principle, just as mass is a first principle, without exception or transgression. All becoming is within the cycle and mass.' One of the most detailed passages in the late sketches[26] gives a clear picture of this. There is small interest for us in Nietzsche's allegedly scientific arguments, which count for as little as his other forays into this field.

Far more important are his conclusions; Nietzsche regards as theologians all who acknowledge something new in the world.

> This notion – that the world intentionally avoids a goal and even knows artifices for keeping itself from entering into a circular course – must occur to all those who would like to force on the world the ability for *eternal novelty*, i.e., on a finite, definite, unchangeable force of constant size, such as the world is, the miraculous power of infinite novelty in its forms and states. The world, even if it is no longer a god, is still supposed to be capable of the divine power of creation, the power of infinite transformations; it is supposed to consciously prevent itself from returning to any of its old forms; it is supposed to possess not only the intention but the *means* of avoiding any repetition . . .[27]

We have laid stress on the 'becoming' in Nietzsche's ethics. This, we believe, is right because it contains the immediate reasoning behind these ethics and particularly their revolutionary gestures, such as the transvaluation of all values. In order to break the old moral 'tablets' on which 'eternal laws' of morality were inscribed, Nietzsche used the concept of becoming – which he often traced back to Heraclitus – as a philosophical battering ram. The 'innocence of becoming' was the immediate prerequisite for Nietzsche's activism, his reactionary militancy, his conquest of Schopenhauerian passivity. Hence the Nietzschean concept of becoming had to surpass Schopenhauer's wholly senseless, patently superficial agitation about 'the world of appearance'. But it is of the very essence of Nietzschean philosophy that all this can be only a prelude. Let us recall the structure of *Zarathustra*, where the idea of becoming reigns supreme in the first part, e.g., in the call to create the Superman, but where the same type's recurrence forms a crowning conclusion in the 'Drunken Song'. [. . .]

Nietzsche's myth of eternal recurrence as the highest fulfilment of the will-to-power combines, we might say, hard antagonism and picturesquely blurred eclecticism. The two extremes, however, perform a single function from the viewpoint of his central polemical stance, his fight against socialism and for imperialist barbarity. They have the function of removing all moral restraints with a view to the ruthless termination of this social conflict. As we have noted, Nietzsche's boundless freedom created for the 'lords of the earth' the principle that everything is permitted; fatalistic necessity led, in his view, to the same result. In the *Twilight of the Idols* he unequivocally posed this question:

> What alone can *our* teaching be? – That not one *gives* a human being his qualities: not God, not society, not his parents or ancestors, not *he himself* . . . No *one* is accountable for existing at all, or for being constituted as he is, or for living in the circumstances and surroundings in which he lives. The fatality of his nature cannot be disentangled from the fatality of all that which has been and will be . . . One is necessary, one is a piece of fate, one belongs to the whole, one *is* in the whole . . . *But nothing exists apart from the whole!*[28]

And the indirectly apologetic, moral function of eternal recurrence is exactly the same. In *Zarathustra*, in fact, by way of introducing the crucial proclamation of eternal recurrence, the ugliest man suddenly voices as an inspiration the Nietzschean wisdom:

> 'My friends, what do you think? Do you not want to say to death as I do: Was *that* life? For Zarathustra's sake! Well then! Once more!'[29]

NOTES

All notes are by Lukács, unless otherwise indicated, but publication details are for recent editions of cited works where appropriate.

1 Nietzsche, *Twilight of the Idols* and *The Anti-Christ*, tr. R. J. Hollingdale (Penguin, 1990), 'Maxims and Arrows', no. 26.
2 Marx to Lassalle, 31 May 1858, Ferdinand Lassalle's posthumous *Letters and Writings*, ed. G. Mayer (Berlin, 1922), vol. 3, p. 123.

[3] Elizabeth Forster-Nietzsche, *Der einsame Nietzsche* (Leipzig: Kroner, 1914), pp. 433f. [Ed: An English translation of this work appeared as *The Lonely Nietzsche*, tr. by P. V. Cohn.]

[4] Letter to Carl von Gersdorff, 21 June 1871.

[5] *The Complete Works of Friedrich Nietzsche*, 18 vols., ed. Oscar Levy (New York 1909–11, reissued 1964), vol. 3, pp. 64–5.

[6] *Ibid.*, vol. 2, p. 9.

[7] Nietzsche, 'Homer's Contest' in *Nietzsche: Selections*, ed Richard Schacht (New York: Macmillan, 1993), p. 42.

[8] Nietzsche, *Ecce Homo*, tr. R. J. Hollingdale (Penguin, 1992), p. 52.

[9] Nietzsche, *The Birth of Tragedy and the Geneology of Morals*, tr. Francis Golfing (New York: Doubleday, 1956).

[10] Nietzsche, *Ecce Homo*, p. 49.

[11] [Ed. The *Meditations* appeared separately: the first two, 'David Strauss, the confessor and the writer' and 'On the use and disadvantage of history for life' in August 1873 and October 1874 respectively, the other two, or what Lukács refers to as the second, 'Schopenhauer as educator' and 'Richard Wagner in Bayreuth' in October 1874 and July 1876 respectively. Although Nietzsche writes a vigorous defence of them in *Ecce Homo*, they were not included among the books he himself re-published; and it was not until 1893, some four years after his mental breakdown, that they were collected in the book form in which they are familiar to us.]

[12] Nietzsche, *The Gay Science*, tr. Walter Kaufmann (New York: Vintage Books, 1974), section 125.

[13] Nietzsche, *The Will to Power*, ed. Walter Kaufmann (New York: Vintage Books, 1968), section 120.

[14] Karl Jaspers, *Nietzsche: Einführung in das Verständnis seines Philosophierens* (Berlin, 2nd ed., 1947), pp. 431ff.

[15] Alfred Baeumler, *Nietzsche, Der Philosoph und Politiker* (Leipzig, 1931), p. 103. [Ed. Baeumler was a Nazi and became a professor of philosophy in Berlin after Hitler came to power. His views on Nietzsche were accepted by many of Nietzsche's detractors outside Germany. For instance, Ernest Newman had acknowledged in the fourth volume of his *Life of Richard Wagner* that his account of Nietzsche relies heavily on Baeumler's 'masterly epitome' of Nietzsche's thinking, *Nietzsche, der Philosoph und Politiker* (The Philosopher and Politician).]

[16] Nietzsche, *Ecce Homo*, pp. 103–4.

[17] Nietzsche, *The Anti-Christ*, tr. R. J. Hollingdale (Penguin, 1990), section 43.

[18] *Ibid.*, section 54.

[19] Marx criticizes Social Darwinism with annihilating acuteness in the letter to Kugelmann (27 June 1870), Engels at length in the letter to Lavrov (17 November 1875). Engels emphasizes that the Social Darwinists should be criticized in the first place as bad economists, and only then as bad natural philosophers.

[20] [Ed. David Strauss, the celebrated author of *Life of Jesus* and *The Old and New Faith*, is the object of Nietzsche's wrath in his *Untimely Meditations*.

What enraged Nietzsche most was Strauss's comfortable and untroubled renunciation of Christianity, coupled with an easy conviction that Darwin was one of mankind's greatest benefactors. As Nietzsche put it, 'With a certain rude contentment he covers himself in the hairy cloak of our ape-genealogists and praises Darwin as one of the greatest benefactors of mankind – but it confuses us to see that his ethics are constructed entirely independently of the question: "What is our conception of the world?" ' Nietzsche, *Untimely Meditations*, tr. R. J. Hollingdale (Cambridge: Cambridge University Press, 1983), p. 29.]

21 Nietzsche, *The Gay Science*, section 349.

22 Nietzsche, *Twilight of the Idols*, section 14.

23 *Ibid.*

24 Nietzsche, *The Will to Power*, section 684.

25 *Ibid.*, section 684.

26 [Ed. Lukács refers to 'The Eternal Recurrence' which forms the concluding part of *The Will to Power*.]

27 *The Will to Power*, section 1062.

28 Nietzsche, *Twilight of the Idols*, p. 64.

29 Nietzsche, *Thus Spoke Zarathustra*, tr. Walter Kaufmann (Penguin, 1966), p. 318.

21

Martin Heidegger

The grim years of the First World War, which were full of abrupt changes of fortune, and the ensuing period, brought a marked changed of mood [in the German intellectuals' philosophical outlook]. The subjectivistic tendency remained, but its basic nature, its atmosphere was completely altered. No longer was the world a great, multi-purpose stage upon which the I, in ever-changing costumes and continually transforming the scenery at will, could play out its own inner tragedies and comedies. It had now become a devastated area. Before the war, it had been possible to criticize that which was mechanical and rigid about capitalist culture from a lofty vitalistic angle . . . Since the downfall of the Wilhelminische regime the social world had begun to constitute something alien to this subjectivism; the collapse of the world which subjectivism was continually criticizing, but which formed the indispensable basis of its existence, was lurking at every door. There was no longer any firm means of support. And in its abandoned condition, the solitary ego stood in fear and anxiety. [. . .]

Now wonder that now, when this depressed mood was already starting to make itself felt – years ahead of the actual crisis – as a foreboding of future gloomy events, a renaissance of Kierkegaard's philosophy was proclaimed by the then leading minds, Husserl's pupil Heidegger and the former psychiatrist Karl Jaspers. Of course they did so with up-to-date modifications. Orthodox Protestant religiosity and Kierkegaard's strictly Lutheran faith in the Bible were of no use to present needs. But Kierkegaard's critique of Hegelian philosophy, as a critique of all those striving to find objectivity and universal validity by reasoned thought, and of all concepts of historical progress, acquired a very strong contemporary influence. So did Kierkegaard's development of 'existential philosophy' from the deepest despair of an extremely self-mortifying subjectivism which sought to justify itself in the very pathos of despair, and his professed exposure of all ideas of socio-historical life as mere vapid and vain ideas, in contrast to the subject which alone existed.

The power of these ideas lay chiefly in the fact that Kierkegaard's philosophy attacked the bourgeois idea of progress, and Hegel's idealistic dialectics, whereas the supporters of existential philosophy were already at odds principally with Marxism, although this seldom found overt and direct expression in their writings; at times they attempted to exploit the reactionary aspects of Hegelian philosophy on behalf of this new campaign. That Kierkegaard's existential philosophy was already no more than the ideology of the saddest philistinism, of fear and trembling, of anxiety, did not stop it conquering wide intellectual circles in Germany on the eve of Hitler's seizure of power, during the nihilistic period of so-called heroic idealism. On the contrary: this pretentiously tragic philistinism was precisely the socio-psychological reason for the influence of Heidegger and Jaspers.

It was this mood of despair, and not deep-seated programmatic differences, which distinguished existential philosophy from the rest of vitalism. Admittedly it was more than a matter of chance or mere terminology that the emphatically used catchword 'life' was succeeded by an emphasis on 'existence'. Although the difference was one of mood far more than philosophical method, it nevertheless expressed something new in content and not trivial: the intensity of the loneliness, disappointment and despair created the new content. The emphatic stress on 'life' signified the conquest of the world through subjectivism; hence the fascist activists of vitalism, who were about to succeed Heidegger and Jaspers, revived the catchword, although they gave it yet another content. [. . .]

Despite this heightening of subjectivistic tendencies, Heidegger represented perhaps even more strongly than his predecessors the philosophical 'third way': the claim to be above the antithesis of idealism and materialism (which he terms 'realism').

> *Dasein* is an entity which, in its very Being, comports itself understandingly towards that Being. In saying this, we are calling to the formal concept of existence. *Dasein* exists. Furthermore, *Dasein* is an entity which in each case I myself am.[1]

This epistemological hocus-pocus, so typical of the whole imperialist period, was perpetrated by Heidegger by means of his systematic use of the term 'existence' (*Dasein*), which gave the impression of an objectivity independent of human consciousness, although by 'existence' he meant nothing more than human existence – indeed only, in the final analysis, its manifestation in the consciousness.

Heidegger solved this crucial question of the philosophical 'third way' on the basis of apodictic statement and 'essential intuition'. He himself was obliged to see that through his position, he was approaching that vicious circle which Dilthey had perceived with alarm in the early vitalism.

> Dilthey's own researches for laying the basis for the human sciences were forced one-sidedly into the field of the theory of science; and it was of course with a regard to such discussions that his publications were often oriented in this direction. But the 'logic of human sciences' was by no means central for him – no more than he was striving in his 'psychology' 'merely' to make improvements in the positive science of the psychical.[2]

But whereas Dilthey paused to regard the circle with scientifically honest alarm, Heidegger resolutely cut the knot with the aid of 'essential intuition' (with which, because of its irrationalistic arbitrariness, anything at all can be sought out, especially by means of an ontological transition of Being).

> [The] circle of understanding is not an orbit in which any random kind of knowledge may move; it is the expression of the existential *fore-structure* of *Dasein* itself . . . Because understanding, in accordance with its existential meaning, is Dasein's own potentiality-for-Being, the ontological presuppositions of historiological knowledge transcend in principle the idea of rigour held in the most exact sciences. Mathematics is not more vigorous than historiology, but only narrower, because the existential foundations relevant for it lie within a narrower range.[3]

We shall discuss later the special significance of the historical in Heidegger. Here it is only important to establish that Heidegger's 'ontologically' smuggled 'understanding', i.e., a procedure governed purely by consciousness, into objective Being is just as ambiguous a contrast between subjectivity and objectivity as that of Mach with regard to the sphere of apprehension. Both, in reality, were carrying out the same translation – though in a different form, as befitted their different intentions – of purely subjective – idealistic positions into objective (i.e., pseudo-objective) ones. It is just that the Machists were far more open and straightforward in translating direct observations into the only (pseudo-objective) reality accessible to us, whereas Heidegger was presenting the project of a – professedly – special science of pure objectivity, of ontology.

To be sure he was no more successful than the earlier phenomenologists in showing how to find a way from objective reality 'set in parentheses' to genuine objectivity independent of consciousness. On the contrary: he posited a close and organic connection between phenomenology and ontology, allowing the latter to grow out of the former without further ado.

'Phenomenology is our way of access to what is to be the theme of ontology, and it is our way of giving it demonstrative precision. *Only as phenomenology, is ontology possible.*'[4] That his approach had to do with the intuitive (and hence irrationalist) arbitrariness of 'essential intuition' is indicated by the definition of the object which directly precedes this:

> Manifestly, it is something that proximally and for the most part does *not* show itself at all: it is something that lies *hidden*, in contrast to that which proximally and for the most part does show itself; but at the same time it is something that belongs to what thus shows itself, and it belongs to it so essentially as to constitute its meaning and its ground.[5]

This is the very '*Being (Sein)* of that which-is-in-being (*Seienden*)': the object of ontology.

The advance in Heidegger's proposition as against Machism lies in the fact that he zealously made the difference between essence and phenomenon his central concern, whereas Machism could only draw overtly subjectivistic ('thought-sparing') distinctions in the phenomenal world. But the advance, which contributed much to Heidegger's influence in a period hankering after objectivity, promptly defeated its own ends in the manner of his answers. For in this method, 'intuition of the essence' alone can decide what is to be comprehended as 'concealed essence' in immediate present reality perceived directly by the subject. Thus with Heidegger too, the objectivity of the ontological materiality remained purely declarative, and the proclamation of ontological objectivity could lead only to a heightening of the pseudo-objectivism and – owing to the intuitive selection principle and criterion – irrationality of this sphere of objectiveness.

But the terminological camouflaging of subjective idealism was exposed each time that Heidegger came to speak of concrete questions. Let us quote just one example:

> *There is truth only in so far as Dasein is and so long as Dasein is.* Entities are uncovered only *when Dasein is*; and only as long as *Dasein is*, are they disclosed. Newton's laws, the principle of contradiction, any truth whatever – these are true only as long as *Dasein is*. Before there was any Dasein, there was no truth; nor will there be any after *Dasein* is no more. For in such a case truth as disclosedness, uncovering, and uncoveredness, *cannot* be.[6]

This juggling with quasi-objective categories on an extremely subjectivistic basis pervades Heidegger's entire philosophy. Kierkegaard's conscious subjectivism first reversed the philosophical hierarchical positions and placed possibility higher than reality in order to create room – a vacuum – for the free decision of the individual concerned with absolutely nothing beyond saving his soul. Heidegger followed Kierkegaard in this, albeit with a difference which very much impaired the logic and honesty of his philosophizing. For in contrast to his master on this point, he still avowed the objectivity of the categories thus arising (the so-called existentials).

The claim of objectivity is even more marked with Heidegger than with Scheler, and yet he made the subjectivistic character of phenomenology far more salient. And the Husserlian tendency towards a strictly scientific approach had now already faded completely. In striving to argue an objective doctrine of Being, an ontology, Heidegger needed to draw a sharp dividing-line between it and anthropology. But it is clear that when dealing with central problems and not engaged in pure, detached methodology, his ontology is in actual fact merely a vitalistic anthropology with an objectivistic mask. Characteristic, for example, are his efforts to prove the underlying anthropological bias in Kant's 'transcendental logic', efforts intended to make Kant just as much a forerunner of existential philosophy as Simmel had claimed he was of vitalism.

Over and above his reading of Kant, however, Heidegger expressed this tendency at every point. Anthropology today, in his view, is 'no longer just the name for a discipline, nor has it been for some time. Instead, the word describes a fundamental tendency of man's contemporary position with respect to himself and to the totality of beings . . . Anthropology seeks not only the truth about human beings, but instead it now demands a decision as to what truth in general can mean.'[7] And he clarified this attitude, which implied a factual identity between his ontology and anthropology, by saying that while no age had known as much about man as the present one, it was also true that 'no age knew less what man is than the present age. To no age has man become so questionable as to ours.'

This plainly expresses the negativity of Heidegger's philosophical tendencies. For him philosophy was no longer the detached 'strict' science of Husserl, but also no longer the path to a concrete world outlook, as vitalism from Dilthey to Spengler and Scheler had been. Its task was rather: 'to keep the investigation open by means of questions'. With a pathos reminiscent of Kierkegaard, Heidegger expounded his position as follows:

> Does it make sense, and is there a justification for grasping man on the grounds of his innermost finitude – that he requires 'Ontology,' i.e., understanding of Being – as 'creative' and consequently as 'infinite',

where indeed there is nothing which even the idea of an infinite creature recoils from as radically as it does from an ontology? At the same time, however, is it permissible to develop the finitude in *Dasein* only as a problem, without a 'presupposed' infinitude? . . . What does the infinitude which is so 'composed' mean? Will the Question of Being, in all its elementary weight and breadth, free itself from all this questionableness? Or have we already become so much the fools of the organization, of the hustle and bustle, that we are no longer able to befriend the essential, the simple, and the constant?[8]

Thus what Heidegger termed phenomenology and ontology was in reality no more than an abstractly mythicizing, anthropological description of human existence; in his concrete phenomenological descriptions, however, it unexpectedly turned into an – often grippingly interesting – description of intellectual philistinism during the crisis of the imperialist period. Heidegger himself admitted this to a certain degree. His programme was to show that which-is-in-being, 'as it *immediately and mostly* is, in its average *everyday state*'. Now what is really interesting about Heidegger's philosophy is the extremely detailed account of how 'the human being', the supporting subject of existence, 'immediately and for the most part' dissipates and loses himself in this everyday state.

Here reasons of space, apart from anything else, prevent us from detailing this. Let us stress just one element, namely that the inauthenticity of the Heideggerian everyday existence, that which he calls the 'fallen state' (*Verfallensein*), is caused by social being. According to Heidegger, man's social character is an 'existential' of existence, which he regards as a term in the sphere of existence equivalent to categories in thinking. Now, social existence signifies the anonymous dominance of 'the one' (*das Man*). We need to quote at some length from this account in order that the reader can receive a concrete picture of Heidegger's ontology of the everyday state:

The 'who' is not this one, not that one, not oneself, not some people, and not the sum total of them all. The 'who' is the neuter, the '*they*' [*das Man*] . . . In this inconspicuousness and unascertainability, the real dictatorship of the 'they' is unfolded. We take pleasure and enjoy ourselves as *they* [*man*] take pleasure; we read, see, and judge about literature and art as *they* see and judge; likewise we shrink back from the 'great mass' as *they* shrink back; we find shocking what *they* find shocking. The 'they', which is nothing definite, and which all are, though not as the sum, prescribes the kind of Being of everydayness . . . Everyone is the other, and no one is himself. The 'they', which supplies the answer to the question and the '*who*' of everyday *Dasein*, is the *'nobody'* to whom *Dasein* has already surrendered itself in Being-among-one-another [*Untereinandersein*].

In these characters of Being which we have exhibited – everyday Being-among-one-another, distantiality, averageness, levelling down, publicness, and disburdening of one's Being, and accommodation – lies that 'constancy' of *Dasein* which is closest to us . . . In these modes one's way of Being is that inauthenticity and failure to stand by one's Self. To be in this way signifies no lessening of *Dasein's* facticity, just as the 'they', as the 'nobody', is by no means nothing at all. On the contrary, in this kind of Being, *Dasein* is an *ens realissimum*, if by 'Reality' we understand a Being that has the character of *Dasein*.

Of course, the 'they' is as little present-at-hand as *Dasein* itself. The more openly the 'they' behaves, the harder it is to grasp, and the slier it is, but the less is it nothing at all. If we 'see' it ontico-ontologically with an unprejudiced eye, it reveals itself as the 'Realest subject' of everydayness.[9]

Such descriptions constitute the strongest and most suggestive parts of *Being and Time*, and in all likelihood they formed the basis of the book's broad and profound effect. Here, with the tools of phenomenology, Heidegger provided a series of interesting images taken from the inner life, from the world view of the dissolute bourgeois mind of the post-war years. These images are suggestive because they provide – on the descriptive level – a genuine and true-to-life picture of those conscious reflexes which the reality of post-war imperialist capitalism triggered off in those unable or unwilling to surpass what they experienced in their individual existence and to go further towards objectivity, i.e., towards exploring the socio-historical causes of their experiences. With these tendencies, Heidegger was not alone in his time; similar tendencies were expressed not only in Jaspers's philosophy, but also in a large part of the imaginative literature of the period (it will suffice, perhaps, to mention Céline's novel, *Journey to the End of the Night*, and Joyce, Gide, Malraux, etc.). However, even if we acknowledge the partial accuracy of these accounts of spiritual states, we must ask how far they square with objective reality, how far their descriptions go beyond the immediacy of the reacting subjects. Of course this question is chiefly of philosophical moment; imaginative literature operates within far more elastic limits, although its stature is still determined by its comprehensive concreteness and depth of the representation of reality . . .

Heidegger's descriptions are related to the spiritual conditions that were prompted by the crisis of post-war imperialistic capitalism. There is evidence for this not only in the influence exercised by *Being and Time*, far beyond the sphere of the really philosophically-minded – and it was repeatedly singled out for praise and censure by philosophical critics. What Heidegger was describing was the subjective-bourgeois, the intellectual reverse side of the economic categories of capitalism – in the form, of course, of a radically idealistic subjectifying and hence a distortion. In this respect Heidegger was carrying on Simmel's tendency 'to construct a basement underneath historical materialism', professedly in order to render visible the philosophical, indeed metaphysical hypotheses of this doctrine. The difference, however, tells us more than the affinity. It is a difference expressed both in the methodology and the mood of Heidegger's work. Methodologically, in the fact that, in contrast to Simmel who was expressly criticizing historical materialism and trying to 'deepen' it through personal reinterpretation, Heidegger did not give the least indication of doing anything similar. Not only is the name of Marx absent from *Being and Time*, even from allusions where it is patently relevant, the content also dispenses with all objective categories of economic reality.

Heidegger's method was more radically subjectivistic: without exception his descriptions pertain to spiritual responses to socio-economic reality. Here we have, displayed in practice, the inner identity of phenomenology and ontology, the purely subjective character of even the latter in spite of all declared objectivity. Indeed it is even manifest that this shift to ontology – an allegedly objective ontology – rendered the philosophical view of the world still more subjectivistic than it was at the time of the overtly radical subjectivism of a thinker like Simmel. For in the latter, there are at least glimmers of objective social reality with its contours distorted, whereas in Heidegger this reality is reduced to a series of purely spiritual states described phenomenologically. This shift of method is intimately connected with the change in the basic mood. Simmel was philosophizing in the very hopeful early days of vitalism. Despite establishing a 'tragedy of culture', and for all his critique of capitalist civilization, he still considered money, as we may recall, the guardian of inwardness.

In Heidegger, these illusions had crumbled long ago. The individual's inner life had long since renounced all world-conquering plans; no longer was its social environment regarded as something problematical in itself, but as a *locus* in whose domain pure inwardness could none the less lead a free life. The surrounding world was now an uncanny, mysterious permanent threat to everything that would constitute the essence of subjectivity. This again, to be sure, was not a new experience for bourgeois man under capitalism; Ibsen, for example, had portrayed it many decades earlier in the famous scene where his Peer Gynt – symbolizing the problem of the essentiality, or lack of it, in his own life – peels an onion and finds no core, only skin In Heidegger this refrain of the ageing and despairing Peer Gynt became the determining maxim of his descriptions. [. . .]

Heidegger's complicated trains of thought, his laborious phenomenological introspections struck upon the material of experiences widespread among this class and found an answering chord. Heidegger was here preaching a retreat from all social dealings just as much as Schopenhauer, in his time, had proclaimed a withdrawal from the bourgeois idea of progress, from the democratic revolution. Heidegger's retreat, however, implies a reactionary stand far stronger than that to be found in Schopenhauer's quietism. At the height of the revolution, to be sure, even this quietism could, within the thinker advocating it, all too easily tilt over into counter-revolutionary activity, and Nietzsche demonstrated how easily a counter-revolutionary activism could be evolved from Schopenhauer's hypotheses on the philosophical level as well. One may say without undue exaggeration that in the period of the imperialistic bourgeoisie's struggle against socialism, Heidegger was related to Hitler and Rosenberg as Schopenhauer, in his own day, was related to Nietzsche.

All the same, events never repeat themselves mechanically – not even in the history of philosophy. The human emotional emphasis in the process of retreat was totally different, indeed opposed, in Schopenhauer and Heidegger. With the latter, the feeling of despair no longer left the individual free scope for a 'beatific' aesthetic and religious contemplation as in Schopenhauer. His sense of peril already encompassed the whole realm of individual existence. And although the solipsism of the phenomenological method may have distorted the depiction of it, it was still a social fact: it was the inner state of the bourgeois individual (especially the intellectual) within a crumbling monopoly capitalism, facing the prospect of his own downfall. Thus Heidegger's despair had two facets: on the one hand, the remorseless baring of the individual's inner nothingness in the face of the imperialistic crisis; on the other – and because the social grounds for this nothingness were being fetishistically transformed into something timeless and anti-social – a feeling, to which it gave rise, which could very easily turn into desperate revolutionary activity. It is certainly no accident that Hitler's propaganda continually appealed to despair. Among the working masses, admittedly, the despair was occasioned by their socio-economic situation. Among the intelligentsia, however, that mood of nihilism and despair from whose subjective truth Heidegger proceeded, which he conceptualized, clarified philosophically and canonized as 'authentic', created fertile ground for the spread of Hitlerian agitation.

This everyday state of being, dominated by 'the one', was therefore actually a non-being. And in fact Heidegger defined Being not as immediately given, but as extremely remote: 'The state of being (*das Seiende*) in which each of us rests is ontologically the remotest state.' This most intrinsic part of man, he maintained, was forgotten and buried in everyday life; and it was precisely the task of ontology to rescue it from oblivion.

This programmatic attitude to life (the social life of his period) determined Heidegger's whole method. We have already indicated, more than once, the unsurmountable subjectivism of the phenomenology, the pseudo-objectivity of the ontology. But only now that Heidegger's world picture stands before us in a certain concreteness with regard to both content and structure is it plain that this method, for all its objective fragility, was the only possible one for his purposes. For in Heidegger's conception, man's life in society was a matter not of relation between subjectivity and objectivity, not of a reciprocal relationship between subject and object, but of 'authenticity' and 'inauthenticity' within the same subject. Only in appearance, in the methodological expressions, did the ontological surpassing of objective reality 'set in parentheses' tend towards objectivity; in actual fact it was turning to another, purportedly deeper, layer of subjectivity. Indeed it may be said that with Heidegger, a category (an existential) expressed Being all the more genuinely and came all the closer to Being the less it was encumbered by the conditions of objective reality. For that reason his defining terms (mood, care, fear, summons, etc.) were without exception of a decidedly subjective character.

But for that very reason, Heidegger's ontology was bound to grow more irrationalistic the more it developed its true nature. Admittedly, Heidegger was constantly trying to shut himself off from irrationalism. Here too it was his aim to elevate himself above the antithesis of rationalism and irrationalism, to find a philosophical 'third road', just as in the question of idealism and materialism. But for him it was impossible. He repeatedly criticized the limits of rationalism, but would then add to his critique: 'However the phenomena are no less falsified when they are banished to the sanctuary of the irrational. When irrationalism, as the counterplay of rationalism, talks about the things to which rationalism is blind, it does so only with a squint.'[10] But since, in Heidegger's eyes, this blindness lies in the fact that rationalism takes into account the observable facts and laws of objective reality, a loss of all real possibility results from his exclusion of irrationalism. For if one removes from a concrete state every condition relevant to observable reality, if this concrete state arises solely in the inner life, it is inevitable that the consequent findings will take on an irrationalist character.

This was already so with Kierkegaard. The latter, however, although able to work with theological categories and hence to attain a quasi-rationality or quasi-dialectic, did not shrink from the most extreme conclusions and spoke, with regard to precisely the decisive questions of 'existence', of the paradox, i.e., of irrationality. Heidegger lacked, on the one hand, the possibility of resorting to overtly theological categories and, on the other, the courage openly to declare his allegiance to irrationalism. Yet every one of his ontological statements shows that the dereification of all conditions of objectivity in reality – however we may phrase it – leads to irrationalism. Let us give a single example. Heidegger writes of 'mood' (*Stimmung*). This is realized in principle in its 'why', 'whence' and 'whither'.

> In an *ontologico*-existential sense, this means that even in that to which such a mood pays no attention, *Dasein* is unveiled in its Being-de-livered-over to the 'there'. In the evasion itself the 'there' *is* disclosed. This characteristic of *Dasein*'s Being – this 'that it is' – is veiled in its 'whence' and 'whither', yet discloses in itself all the more unveiledly; we call it the *'throwness'* (*Geworfenheit*) of this entity into its 'there'; indeed, it is thrown in such a way that, as Being-in-the-world, it is the 'there'. The expression 'throwness' is meant to suggest the *facticity of its being delivered over*. [But] *Facticity is not the factuality of the* factum brutum *of something present-at-hand, but a characteristic of* Dasein's Being – one which has been taken up into existence, even if proximally it has been thrust aside.[11]

As long as Being – in Heidegger's 'project' – intervenes or intends to intervene, the findings (and the road to obtaining them) can only be irrationalistic. The road to Being means a casting aside of all objective conditions of reality. At all times, Heidegger's ontology imperiously demands this in order that man (subject, existence) might escape the power of 'the one' that rendered him inauthentic and took away his essence.

We thus see that, inadvertently, Heidegger's ontology has turned into a moral doctrine, indeed almost a religious sermon; this ethico-religious epistemological shift also shows the determining influence of Kierkegaard on Heidegger's propositions and method. The gist of the sermon is that man should become 'essential' and make ready to hear and understand 'the call of conscience' in order to mature to 'resolution'. Heidegger gave a very detailed account of this process too; again, we can give only a brief outline of it here. The disclosure of the nothingness concealed in the 'fallen state' (*Verfallensein*) is achieved through ontology: 'The essence of the originally nullifying nothing lies herein: it begins by putting being-there (*Da-sein*) before the state of being (*das Seiende*) as such . . . Being-there means: bound immanency (*Hineingehaltenheit*) in nothingness.'

That is the essence of Heidegger's 'existence', and men were deemed to differ merely in respect of whether or not they were conscious of it. The attainment of awareness took place through the conscience. 'Conscience attests not by making something known in an undifferentiated manner, but by calling forth and summoning us to Being-guilty . . . Understanding the call discloses one's own *Dasein* in the uncanniness of its individualization.'[12]

The understanding of this summons brought man to a state of resolution. Heidegger stressed the significance of this 'existential' with great pathos. After what has gone before, it comes as no surprise when he strongly denies that 'resoluteness' (*Entschlossenheit*) in respect of man's surroundings might bring about even the slightest change; not even the dominance of 'the one' is disturbed.

> The 'world' which is ready-to-hand does not become another one 'in its content', nor does the circle of Others get exchanged for a new one; but both one's Being towards the ready-to-hand understandingly and concernfully, and one's solicitious Being with Others, are now given a definite character in terms of their ownmost potentiality-for-Being-their-Selves . . . The irresoluteness of the 'they' remains dominant notwithstanding, but it cannot impugn resolute existence.[13]

Here, the methodology and content of Heidegger's philosophy are expressing in an extremely complicated (but above all, mannered) terminology the intellectual philistine's feelings in a time of severe crisis: the threat to personal 'existence' is so deflected as to prevent its giving rise to any obligation to alter one's external living conditions or indeed to collaborate in transforming objective social reality. Difficult though Heidegger may be to grasp, this much was correctly read out of his philosophy.

So the only result arrived at here was the insight that existence as such is to blame. And the authentic life of the resolute man now constituted a preparation for death; 'a foreshadowing of the possibility', in Heidegger's terminology. Here again there are traces of Kierkegaard, though without his pronounced Protestant theology.

Like every vitalistic philosophy, this Heideggerian theology without positive religion or a personal God was, of course, bound to contain a new doctrine of time of its own. This too was a methodological necessity. For the rigid opposition of space and time was one of the weakest points of undialectical rationalism. But whereas a true way of surmounting that opposition must lie in the dialectical interaction of space and time founded in objective reality, irrational vitalism had always directed its sharpest attacks against the rationalistic concept of time, taking time and space – like culture and civilization in the realm of social philosophy – as diametrically opposed, indeed warring principles. To conquer time was very important to vitalism in a positive respect – this is the reverse side of the aforesaid polemical intention – because the identification of experience and life (existence) crucial to its pseudo-objectivism was only possible if there was a subjectified, irrationalist conception of time to meet this demand.

Heidegger laid much weight on this. He sharply divorced himself from Bergson whom he condemned – along with Aristotle and Hegel – as representing a 'vulgar' view of time. In this 'vulgar' time it was accepted that one knew past, present and future; the time of the 'fallen' world of the 'one', the time of measurement, clock-time, etc. Genuine time, on the contrary, knew no sequentiality.

> The character of 'having been' arises from the future, and in such a way that the future which 'has been' (or better, which 'is in the process of having been') releases from itself the Present. This phenomenon has the unity of a future which makes present in the process of having been; we designate as *'temporality'*.[14]

[. . .] In view of this interpretation of time Heidegger's second chief programmatic point, proof of the elementary historicality of 'existence' as the basis for comprehending history, turns out to be pure shadow-boxing. Heidegger was right in making a stand against the neo-Kantians who were trying to argue historicality from a subjective 'setting', and in indicating that Being must be historical in order for there to be any historical science. As on many points, vitalism was here pre-empting the collapse of undialectic idealism. But Heidegger still lagged far behind the neo-Kantians in the concrete definition of the 'existential' historicality. As a consequence the primary phenomenon of history was, for him, existence, i.e., the life of the individual, the 'universal coherence of life between birth and death'. And this too – quite in accordance with the Diltheyan vitalistic method – was defined from experience. 'It [this coherence] *consists of* a sequence "within time".'

The result was a double distortion. Firstly, Heidegger did not take the historical data in nature as the 'originals' (Kant–Laplace theory,

Darwinism, etc.) but presented the coherence of human experiences, far removed from the 'original state', as the starting point, the 'primordial phenomenon'. Secondly, he failed to observe that his 'primordial phenomenon' was derivative: a consequence of that social Being and praxis of men in which alone such a 'coherence' of experience could come about at all. As far as he did notice a link, he rejected it as belonging to the domain of the 'one'. In so doing, he not only isolated a distorted derivative of social human praxis – as a historical 'primordial phenomenon', as 'original' – from real history, but also set them up as antinomies. The tendency to falsify the structure of reality in this way graphically expressed the pre-fascist character of Heidegger's thinking. Now since the primary historicality was 'ontologically founded' on this basis, the automatic product of it was Heidegger's crucial distinction between 'authentic' and 'inauthentic' history . . .

But according to Heidegger's reading of history, it is precisely real history which is inauthentic, just as real time is the 'vulgar' kind. In giving history an apparently ontologically reasoned basis, Heidegger actually took away any kind of historicality, while acknowledging as historical only a philistine's moral 'resoluteness'. In his analysis of everyday existence, Heidegger had already rejected all human orientation towards objective factors or trends in socio-historical life. There he stated:

> In having a mood, *Dasein* is always disclosed moodwise as that entity to which it has been delivered over in its Being; and in this way it has been delivered over to the Being which, in existing, it has to be. 'To be disclosed' does not mean 'to be known as this sort of thing'. And even in the most indifferent and inoffensive everydayness the Being of *Dasein* can burst forth as a naked 'that it is' shows itself, but the 'whence' and the 'whither' remain in darkness . . . In an *ontico*-existential sense, this means that even in that to which such a mood pays no attention, *Dasein* is unveiled in its Being-delivered-over to the 'there'. In the evasion itself the 'there' *is* something disclosed.[15]

The illumination of existence can come only from within, for every (to Heidegger's mind: purported) objectively directed perception brings about a casting down (*das Verfallen*), a state of surrender to the 'one' and inauthenticity. Thus it was only logical for Heidegger, in positing the historicality of existence, to refute equally firmly everything objectively historical; Heidegger's historicality, then, has nothing to do with the point 'that existence occurs in a "world-history"'.[16] Here he was polemicizing – quite rightly to some extent – against the old idealistic argumentation of the theory of history.

Even if the problem of 'history' is treated in accordance with a theory of science, not only aiming at the 'epistemological' clarification of the historiological way of grasping things (Simmel) or at the logic with which the concepts of historiological presentation are formed (Rickert), but doing so with an orientation towards 'the side of the object', then, as long as the question is formulated this way, history becomes in principle accessible only as the *object* of a science. Thus the basic phenomenon of history, which is prior to any possible thematizing by historiology and underlies it, has been irretrievably put aside. How history can become a possible *object* for historiology is something that may be gathered only from the kind of Being which belongs to the historical – from historicality, and from the way it is rooted in temporality.[17]

Here again Heidegger was pre-empting the collapse of idealism, not unskilfully, by giving the impression that he planned to make the historical nature of existence itself the starting point of history. But in one breath he was giving this existence itself, as we have observed, a thoroughly subjectivistic definition, while in the next he radically 'purged' the original historicality of existence of all relation to real, objective history . . .

This, of course, implies the positing of an 'inauthentic' historicality as well. And here, in accordance with the main substance of his conception, Heidegger almost compromised himself. For if the sole historical issue at stake is that of what one might – in theological language – term 'saving the soul', then there is no clear reason why everything else, whose role cannot be more than, at most, a distraction from Being in history, should likewise have a historical character. But sometimes Heidegger acknowledged a primary and secondary, and sometimes an authentic and inauthentic historicality.

Do not equipment and work and every thing which *Dasein* dwells alongside, belong to 'history' too? If not, is the historizing of history just the isolated running-off of 'streams of experience' in individual subjects? . . . But even Nature is historical. It is *not* historical, to be sure, in so far as we speak of 'natural history'; but Nature is historical as a countryside, as an area that has been colonized or exploited, as a battlefield, or as the site of a cult.[18]

So not much more emerges from Heidegger's 'inauthentic' history than a Spenglerian 'historicality' (*Geschichtlichkeit*). But whereas, with Spengler, this was an organic part of his conception, with Heidegger it damaged the basic idea and was, in the last analysis, unnecessary ballast. In part it arose from Heidegger's reluctance openly to conform to radical irrationalism, to the radical rejection of any scientific approach; and in part it was a legacy – no longer organic – of the basic theological conception of Heidegger's path to saving the soul, a path which in Heidegger – godless and soulless – had lost its earlier guiding principles.

This brings to light an important factor in Heidegger's relationship to Kierkegaard. For Heidegger arrived at this twofold view of history as authentic and inauthentic under the influence of Kierkegaard's polemics against Hegel. But as always in history, the reactionary thinker at the less advanced stage was more candid, forthright and rigorous than his imperialistic epigone. Kierkegaard acknowledged no world history save in the eyes of God. For man, who in his view – significantly enough – could be only a spectator in history, there is no history but only an individual moral-cum-religious development. [. . .]

In Heidegger we find a problem-complex similar to that found in Kierkegaard but, lacking a God, Christ or soul, Heidegger wanted to create a theological philosophy of history on behalf of 'religious atheism'. Hence the disappearance of all the substantial elements of theology, even Kierkegaard's, with only the now totally empty theological framework remaining. For Kierkegaard too, such categories of the forlorn life of the isolated individuality as anxiety, care, guilt-feelings, resolutions, etc., were the 'existentials' of 'authentic' reality. But Kierkegaard – because of the residue of a theological philosophy of history positing, to his mind, a real history for God – was capable of radically denying historicality for the individual man working out his own salvation. Heidegger, on the other hand, had to disguise this unhistorical existence as 'authentic' history in order to achieve a contrast to the denial of real history (the 'inauthentic').

Again the socio-historical content was the deciding factor in this antithesis. Kierkegaard, whose thinking rejected bourgeois democratic progress, could still envisage a way back into the feudal religious world; even if this conception was already susceptible in his work to a decadent, bourgeois isolation. Heidegger, who wrote during the crisis of monopoly capitalism and in the vicinity of a socialist state ever gaining in strength and appeal, could evade the consequences of this crisis period only by disparaging real history as 'inauthentic'. This also meant acknowledging as 'authentic' history only such a spiritual development as would, through care, despair and so forth, lead men away from social actions and decisions, at the same time confirming them inwardly in such a state of disorientation and perplexity as would encourage to the utmost a switch to reactionary activism of the Hitlerian variety.

NOTES

All notes are by Lukács, but publication details are from recent editions of cited works where appropriate.

1 Martin Heidegger, *Being and Time*, tr. John Macquire and Edward Robinson (New York: Harper and Row, 1962), p. 78.

2 *Ibid.*, p. 450.

3 *Ibid.*, p. 195.

4 *Ibid.*, p. 60.

5 *Ibid.*, p. 59.

6 *Ibid.*, p. 269.

7 Martin Heidegger, *Kant and the Problem of Metaphysics*, tr. Richard Taft (Bloomington: Indiana University Press, 1990), p. 143.

8 *Ibid.*, p. 168.

9 Heidegger, *Being and Time*, pp. 164–6.

10 *Ibid.*, p. 175.

11 *Ibid.*, p. 174.

12 *Ibid.*, pp. 341–2.

13 *Ibid.*, pp. 344–5.

14 *Ibid.*, p. 374.

15 *Ibid.*, pp. 173–4.

16 *Ibid.*, p. 440.

17 *Ibid.*, pp. 427–8.

18 *Ibid.*, p. 440.

Bibliography

There is no complete, definitive edition of Lukács's writings. The two standard editions, in German and Hungarian, remain incomplete. The best known is the standard German edition, *Georg Lukács Werke*, ed. Frank Benseler, Neuwied and Berlin: Hermann Luchtherhand Verlag (1962–86). This is followed by the more complete Hungarian edition, *Complete Works of György Lukács*, Budapest: Magvetö Kiadó (1971–94), which currently stands at 17 volumes.

LUKÁCS'S MAJOR WORKS

1910 *A lélek és a formák. Kisérletek*, Budapest: Franklin. (*Soul and Form*, tr. Anna Bostock, Cambridge, MA: MIT Press, 1974.)

1911 *A modern dráma fejlödésének története* [History of the development of modern drama], 2 vols, Budapest: Franklin.

1919 *Taktika és etika*, Budapest: Közoktatási Népbiztosság Kiadása, (*Tactics and Ethics: Political Essays, 1919–1929*, tr. Michael McColgan and ed. Rodney Livingstone, New York: Harper and Row, 1972.)

1920 *Die Theorie des Romans*, Berlin: Paul Cassirer. (*Theory of the Novel*, tr. Anna Bostock, Cambridge, MA: MIT Press, 1971.)

1923 *Geschichte und Klassenbewusstsein: Studien über Marxistische Dialektik*, Berlin: Malik Verlag. (*History and Class Consciousness*, tr. Rodney Livingstone, Cambridge, MA: MIT Press, 1971.)

1924 *Lenin: Studie über den Zusammenhang seiner Gedanken*, Berlin: Malik Verlag. (*Lenin: A Study on the Unity of His Thought*, tr. Nicholas Jacobs, Cambridge, MA: MIT Press, 1971)

1937 *Literaturnii teorii xix veka i marxizma* [Marxism and nineteenth-century literary theory], Moscow: Gos. Izd. Chudozestvennaja.

1944 *Irástudók felelösége* [The responsibility of writers], Moscow: Idegennyelvü Irodalmi Kiadó.

1945 *Balzac, Stendhal, Zola*, Budapest: Hungária.
Studies in European Realism, tr. Edith Bone, London: Hillway Publ. Co., 1950.
Irodalom és demokrácia [Literature and democracy], Budapest: Szikra.

1947 *A történelmi regény*, Budapest: Hungária. (*The Historical Novel*, trs Hannah Mitchell and Stanley Mitchell, Boston: Beacon Press, 1962.)
A polgár nyomában: a hetvenéves Thomas Mann, Budapest: Hungária. (*Essays on Thomas Mann*, tr. Stanley Mitchell, New York: Grosset and Dunlap, 1965.)
Goethe und seine Zeit, Berne: Francke. (*Goethe and His Age*, tr. Robert Anchor, New York: Howard Fertig, 1978.)

1948 *Der junge Hegel*, Zurich: Europa Verlag, (*The Young Hegel*, tr. Rodney Livingstone, Cambridge, MA: MIT Press, 1976.)
Existentialisme ou marxisme?, Paris: Nagel.
Essays über Realismus, Berlin: Aufbau Verlag. (*Essays on Realism*, tr. David Fernbach and ed. Rodney Livingstone, Cambridge, MA: MIT Press, 1981.)

1949 *Ady Endre*, Budapest: Szikra.

1951 *Deutsche Realisten des neunzehnten Jahrhunderts*, Berlin: Aufbau Verlag.

1952 *Der russische Realismus in der Weltliteratur*, Berlin: Aufbau Verlag.
Balzac und der französische Realismus, Berlin: Aufbau Verlag.
Studies in European Realism, introduction by Alfred Kazin, New York: Grosset and Dunlap, 1964. (Essays from *Der russische Realismus in der Weltliteratur* and *Balzac . . .* translated into English.)

1954 *Die Zerstörung der Vernunft*, Berlin: Aufbau Verlag. (*The Destruction of Reason*, tr. Peter Palmer, Atlantic Highlands, NJ: Humanities Press, 1981.)
Beitrage zur Geschichte der Aesthetik, Berlin: Aufbau Verlag.

1955 *Probleme des Realismus*, Berlin: Aufbau Verlag. (*Realism in Our Time*, trs John Mander and Necke Mander, with a preface by George Steiner, New York: Harper and Row, 1964.)

1958 *Wider den missverstandenen Realismus*, Hamburg: Claasen.

1963 *Die Eigenart des Asthetischen*, 2 vols, Neuwied and Berlin: Luchtherhand.

1969 *Solzhenitsyn*, Neuwied and Berlin: Luchtherhand. (*Solzhenitsyn*, tr. William David Graf, Cambridge, MA: MIT Press, 1971.)

1974 *Die Heidelberger Philosophie der Kunst (1912–1914)*, hrsg. György Márkus und Frank Benseler, Neuwied and Darmstadt: Luchtherhand. *Georg Lukács Werke*, Band 16.
Heidelberg Asthetik (1916–1918), hrsg. György Márkus and Frank Benseler, Neuwied and Darmstadt: Luchtherhand. *Georg Lukács Werke*, Bank 17.

1981 *Moskauer Schriften*: Zur Literaturtheorie und Literaturpolitik (1934–1940), hrsg. Frank Benseler, Frankfurt am Main: Sendler.

SELECTED WORKS ON LUKÁCS

Arato, Andrew and Breines, Paul, *The Young Lukács and the Origins of Western Marxism*, New York: Seabury Press, 1979.

Bahr, Erhard, *Georg Lukács*, Berlin: Colloquium, 1970.

Bernstein, J. M., *The Philosophy of the Novel: Lukács, Marxism and the Dialectics of Form*, Minneapolis: University of Minnesota Press, 1984.

Colletti, Lucio, *Marxism and Hegel*, London: NLB, 1973.

Congdon, Lee, *The Young Lukács*, Chapel Hill: University of North Carolina Press, 1983.

Deutscher, Isaac, *Marxism in Our Time*, Berkeley, CA: The Ramparts Press, 1971.

Eagleton, Terry, *Marxism and Literary Criticism*, Berkeley, CA: University of California Press, 1976.

Eagleton, Terry, *The Ideology of the Aesthetic*, Oxford: Basil Blackwell, 1990.

Feenberg, Andrew, *Lukács, Marx and the Sources of Critical Theory*, New York: Oxford University Press, 1986.

Gluck, Mary, *Georg Lukács and His Generation 1900–1918*, Cambridge, MA: Harvard University Press, 1985.

Goldmann, Lucian, *Lukács and Heidegger: Toward a New Philosophy*, tr. William Q. Boelhower, London: Routledge and Kegan Paul, 1977.

Heller, Agnes (ed.), *Lukács Reappraised*, New York: Columbia University Press, 1983.

Hughes, Stuart, *An Essay for Our Time*, New York: Knopf, 1950.

Hyppolite, Jean, *Studies on Marx and Hegel*, New York: Basic Books, 1969.

Jameson, Fredric, *Marxism and Form*, Princeton: Princeton University Press, 1971.

Jay, Martin, *Marxism and Totality: The Adventures of a Concept from Lukács to Habermas*, Berkeley, CA: University of California Press, 1984.

Kadarkay, Arpad, *Georg Lukács: Life, Thought and Politics*, Oxford: Basil Blackwell, 1991.

Kiralyfalvi, Bela, *The Aesthetics of György Lukács*, Princeton: Princeton University Press, 1975.

Kolakowski, Leszek, *Main Currents of Marxism*, tr. P. S. Falla, 3 vols, New York: Oxford University Press, 1981.

Levin, Harry, *Refractions*, New York: Oxford University Press, 1966.

Lichtheim, George, *Georg Lukács*, New York: Viking Press, 1970.

Löwy, Michael, *Georg Lukács: From Romanticism to Bolshevism*, London: NLB, 1979.

MacIntyre, Alasdair, *Against the Self-Images of the Age*, New York: Schocken Books, 1971.

Marcus, Judith, *Georg Lukács and Thomas Mann*, Amherst: University of Massachusetts Press, 1987.

Matassi, Elio, *Il Giovane Lukács: saggio e sistema*, Naples: Guida, 1979.

Mitzman, Arthur, *The Iron Cage: An Historical Interpretation of Max Weber*, New York: Knopf, 1969.

Raddatz, Fritz, *Georg Lukács*, Berlin: Colloquium, 1970.

Steiner, George, *A Reader*, New York: Oxford University Press, 1984.

Wellek, René, *Four critics: Croce, Valéry, Lukács and Ingarden*, Seattle: University of Washington Press, 1981.

Index